THE MURDERING MIND

Books by David Abrahamsen, M.D.

THE MURDERING MIND
OUR VIOLENT SOCIETY
THE EMOTIONAL CARE OF YOUR CHILD
THE PSYCHOLOGY OF CRIME
THE ROAD TO EMOTIONAL MATURITY
WHO ARE THE GUILTY?
102 SEX OFFENDERS
MIND AND DEATH OF A GENIUS
MEN, MIND AND POWER
CRIME AND THE HUMAN MIND

THE
MURDERING
MIND

David AbrahAmsen, M.D.

DISCARD

HARPER & ROW, PUBLISHERS
New York · Evanston · San Francisco · London

FIRST EDITION

Designed by Linda Dingler

Library of Congress Cataloging in Publication Data

Abrahamsen, David, 1903–
  The murdering mind.
  Bibliography: p.
    1. Criminal psychology. 2. Murder—United
States. I. Title. [DNLM: 1. Criminal psychology.
2. Homicide. HV 6515 A159m 1973]
HV6080.A315   364.1'523'019   72–9742
ISBN 0–06–010022–2

Acknowledgments

This book follows the fundamental views of Sigmund Freud, without whose indomitable research into the working of the human mind it could not have been written. While the actual writing of the manuscript only took about two years, the experience of over thirty years in the field of psychopathology and the presentation of expert testimony in court has gone into its making.

My friend and legal adviser, Albert Gaynor, formerly chief of the Criminal Division of the United States District Court, Southern District of New York, has been very helpful in reading the manuscript and particularly in giving valuable advice about court proceedings. I would also like to thank my secretary, Louise Kragelund, for her many retypings of the manuscript; Gay Stebbins, associate dean of admissions at the University of Pennsylvania, for her many excellent editorial suggestions; Joan Kahn, senior editor at Harper & Row, for her stimulating interest; and last but not least my wife, Lova, for her patient encouragement.

David Abrahamsen, M.D.

CONTENTS

Dimensions of the Murderer

To write about murder is very difficult. The subject is repellent; it goes against the grain of our life-preserving instincts. Yet we have to explore homicide because not only is it an important reality of life, but it is also salutary to inquire into murder to find out its nature. If there is truth to Pope's words "The proper study of mankind is man," then the study of murder should be given a high priority.

What is it like to be a psychiatrist probing the human mind? Even the most accomplished psychiatrist does not pretend to know its full dimensions—nor can the often distorted mind of a murderer be fitted into clinically defined categories. The truth is that the impulse to murder is within us all; we all have dimensions of turbulence and sickness which grow out of our past. Can we indeed learn to know the mind of the murderer? How much is this mind the product of strong emotional forces present both in childhood and in adult life? What is it that distinguishes the murderer from all those people who feel rage, anger and frustration and who fantasize about killing but who do not carry out the act of murder? This complex problem touches us in every aspect of human and social behavior.

Writing specifically about the mind of the murderer takes me back to my native Norway some thirty years ago, where in addition to my private psychiatric practice I worked in the Department of Justice. Murders were very rare in Norway, maybe one or two, possibly five a year. With the incidence of murder so low,

I was able to study in depth the psychological makeup of the various murderers, each with his individual characteristics and unique background. When I came to America, a country whose population is fifty times that of Norway and whose social system is radically different, I found a greatly increased incidence of murder and my experience in dealing with homicide grew accordingly.

Through psychiatric and consultative work in many parts of this country I have come to know intimately hundreds of people exhibiting neurotic or psychotic symptoms in all their variety, including murderous impulses. I have also come to know, more or less intimately, many persons who have murdered. Some of these individuals have been gassed, hanged or electrocuted. Others died of natural causes. Many through good fortune—if it can be called that—have survived and are still in prison. There are a few who are free, having been given a suspended sentence, and are on probation, or have served their sentence.

My original impression, based on my work in psychiatric hospitals, in prisons and in state and federal courts, as well as in my private practice, was that most people who killed could be typed by the "casebook"—that is, they shared certain well-established characteristics. Most conspicuous among these were difficulty in communicating, rebellion against parents, little or no male identification, a rich fantasy life, a feeling of unworthiness, the wish for revenge, fears, frustration and depression.

But as I dealt with an ever greater variety of cases, I was surprised to discover that many law-abiding people who came to seek my help shared with murderers many psychological symptoms and deviations in personal behavior. Although these private patients were plagued by more or less the same troubles, they could not and did not commit murder. What made the crucial difference between the mind that murdered and the one that did not? Did the answer lie in the psychiatric help I could give my patients by enabling them to relieve their fears, anxieties and frustrations? While therapy was indeed important, this could not be the whole story.

One important insight I have gained in my many years of psychiatric work is that there is more to the homicide than the murderer's own violent act. As important as it is to probe the deepest recesses of the murderer's mind in order to clarify his motivation, it is just as important—and fascinating—to study the victim and the often perplexingly close tie between killer and victim, a relationship which often illuminates the character of each. This link is an aspect of the murdering mind which is most often overlooked or simply omitted when a case comes to trial.

The law assumes that the criminal is always the perpetrator in the crime and that the victim is always innocent. The law does not give much consideration in its verdict when the culprit has been deliberately provoked. The usual psychiatric examination does not seek out the role of the victim in the crime. Yet my experience as a psychoanalyst has convinced me that the murdered person often plays an unconscious part in his own death. For a long time I have advocated that we scrutinize what, if any, relationship existed between the killer and his victim in order to assess more accurately the part each one played in the events leading up to the final act of murder.

Perhaps in the practice of criminal justice we should introduce a new discipline, a *comprehensive victimology*, which would cover *all* aspects of the relationship between the criminal and his victim. While there have been scattered sociological and legal discussions of the problem, they have been mostly in terms of financial compensation and insurance, which although important are only a small part of this complex relationship. More important is the tie between the protagonists.

Fundamentally victimology would encompass the scientific study of the personality, giving special attention to the pertinent factors of the emotional and social development of a person (or group) who becomes the *victim* of a crime. The central focus of this approach to criminal behavior would be to explain how the victim himself, or herself, contributes to his own murder, or to another crime, and how in the end the tables are turned and the criminal becomes his own victim. (Another aspect of this study would be group victimology—the analysis of victims in prisons, concentration camps, labor camps—which is outside the scope of this book.)

Only rarely is the human mind obsessed with the total impulse to murder. Instead, in my experience, homicide is in many instances provoked or stimulated unconsciously by the victim. As a student of Freud, I strongly believe that the mind of the murderer is charged with a turbulence of emotions stored from early childhood. When these often repressed emotions are tantalized, made hot, stirred up or activated, the mind, particularly when aroused or frustrated, becomes violent. And so it is that a person who may appear quite normal and well-adjusted on the surface becomes possessed by a mind that murders.

It is this synergism between murderer and victim which I have tried to make more explicit before the law. In this respect I have been conspicuously unsuccessful. The whole machinery of the law —the prosecution, the indictment, the court and the lawyer, the verdict, the sentence and the imprisonment—is a system rigidly defined in the name of justice. But justice or, as I would rather like to term it, "fairness" can be arrived at only when we know not only the conscious "case history" but also and more importantly the *unconscious* mind of the murderer which relieves him of the sense of guilt that would arise from a deliberate act of murder.

The first part of this book endeavors to show the variety of the murderer, the complex emotions present in him generally—specifically in the political assassin—his early symptoms, his fear of death, the closeness between love and hate, just to name a few aspects.

The second and third parts of the book describe a selective case study of a man called Tiger. Here, in part, I have modified my professional attitude as a psychiatrist in order to convey to you my human interest in the protagonist. The story of Tiger's troubled childhood and his complicated love is both human and tragic. His case has helped me to understand better this tie between the murderer and the victim and between him and his crime. In *reconstructing* this case history, I hope to provide the reader with psychological insight into the mind that murders. He may also share with me some of the frustrations the psychiatrist encounters in the courtroom. There are in this book many pages reconstructed from the courtroom to illustrate, with the ring of real-life dialogue, the often acrimonious battle between the district attorney and the defense lawyer. One of the most difficult problems the psychiatrist has stating his findings in court is that the law functions on the level of facts, or presumed facts, while psychiatry works on the conscious and unconscious levels, and of the latter type, involving feelings and moods, fantasies and dreams. It requires interpretation which may sound unreal, if not unbelievable. Nonfiction, whether we like it or not, is bound by time and has a tendency to become dated. In contrast, fiction is timeless and surpasses reality. If this case sometimes sounds too strange to be true, reality at times *is* stranger than fiction.

I have endeavored to put into straightforward form any psychiatric findings that I consider applicable to the law. In my effort to avoid technical language, which the psychoanalyst enjoys and the layman dislikes, some unavoidable oversimplification may have occurred.

One further point. Most murder cases described here are a matter of public record. In order to protect individual privacy— a person's most precious right—I have disguised identities, sometimes by making a composite picture, at others by intensifying certain actions of psychiatric importance in order to place the murderer in sharper relief in terms of his psychic nature. It is also true that the many long interviews with the accused often cannot do justice to the intricacies of his mind and behavior, particularly when compressed into the court proceedings. Trying to honor one's professional commitment and still do justice to the accused in court is like navigating between Scylla and Charybdis. In the case of Tiger I have made a composite picture, transposed details of interviews from office to jail, telescoped certain events in time, added court deliberations and changed names, times and places in order to conceal identities.

In following the unfolding of this complex study, the reader may be drawn to identify with Tiger; he may share with him many traits and feelings. Or he may well recognize some of the other murderers described here, or people who have been on the brink of killing, and find some traits in them that strike a chord in himself.

But this is only to say, in effect, that we are all human beings made of similar clay. The only and essential difference is in the varying *composition* of our personality style and emotions, and the *way* we try to cope with our conflicting situations. The reader must not seek explanations fitted to particular situations. If he wants to find answers for his own difficulties, he has to find them *within* himself.

PART ONE

THE MIND OF THE MURDERER

"What I have been trying to do in fiction you have done in science." Letter from Theodore Dreiser to author, 1944

Murder emerges from the intensity of death wishes that coexist with our life-serving emotions, just as love and hate live in us. Murder, despite our reluctance to admit it, is part of our humanity because it is rooted in human emotions. It is this frail and cruel side of our behavior which makes many of us more capable than we realize of committing murder.

Through my many years of experience, I have learned that there are three main intertwining psychological elements which may open the mind to murder: frustration, fear, and depression. But the making of the murderer is more complicated than the interaction of these three factors. Having examined hundreds of people who have killed (and I exclude murders committed by organized crime), I have found that homicide usually does not originate because of a clearly defined impulse to murder, but is released by the intensity of inner conflicts. To presume that murderous acts happen chiefly because of the person's homicidal aggressions and death wishes would be to make practically everyone a killer. In examining those who have committed murder, I have found one common characteristic. Although it was very often not easily apparent on the surface, all the murderers were intensely tormented. Deep down, they felt beset, trapped in an intense conflict growing out of the struggle between their sexual and self-preserving feelings on the one hand and their external surroundings on the other. Specifically they were caught up in a *persistent internal conflict* between the environment around them and the world within them—the world of infantile sexual and life-preserving drives. It is these inner drives which shape the aggressive thrust that in a certain situation may trigger murderous impulses resulting in violent acting out to the point of murder.

The conflict I refer to is due to serious traumatic situations, primarily experienced in earliest childhood, before the child is one or two years old. When as children we feel hurt by people's rejection or criticism, we either give vent to it or push away from our mind our real resentment or dislike until we "forget" about them. They become unconscious. When we continue to repress and it becomes a pattern of behavior, without finding any outward expression or release, these hateful emotions accumulate within us. If we are unable to curb these hostile feelings, our ego-protective defenses crumble and murderous acting-out impulses emerge.

Unfortunately, the person afflicted in this way often is not aware of this pattern of repression which has been built up since childhood. Any emotional conflict tends to make him overreact to frustrations which he cannot contain. When subjected to excessive pressure or torment he becomes angry, helpless, revengeful, impulsive.

As a matter of fact, these people who become most violent, or who murder, are those who have difficulty in dealing with their anger or are simply not able to deal with it. Since anger is not socially accepted, they will repress it and become anxious, and this anxiety at times can be more disruptive than the anger. Anyone, if he is *too* fearful and anxious, may violently act out his anger when he is particularly threatened. While human beings like to remember pleasant matters, they are perhaps to a higher degree prone to recall traumatic incidents—when they were deprived, anxious, felt threatened, or were angry. Such memories stay with them throughout their lifetime and influence what they conceive as threats. They may, therefore, when faced with certain people or situations, be predisposed to anxiety and anger that, when frustrated in its expression, may lead them to homicide. When they act out this frustrated anger, they are, as is now quite well known, unconscious of the real motivation underlying their behavior. People do not seem to realize that homicide is—like so many of our other actions—usually brought about by unconscious motivations anchored to some often unremembered emotion strongly experienced in childhood, most often sexual in nature. As a matter of fact, sexual elements are always involved in the violent act.

The most extraordinary case of murder being a substitute for genuine sexual gratification was that of a young man who in the course of a few weeks shot seven people to death. Most of these crimes occurred on his way to or from his mother's house. On the surface his murders looked like robberies, but money was not the real motivation. He had failed in his marriage and felt rejected by his mother. She considered him a little boy, but he vowed that he would show her that he had power, virility. Unaware of the unresolved conflict with his mother, he had a deep yearning for her, and an even deeper desire to rob her. He expressed his long repressed sexual desires in a pattern of robberies in which he discharged a gun—a symbolic substitute for ejaculation—at his victims. By victimizing several strangers he indirectly victimized his mother. The jury found him guilty of murder first degree, and the judge sentenced him to death. Nobody in court understood the underlying crisscrossing unconscious elements responsible for his murders. The functioning of his ego was disrupted. He killed without being aware of the underlying motivation.

As one who experienced an unsolvable conflict (the *ego-disharmonious* type) between his ego and superego (conscience), he was unable to control his death wishes. This psychological limitation led to an altered state of consciousness, a *dissociative reaction*. By this we mean that his ego and superego were split off from the rest of his personality. Consequently he was unable to control his aggressions or feelings of hostility. Lacking the capacity to satisfy his aggressive needs consistently, he could only react in an explosive and violent fashion. The result was murder repeated seven times.

Important to mention is the altered state of consciousness due to alcohol. Alcohol, as a matter of fact, may be more of an influencing element in causing murder than a psychological dissociative reaction.

A second form of homicide is the *psychotic murder*, characterized by a complete break with reality. A third form, the *ego-*

harmonious type, is carried out without much or any disruption in the functioning of the ego; the killing is rational and consciously acceptable to the perpetrator.

Many of these people have lived in a subculture where direct hostile aggression and violence have become the order of the day. Dr. Emanuel Tanay (in a paper, "Psychiatric Aspects of Homicide Prevention," *American Journal of Psychiatry* 128 [January 1972]: 815–18) has suggested three different types of murderers: the ego-syntone, ego-dystone and psychotic types.

Obviously murder displays itself in many forms. Some murders are committed on the spur of the moment with strong, largely unconscious emotional involvement. Others can be and are thought of, planned for and prepared, as is the case with a cunning killer or with organized crime. Such homicides—with which the law has been chiefly concerned—take place by and large without any emotional implication. Yet the majority of homicides are committed by people of the ego-disharmonious type.

The law's relative indifference to this most prevalent type of murderer can be in part attributed to profound ignorance of his psychological makeup. Not only have lawmakers shown great resistance to understanding the murderer's attitude, but they have also shied away from trying to figure out the murdering mind. The mind of the murderer is complex, but the law has tended to minimize its complexity by asserting that the overwhelming majority of murders were committed by people without personality conflict—the ego-harmonious type—which is directly contrary to the facts.

While these emotional conflicts are found in people suffering from a deep-seated mental disease, they are predominant in many murderers and/or in other criminals. It is by the enlarged constellation and marked intensity of certain of these features, such as revenge, search for power, a lack of self-esteem, and fears that we may distinguish the murderer and the potentially disturbed person. When we study the experiences many murderers have met with, we find a great deal of sexually overstimulating incidents. For instance, they may have observed sexual intimacies between their parents which have been instrumental in the development of deep-seated psychosexual disturbances, a symptom of which is frequently passivity. In trying to fight off their passivity, they try to defend themselves against the resultant feelings of helplessness by hostile acting out.

Interestingly, we often find in murderers a visual hypersensitivity and defects in speech and spelling, developed in early childhood,[1] which come as a result of a disturbed thought process.

Since the ego of the murderer is weak, he has few emotional interests, and is preoccupied and withdrawn from the outside world. This withdrawal into himself, which is found in depressed people as well as criminals, mobilizes feelings of vengefulness. Being unable to forget the hurt he has once suffered, he begins to fantasize about taking revenge, and singles out either his father or a father substitute in the Oedipal situation; or, making murder more of a mystery, he selects his mother. This extreme form of vengefulness we most often find in the murderer who is capable of killing more than one person.

The prime marks of the murderer are a sense of helplessness, impotence and nagging revenge carried over from early childhood. Intertwined with this core of emotions which color and distort his view of life and all his actions are his irrational hatred for others, his suspiciousness and his hypersensitivity to injustices or rejection. Hand in hand with these go his self-centeredness and his inability to withstand frustration. Overpowered by frequent uncontrollable emotional outbursts, he has a need to retaliate, to destroy, to tear down by killing.

We recognize these symptoms more readily in the person who kills his beloved in a fit of passion. Being in love, which, as Freud put it, "at times takes the form of a mild psychosis," he is unable to tolerate his intensely jealous and tortured feelings of being rejected. He must retaliate immediately through acting out to the point of murder in order to satisfy his ungratified love feelings.

We find these passions of love particularly in adolescents or in people who are emotionally immature. Being preoccupied, idealistic and selfless, they go more than out of their way to accommodate their beloved, even to the point of self-sacrifice. While such

1. Phyllis Greenacre, *Trauma, Growth and Personality* (New York: Norton, 1952), p. 227.

passionate feelings in an adult person may well reflect his emotional immaturity, they may also be present, but to a lesser degree, in so-called well-adjusted people.

The jilted lover, overcome by his passions toward his loved one and feeling rejected by her, has three courses open. He may kill the girl, commit suicide, or try to overcome his suffering by the avoidance of self-pity. The outcome will to a large extent depend upon his age. The older man is apt to kill his rival, compared to whom he feels sexually inadequate, while the younger man will kill the girl. If he doesn't kill her, he may kill himself. Such suicidal wishes, though, may take on a passive form characterized by withdrawal from all activities, preoccupation with the memory of his loved one, indulgence in self-pity and the feeling that the world has come to an end. He remembers the places they used to visit together, their private jokes, and when he hears "their" song he experiences a profound feeling of loss. Ideas of revenge may race through his brain and fantasies of becoming a hero take shape in his longing mind, and for a while he almost feels better; then, brutally, everything seems hopeless again. Unable to bear the intensity of his tortured feelings, he finally succumbs to his suicidal or murderous emotions and must discharge them immediately.

These same feelings, twisted and tortured, although much more disguised, are operative in murderers who seem more self-centered, more withdrawn and calculating. When these people are unable to inhibit their hateful emotions, their ego defenses are disrupted so that murderous acting-out impulses appear. By repressing any awareness of their intolerable reality situation, they avoid experiencing what they would otherwise feel. The level of danger is reached when no more outlets exist for their violent aggressions. If they do not find any gratification, their emotions will burst through, leading to murder.

To explain a murder theoretically seems to be easy. But when it comes to trial, it is more involved. First, the court does not necessarily require the presence of motivation in order to obtain a conviction. Secondly, in itself the homicide may remain a mystery, not only because of the many unconscious emotions that go into its making. Murder is a mystery also because death is beyond the experience of any living person. Trying to fathom death, we fear it (though many wish for it), but we cannot experience death as an ultimate. We are attracted to it, as an unknown, we yearn to seek it out—to discover what is in this twilight of shadow and mist. But at the same time, frightened by it, we want to push it out of our minds. Whether unafraid of or frightened by death, we still are curious about it. But death, despite our most ingenious efforts, guards its secret, and this secret is in part the reason for our fascination with murder.

Murder fascinates and intrigues most of us, as is clearly reflected in our persistent interest in the murder story. The many killings reported in the papers, usually on the first page, hardly satisfy the large number of people who in their fantasy again and again wish to reenact murder. We read murder mysteries as an acknowledged and respected form of relaxation. We try to discover the murderer and his motivation and, becoming engrossed, experience an almost sexual excitement, which mounts and sinks in our mind. The curiosity many people exhibit when they try to solve a mystery story is similar to the child's curiosity about the secret, forbidden things that happen behind the closed door of his parents' bedroom. Wanting to intrude upon the mystery of sex between his parents—although this is not true of every child—he conceives their sexual intimacy as a violent fight between his father and mother in which the man injures the helpless woman and makes her suffer. In the mind of the child his mother is hurt, and he even imagines that she may be killed. To him sex is like violence, sexual intercourse like a bloody crime. It is forbidden to watch, but its secrecy stimulates his curiosity. And so the child's fascination with the sexual mystery becomes that of the adult with the murder mystery, and his captivation stems in part from the reactivation of his forgotten childhood fantasies about defloration, bloody and violent sexual intercourse, pregnancy and birth, life and death.

Our fascination with murder is also rooted in our conscious or unconscious hateful and murderous wishes. While its evil repels us, it attracts us irresistibly. To a great many people murder is daring and shocking because the killer has violently transgressed the age-old moral boundaries of society. But at the same time, many a law-abiding citizen, secretly attracted to evil, would like to transgress these boundaries himself if only he dared.

For the vast majority, for those who at times have felt angry enough to kill, the deed is hatched only in fantasies, in wishes or dreams. What remains from these fantasies is a *secret* admiration for the murderer, who has dared to do what the average individual himself cannot, will not do in actuality. Harboring this hidden fascination for the murderer, he cannot help but feel sympathy—which leads him to condone and forgive the murderer. At the same time, because he must push away his own unconscious murderous and destructive impulses, he *publicly* denounces him, and requests that in keeping with the biblical proverb "an eye for an eye, and a tooth for a tooth," the murderer be sent to the gallows, the gas chamber, the electric chair, or the firing squad. He is unaware that his guilt feelings about his own murderous wishes have played a trick on him. In denouncing the killer he repudiates his own homicidal desires and his guilt so that he now can join righteously the outcries of his fellow citizens in condemning the murderer to his fate.

Murder, then, mobilizes in us a web of unconscious contradictory emotions. While the murderer and his victim are the protagonists, the public gets into the act with unashamed excitement. Behind this excitement is the conscious or unconscious death wish which the person tries to counteract by becoming righteous, smug or hypocritical. The death wish, rooted in the death instinct, which extends from unconsciously harming someone to causing his ultimate death, varies in strength. But it is at times so strong that I can venture the idea that if everyone carried out his death wishes, there would be no human beings left alive.

The death wish is originally directed against the person's own self, but the murderer, afraid of killing himself, kills somebody else. The hateful and murderous impulses play havoc in a man or woman in periods of emotional torture and unhappiness. The homicidal and suicidal impulses become intertwined. Every homicide, we can say, is unconsciously a suicide, and every suicide in a sense is a psychological homicide. Both acts are caused by the perpetrator's sudden and acute loss of self-esteem. The man who kills oscillates between suicide and homicide because he is afraid of people, afraid of himself and afraid of dying. He is unconsciously trying to rid himself of the fear of his own death.

A case markedly illustrating this point was that of a nineteen-year-old youth who shot his father to death. The boy had been raised in a family in which there was much quarreling and violent fighting, and where daily beatings and neglect were the norm. He grew up in turmoil. He had temper tantrums, was a bedwetter, did poorly in school despite his high intelligence. He falsified his school records and was withdrawn, angry and defiant. For a short while he received psychiatric treatment. The relationship between him and his parents remained hateful and explosive. After being hit by his father one night, the youth took a shotgun and killed him. But behind this dramatic act was a fear of people and a *fear of himself*. Even if he was aware of the fear, brought on by his father's long-time abuse, a trait prominent in the battered-child syndrome, he was not cognizant that he feared for his own life. *He* was holding the gun when he walked into his father's bedroom, yet he was afraid for *his own life*.

Some people may think it strange for a nineteen-year-old boy to be concerned about death. But this is just the age when suicidal thoughts reach one of their peaks. Among adolescents in America, suicide is the third highest cause of death. This parricide, like many confused youngsters, feared the wild impulses in the dark regions of his mind—as well as his death. In killing his father he unconsciously was trying to rid himself of the fear of his own death. He killed because, in part, he was afraid of dying.

This is a significant point. Deep down in us we somehow have the feeling that by murdering another human being we try unwittingly to rid ourselves of the fear of death which is always at our heels. As long as human beings consciously or unconsciously have the fear of dying, they will go on killing.

One particular aspect of murder is political assassination, which especially since 1963, along with the dramatic outgrowth of our national violence, has become part of American life. While it would be outside the scope of this book to find out to what extent the political assassinations of the past ten years have changed the course of our history, in our context it is essential to discern what kind of people political assassins are, and if they differ in any way from the run-of-the-mill murderer.

In my study at the United States District Court, Southern District of New York, New York City, based upon psychiatric-psychological examinations of people charged with or suspected of having threatened to kill the president of the United States or other government officials, of people suspected of being capable of such a violent act, and of people who actually have committed such murders, common personality traits were found. Eleven defendants charged with threatening the president or other government officials (of whom I examined eight and studied the records of two others), Lee Harvey Oswald, James Earl Ray, Sirhan Bishara Sirhan and Arthur Herman Bremer—who was convicted for the shooting of Governor George C. Wallace—all showed surprising similarities in their family background, their personality makeup and their pattern of behavior. This was also the case with the killers of Presidents Lincoln, Garfield and McKinley, particularly John Wilkes Booth, who shot Lincoln to death.

The actual or would-be assassins displayed intense and recurrent fantasies of revenge and omnipotence which stimulated their violent impulses into action. Highly characteristic was their personal failure, another expression of the loss of self-esteem so prevalent in murderers. Also predominant was acute self-hate, leading to suicidal ideas, feelings of isolation and, in the case of actual assassins, the belief that they had to fight the whole world. All of the real or would-be assassins grew up in a family where there was poverty, hostility, quarreling and fights; absent, unassuming or neglectful fathers, and domineering mothers.

In general, the political assassin in American history has been a loner, an isolated person incapable of exhibiting genuine humane relationships. He has had unusual ambitions out of proportion to his intellectual and emotional capabilities. Underlying this discrepancy has been his inflated opinion of himself, revealing feelings of omnipotence and the love of demonstrating power.

There was a remarkable similarity in the family constellations of the real and would-be assassins in that none of them had a stable, manly figure with whom to identify. They identified with their mothers. Such a feminine identification was also in part augmented by the mothers, who openly conveyed to their sons angry and revengeful threats against the husbands who had neglected or deserted them. Having a father who had been neglectful, had left home, or had died, the actual and would-be assassins felt they had to "protect" their mother and at the same time ward off their own sexual feelings toward her. The mother was forbidden—and forbidding—territory. But being unable to overcome their sexual yearnings for her and unable to accept their own sexual aggressions, they had to find an outlet. This need was to no small extent stimulated by their idea that they had to "protect" their mother. Such a fancied protection made them feel important and strong, and filled their childhood with fantasies of omnipotence. Engrossed and obsessed with this type of power fantasy, they came to believe that their omnipotence made them more powerful than anyone else, that through some act they could change the world. Their threats and attacks against officials of the United States government or important political figures were justified in their fantasies; it was a reflection of their feelings of omnipotence.

The distorted identification appeared early in the life of many of the would-be and real assassins. Common signs of serious derangement were loneliness, intense hate, helplessness, dependency, omnipotence, fears, frustrations and murderous death wishes. In particular, the absence of a father in the boy's life was devastating to his emotional well-being. John Wilkes Booth's father took two sons with him and left John at an early age on a Maryland farm with his mother. Since the son was alienated both physically and emotionally from his father, he became close to his mother and she exerted an overwhelming influence upon his early development. Undoubtedly there existed a symbiotic relationship between the mentally deranged mother and John, to whom she transmitted many of her own distorted ideas and fantasies. Being deprived of a father and unable to find a suitable male figure with whom he could identify, the son developed a distorted identification which weakened his feelings of masculinity and made him vulnerable to any threats against his virility and manliness. As a defense he had to outdo his father and his successful older brothers. His killing of President Lincoln, whom he hated, was a displacement of his hate for his father and his brother Edwin, which was rooted in his early childhood. Displacement is a clinical phenomenon we often observe in acts directed against one particular person but unconsciously aimed at someone else.

Lee Harvey Oswald's father died before Lee was born, and the boy was raised by an overprotective, domineering mother who kept him close to her heart. The fathers of Ray and Sirhan struck or beat their sons, and both later left their families to fend for themselves. In the case of Bremer, the father was reported to have been drinking frequently, with resultant arguments and fights in the home. The mother, the doctors reported, was a disorganized person, probably mentally ill, who at times refused to cook meals for her family and locked her husband out of the home. All these cases reveal the absence of a constructive male person with whom these assassins could identify during their childhood, a lack that resulted in a twisted identification and produced in them a lessening of their sense of masculinity to the point that they were unable to defend themselves when they felt threatened by an attack against their manliness.

Unsatisfactory relationships with women, a concomitant of their inadequate masculine identification, were common to Oswald, Ray, Sirhan and Bremer. Oswald's wife, Marina Nicholaevna, openly accused him of being impotent, for which reason she had left him two months before he allegedly killed President Kennedy on November 22, 1963. Her accusation may very well have been an important factor in the assassination of the President. He would show his wife once and for all that he indeed was powerful. In the past he had attempted to prove that he was no weakling by treating both his wife and his children in a brutal manner, crudely striking her on a number of occasions. He frequently left home, returning when impelled by the pressure of his compulsive drives. Although unable to provide his family with the barest necessities because of difficulty in finding and holding jobs, he was nevertheless extravagant when it came to satisfying his own needs. He had his notes on the Soviet Union typed professionally, had circulars printed for his activities in the Committee on Fair Play for Cuba, and bought himself a rifle.[2]

Ray, who killed the Reverend Martin Luther King, Jr., and Sirhan, who killed Senator Robert F. Kennedy, apparently never had a girl friend, and Bremer's relationship with the one girl he was known to date was quite tenuous. At Bremer's trial in August 1972 it was stated that he was a virgin. Such a faulty relationship was natural to a youth who had been unable to develop a firm and constant male identity.

The assassins' distorted relationships with women had serious repercussions for their relations with people in general. They had few if any close friends. They were, as mentioned before—and this applies to the eleven defendants I examined personally—loners. They were fearful and felt threatened, which made it difficult if not impossible for them to trust anyone. It has long been recognized that a child who cannot trust his parents rarely trusts other people.

Other traits common to the people in my study included antisocial or criminal records and histories of mental disturbance. They all had performed poorly in school and had frequent absences.

Their inability to distinguish between reality situations and their own fantasies was striking. Following the killing of President Lincoln, John Wilkes Booth thought he would be considered a hero. On the night before he shot Lincoln at Ford's Theater, he went into Taltavel's Tavern for a drink. He was accosted by an intoxicated man who told him, "You'll never be the actor your father was." Booth easily replied, "When I leave the stage, I will be the most famous man in America."[3]

And Leon Czolgosz, who shot President McKinley to death on

2. David Abrahamsen, "A Study of Lee Harvey Oswald: Psychological Capability of Murder," *Bulletin of the New York Academy of Medicine, Second Series,* vol. 43, no. 10 (October 1967), pp. 861–88.

3. David Abrahamsen, *Our Violent Society* (New York: Funk & Wagnalls, 1970), p. 177. Quote taken from Philip Weissman, "Why Booth Killed Lincoln: A Psychoanalytic Study of a Historical Tragedy," in *Psychoanalysis and the Social Sciences*, vol. 5, edited by Warner Muensterberger and Sidney Axelrod (New York: International Universities Press, 1958).

September 6, 1901, complained bitterly about the way he was treated after he had shot the president:

"After I shot twice they knocked me down and trampled on me. Somebody hit me in the face."[4]

Oswald, who had expected to be welcomed as a hero when he secretly went off to the Soviet Union, was shattered when he discovered that the Russians were not very keen on having him in their country. He did not consider himself a Marxist, but rather a Marxist philosopher.

Sirhan dreamed of becoming a diplomat, but he didn't have the ability to complete college, so he decided to become a famous jockey, found himself an exercise boy and suffered an apparent concussion of the brain after being thrown from a horse. That was the end of that dream.

After being in and out of prisons for some time, Ray developed a fancy for the law. He became a "prison lawyer," writing briefs, but when it came to preparing his own case, he handled it in a self-damaging manner and lost.

A study of Bremer's diary indicates that he fantasized about becoming a great photographer or writer, though he was able to get jobs only as a janitor or a busboy.

One prominent difference between the real and would-be political assassins and murderers in general was that the former were more concerned about society and world events than the latter, although there may be some overlapping in these tendencies. Most of the assassins and would-be assassins were strongly interested in the government. They read and studied newspapers, magazines and books, and perceived the world as a place of chaos and ugliness. They saw the world around them as ugly because their own inner world was ugly, but this they were unable to conceive, as it was unconscious. That the world was being threatened by political subversion was a reflection of their feeling that they themselves were being threatened. They therefore could rationalize their violent deed, give some political or moral reason for it, as was the case with Czolgosz and Booth. Those who threaten government offi-

4. L. Vernon Briggs, *The Manner of Man That Kills: Spencer-Czolgosz-Richeson* (Boston: Gorham Press, 1921), p. 243.

cials in a way issue a cry for help. Unconsciously they want the government to take care of them, help them out of their misery, support them, meet their dependency needs.

One may ask why the would-be and real assassin shows a predominant concern for the world around him, in contrast to the murderer who directs his deed against the individual. The answer lies in the amount of repressive hostile fantasies and dreams which in the case of the assassin have lost all ego (personality) boundaries and have engulfed the world. This boundless repression of revenge fantasies brings about hatred of the world, which he has to destroy in order to create his own world in his own image. Supported by his regressive fantasies of carrying out grandiose deeds, he strikes out even if it means murder.

It is possible that these fantasies cause political assassins unconsciously to select as victim one who has achieved what they themselves would have wished, but which they could never hope to achieve. Oswald, for instance, who was a Marxist and who once dreamed of becoming premier of Cuba, killed a freedom-loving president who was the leader of a powerful country. When Bremer shot Governor Wallace, it may have been because he wanted to be like the governor but was incapable of it. It was discovered that he also had been following President Nixon and Senator Humphrey around the country on their campaign tours. These two men are powerful figures with whom Bremer could identify but like whom he could never hope to be.

In an ambivalent way the would-be or real assassin identifies with the powerful public figure while simultaneously hating him in order to protect himself against the anxiety that would be stimulated if he formed a constructive attitude toward the government. If he thought positively about the government, he would have to think about himself in a negative way, would have to admit that there might be something wrong with him. He hates the head of the government because the leader not only fails to give the assassin hope, but also releases hatred in him. He acts out his murder of the governmental leader by disguising his childhood hate of his father under a political or social mask.

This may be one reason why the political assassin carries out his crime so desperately, without thinking much of the consequences to himself. Although the same desperate feelings may be and often are present in nonpolitical homicides, the assassin's murder is at once frenzied and singularly goal-directed. It is as if he has nothing to lose, as if nothing more matters. Everything is placed on one card. Overwhelmed by his hate, he is in for the kill. As a patient said to me some time ago, "I must have a killing hatred in me."

This desperate quality in carrying out his frantic act can to some extent be compared to that of the skyjacker, whose acts jeopardize both his own life and the lives of all the people on the airplane. Such a person, at least unconsciously, not only invites danger and likes it, but loves it, just as many people not only have an impulse to see and enjoy violence vicariously, but love it. For the skyjacker risk and peril are a significant, if not the most significant, part of his life. Often he cannot stop himself. This exposure of himself (and others) to danger is intimately connected with his unconscious wish for misery. Paradoxical as it may sound, some people have to remain miserable in order to feel good. For them it is normal behavior to be constantly in trouble and to feel miserable. They can feel well only when acting out their hateful emotions. Their sadistic inclinations serve as a trigger to threaten and inflict harm and death on others. But at the same time these sadistic tendencies are being turned against themselves and deflected in a masochistic direction.

If one were to examine a skyjacker one might find the masochistic tendency manifested as psychosomatic disorders, a disturbance of bodily functions such as allergy, colitis, migraine headaches, peptic ulcer, hypertension, rheumatoid arthritis, skin diseases, proneness to accidents—all of which frequently are closely related to emotional conflicts, often of an unconscious nature. The salient point is that these psychosomatic conditions have been found to be more prevalent in criminals than in noncriminals, as evidenced in a study I made at Columbia University some twenty-five years ago.[5] Most interesting in this respect was that twice as many offenders as nonoffenders whom we examined were prone to acci-

5. David Abrahamsen, *The Psychology of Crime,* 2d ed. (New York: Columbia University Press, 1967), pp. 91–2.

dents,[6] and this is a significant observation since accident-proneness is to the highest degree rooted in masochistic inclinations. These people appeared most often to be of the blundering type who "happened" to have an accident, or "dared" themselves into experiencing such a mishap, apparently associated with pain and self-destructiveness. The masochistically inclined person does not perceive pain, discomfort and distress as unpleasant and uncomfortable, as would be the case with the average man. Rather, he experiences pain as a pleasure or enjoyment, or feels relieved that he has met with some misfortune which unconsciously he senses he deserves. Deep down he feels he has to be punished due to guilt for some actual misdeed he has committed or for some antisocial or criminal act he has contemplated carrying out.

There is of course no direct causal relationship as such between psychosomatic illness and a criminal act. Psychosomatic disturbances by themselves do not bring about crime. Many people suffer from psychosomatic ailments—migraine headaches, peptic ulcer, asthma—who are not criminals and who probably never will be.

What is important to mention, however, is that psychosomatic conditions are frequently found in those who come from homes where family tension is habitually manifested in the form of violent arguments and rivalry. In other words, hatred and violent acts seem to grow in the same constellation of the family syndrome as do psychosomatic disturbances, sometimes even to the point where these disorders, as evidenced from my research,[7] become a substitute for criminal acts.

An accident-prone man exposing himself to danger does not venture again and again into disaster because of ignorance or stupidity. He is motivated by an unconscious need centered around a core of inner pain and self-torture. He tempts fate, takes risks and unwittingly places himself in dangerous situations in order to punish himself. The skyjacker and the assassin utilize the same psychological mechanism. Those who invite danger like to see how far they can go without seriously harming themselves.

---

6. *Ibid.,* p. 94
7. *Ibid.,* p. 95. See also David Abrahamsen, "Psychosomatic Disorders and Their Significance in Antisocial Behavior," *Journal of Nervous and Mental Disease,* vol. 107, no. 1 (January 1948), p. 14.

Behind this test is the unconscious wish to find out how much power they can exercise over themselves and others. The mutual ground shared by the assassin, the skyjacker and the murderer in general is their search for power. The assassin experiences power when through a single bullet he can terminate the life of a president and throw an entire nation into chaos. The skyjacker obtains the opportunity to achieve power both by threats of shooting and bombing and by demands for huge amounts of ransom money. He experiences a real thrill of power when he dictates orders to the crew of the huge aircraft to take him wherever he wants to go and to gratify his every demand.

But this does not mean that he is psychotic. To claim that all skyjackers are mentally ill to the point of being psychotic is not true. In order to prove that they are insane, they, or other people who have committed serious crimes, such as murderers, rapists, drug addicts or bank robbers, try to pretend they are psychotic by "producing" symptoms which superficially may appear to be psychotic in nature. Discovering such malingerers may not always be easy, since they may cleverly fool both lawyers and psychiatrists until they are caught in their own web.

Where a person resorts to violence, it is, in the last analysis, to *achieve power*. By obtaining power, he enhances his self-esteem, which fundamentally is rooted in sexual identity. In the murderer, this sense of true identity is inadequate or lacking. Those who have been unable to develop their genuine sexual role will try to compensate for it by asserting themselves in a field in which they have a special talent and in which they can hope to excel. In this way they attempt to regain vicariously what they have been unable to achieve sexually, a process that takes place mostly on the unconscious level. People who have developed a distorted sense of identity are unable to love genuinely, and therefore feel themselves unloved and unwanted. They react explosively to being sexually rejected, for it threatens their whole sense of self. The outcome may very well be murder.

Sexual inadequacy is a major reason for the intensity of the violence in murder. The degree of violent acting out employed in homicide is usually far greater than is needed to kill the victim, particularly because of revenge. The sexual component reinforces the often overwhelming feelings of revenge in the murderer. This sexual element may also explain the volatile contagiousness of violence and murder in our country in the past decade.

The extraordinary amount of frustration we find in murderers may be baffling at first glance. When checked against the reality of their situation, however, their frustrations are not always rooted in fact. The point is that these frustrations, even if fancied, are nevertheless real to the killer. Notwithstanding his low self-esteem, the murderer often sees himself as someone too good to be frustrated. Unable to tolerate his frustration, he must act out his hate to show his power.

There is an interesting correlation between the need to commit violence and speech or spelling errors. I made this discovery some thirty years ago in Norway during a psychiatric exploration of persons charged with violent crimes including homicide. In checking these criminals' schoolwork, it was baffling to notice that their records, except for spelling, had been in several instances highly satisfactory. At that time I did not fully understand the meaning of this finding, but as I examined more and more cases, the misspelling, although not present in all violent criminals, occurred quite frequently, not only in adults but in juvenile delinquents who were given to violent acts.

I remember well how much discussion my findings caused when I testified before the Presidential Commission on Violence, in particular because I suggested that this tendency to misspell could be used within certain limits as an early diagnostic and preventive sign in youngsters who later on might become violent.

It was interesting to note the frequent misspellings found in the diary of Bremer. However, the most striking case I have examined was that of Lee Harvey Oswald, in whose "Historic Diary," letters and notes I found a number of spelling errors. Following are some examples:

EXAMPLES OF SPELLING ERRORS
IN LEE HARVEY OSWALD'S WRITINGS

complusery	compulsory
kicten	kitchen

yonuge	young
exalant	excellent
tehniction	technician
sptacular	spectacular
divocied	divorced
oppossition	opposition
enviorments	environments
permonet	permanent
admiriers	admirers
habituatated	habituated
quiality	quality
patrioct	patriotic

This misspelling expresses what we call onomatopoiesis—the making of a word or a name from a sound. In these cases the person uses his imagination and spells a word as his fantasy directs him because he wishes the word to be written *his own* way. These people who make spelling errors are not really anxious to communicate. Rather their verbal communication is a means of exhibiting themselves, as in the case of Oswald and other murderers I have seen.

The spelling errors are measurable symptoms which can, if confirmed in large-scale research data, be used as a means of detecting the potentially violent or murderous person. Where in addition we find habitual truancy and other early symptoms, as mentioned before, we must be on the alert for latent violence.

These symptoms also serve as forerunners to the act of murder. In the same way that most illnesses have an introductory —incubation—period of symptoms before their real onset, so there are signs present in the killer before the actual murder.

In the case of measles, for instance, before the appearance of the rash on the face and body there is an incubation period of seven to fourteen days during which the patient complains of fever, cough and conjunctivitis. As for the murderer, many emotional symptoms can be detected prior to his act, sometimes indicating a serious mental condition.

Predominant Characteristics of the Murderer

1. Extreme feelings of revenge and fantasies of grandiose accomplishments which may result in the acting out of hateful impulses.

2. Loneliness, withdrawal, feelings of distrust, helplessness, fears, insignificance, loss of self-esteem, caused by early (pre-Oedipal) childhood experiences.

3. Sexually overstimulating family situation because of primal-scene experiences.

4. Errors of spelling or speech related to emotional disturbances in early (pre-Oedipal) childhood.

5. Tendency toward transforming identification. Blurred self-image; suggestible, impressionable.

6. Inability to withstand frustration and to find sufficient gratification for expressing hostile aggressive feelings through constructive outlets.

7. Inability to change persistent egocentricity, self-centeredness (primitive narcissism) into elements of healthy ideals and conscience (ego ideals and superego elements), resulting in dependency on and contempt for authority.

8. Suicidal tendencies, with depression.

9. Seeing the victim as the composite picture of murderer's self-image.

10. History of previous antisocial or criminal act associated with threatening or committing murder.

It must be emphasized that all the signs listed are also indications of emotional disturbances which may not necessarily result in murder. Psychiatrists are often asked why one person kills while his brother, who apparently had the same family background, grew up in a normal way, married and lived a useful life.

The reason for this difference lies in environmental and constitutional factors. These factors, in particular the environmental ones, are exposed to family or situational pressure which will differ from time to time, depending upon the parents' relationship in the home, and their feelings and attitudes toward their children. There are no two children who have exactly the same upbringing, because the parents unconsciously react differently to them in spite of their most honest efforts to be equally fair to each child. Given an emotional climate in a home which fluctuates in accordance with the pressures placed on the parents, we will encounter children in the same family who will display symptoms and behavior patterns so different that we find it hard to believe that they have the same father and mother.

The most telling example is Lee Harvey Oswald, who had two older brothers (one of them a half-brother), both of whom grew up to live normal lives. Both were gainfully employed, married and raised a family. At the hearings of the National Commission on the Causes and Prevention of Violence, I was asked why Robert Oswald was well adjusted, a great help to the commission; why he not only displayed a splendid character but also excellent judgment. He held a very responsible position in a large concern, and his employers gave him the finest commendation—all this in contrast to Lee Harvey Oswald's disorganized personality and criminal behavior.

Apparently here were two brothers growing up in exactly the same environment. But in actuality they did not grow up in the same environment, for both Robert Oswald and John Pick lived with a father while Lee did not. Furthermore, even though Lee and Robert had the same mother, her difficulties were intensified after she became a widow, in that she had to take care of the baby, Lee, without the financial and emotional support of a husband.

Whether or not a person may become neurotic or psychotic, or have psychosomatic symptoms without acting out his murderous impulses, or become a murderer will in the final analysis depend upon his being relatively free of emotional conflicts, or upon his ability to master emotional conflict. We erroneously have been led to believe that the triggering situation leading to murder must be provocative. Not so. Equal in importance to the precipitating situation—perhaps even more important—is that the hate which has been accumulating gradually over a long period of time becomes a fixed conflict within the mind of the murderer. When because of fear he is unable to establish an emotional relationship in general and a sexual relationship in particular, the aggressive element in his love turns into hate with the result that his love itself turns into hate, which leads him to homicide.

No one is a murderer at birth; the tendency develops within an individual and some people are driven to commit the deed. This is particularly true when the murderer is provoked by the victim. Most of us are fortunate enough not to seek out emotional relationships that evoke the intensity of emotional frustrations which release the impulsive act of murder. But some people do, and if that happens a torment of emotions, conscious and unconscious, latent and manifest, are let loose between aggressor and victim. Usually we do not know what really took place between them. As a matter of fact, while we know little about the murderer, we know even less about the victim. Because of our lack of knowledge about the relationship between attacker and victim, it cannot be brought out in open court; even if such knowledge were available, there are many aspects of a murder which practically never become known to the public. Often a murder is classified as an open and shut case —as is illustrated vividly in the murder I would like to describe now.

"An open and shut case"—that was the consensus. The twenty-three-year-old man had been charged with murder first degree in the death of a forty-three-year-old woman. Both the district attorney and the defense lawyer had stated their case, and the judge had summarized the case for the jury, which by now had retired for its deliberation. After one hour, the jury returned its verdict: Guilty as charged. One month later the judge sentenced the young man to life imprisonment.

I was involved in this case as a psychiatrist, and I suspected that the facts of the case were not as clear-cut as one might suppose at first. Underlying, crisscrossing, unconscious elements are to a large extent responsible for the murderous act. The case was truly clear only to those who had the means to see, to scrutinize, to ponder the many buried and tangled emotions which exist in every homicide.

What had the court, the jury, members of the press and the public chosen to accept as the indicting factors in the case? The young man had picked up a woman twice his age in a bar, and after several drinks there they had gone to her apartment, where they had more drinks. They made love. Once this physical relationship was established—it lasted about six months—he exploited her financially, and then, not knowing how to get rid of her, he murdered her.

Newspapers and magazines most often describe such murders in rather superficial and oversimplified terms with little or no attempt to explain the complex feelings involved. And these accounts become still more confusing when important factual knowledge is lacking or distorted, as I suspected was true in this case.

To understand murder, we must ask a basic question: What is the real motive? To find the answer, we must probe beyond the obvious facts so often cited by the district attorney in the courtroom. What were the unconscious needs and fears of both the murderer and his victim?

Let us return to the original case. In my interviews with the accused I learned that the woman had picked *him* up in the bar, that she had paid for the drinks and had invited him to her expensively furnished apartment. Although much older, she was still good-looking, and they were attracted to each other. She told him that whenever he needed money she would give it to him. After about six months she asked him to go to Florida with her, all expenses paid.

"This was the beginning of the end," he told me. "She was trying to buy me. The idea of being seen in her company—she was twice my age—especially of running into someone I knew, embarrassed me."

"What did you do then?" I asked.

"I told her no. She got angry and said I was ungrateful. She had done so much for me, and I had given her nothing in return. I was selfish—a taker. That really got me. I threw my drink in her face and ran to the door. What did she mean, I gave her nothing in return? I was young and strong and I was her lover. She ran after me, begging me to stay. She wept and carried on. I felt sorry for her, so I did stay. I'm not sure what happened after that. I was sleepy, drunk. We went to bed and made love. But then she started in again about Florida, nagging me. She wanted to show me off. I couldn't take it. I was scared and mixed up. They say I strangled her, but I don't remember what happened."

The case intrigued me. I found myself asking more and more questions about the woman and her role in the murder. Was she the innocent victim of a violent act, or did she provoke it? The relationship between the murderer and the victim had to be examined.

From various sources I had been able to construct a fair impression of the life of the murdered woman. Since her divorce several years before, she had lived handsomely on her alimony. It was known in the neighborhood that she frequented bars where she met men considered to be rather unsavory characters. On one occasion the police had been summoned to her apartment to restore order.

In the words of the defendant, "She was very sexy. She could never get enough of it—a real 'man-eater.' " Before her marriage she had been a singer. Since then she had held various publicity jobs, although she didn't have to work for a living. I asked the accused if he was after money. He denied it. "But you didn't earn anything," I interrupted, "you lived on her money." He said that he was out for a good time. She was alone and needed somebody.

Her only relative was a great-uncle, who could not give much information about her except that she had often been in trouble —minor accidents. This last point interested me, for it suggested that she was accident-prone. I suspected she was the type of person who unconsciously exposed herself to danger. I began to feel that the victim unwittingly inflicted pain on herself—a definite sign of masochism.

As I pursued my investigation, I started to gain a deeper insight into the psychology of this victim. She was lonely and feared losing her attractiveness as a woman. She craved attention and affection, which for the time being she received from her lover— the man who later murdered her. She must have known that she could not hold him forever; he was twenty years younger. Why did she get involved with him in the first place? Didn't she realize that she was using him, and that, in a more obvious way, he was using her?

The answer, in part, lies within the murderer. He was extraordinarily handsome, with blond hair, blue eyes, classic features. His boyish demeanor and strong physique must have struck a responsive chord in the much older woman, who not only wanted to give affection but herself was in desperate need of it.

The young man was an only child who had lived in a home where his father worked at night and slept all day. As a boy he had hardly known his father. His mother, a compulsive cleaner ("she always had a rag in her hand"), preferred to have her son out of the house so that she could keep it spotless and in perfect order. She had few, if any, tender feelings for her son. Most of the time he felt lonely and unwanted. Inwardly he preferred to be with her rather than to play with the boys on the street. "Mother fucker," they called him behind his back. They thought he was a sissy. When he finished school he was unable to find work, and his mother tried to divert him by taking him to the movies. He felt that she was always putting him down, treating him like a child. One day, "all hell broke loose," and in a fit of anger he left home and moved in with the woman he had met in the bar—the woman who was later his victim. She indulged him, always paying his way. Now he had no money worries. She was like a mother and catered to his every whim. "If she was willing to pay for everything, why should I care? It was a real ball for me."

Aggressively self-seeking and self-serving, he became angry and defensive when I tried to question his motive in "using" people. His erratic behavior, a reflection of a neurotic character disorder, convinced him that by cultivating his good looks he could get whatever he wanted. This strategy of using his charm to "con" his victim was complemented by her need to be flirtatious and seductive toward him, which appealed to his weak ego. Unwittingly exposing herself to a dangerous situation, she tantalized him, and he responded until the relationship became a serious matter. He needed her as a sexual object and as a mother, and she needed him as a lover and as a possession. She exerted a tremendous seductive influence on him, overwhelmed him, like a devouring mother, in order to keep him bound to her. It was a mutual dependency, an incestuous Oedipal relationship.

His tremendous need for self-gratification likewise bound him in a situation from which his defective ego knew no way out, except murder. He became a victim of circumstances which he himself had in part created, as she was a victim of her own seductive behavior. In a murder based on a relationship fundamentally sexual in nature, there is never a passive victim. In this case, both individuals participated in the *homicidal process* during which the sadomasochistic relationship between the aggressor and the victim increased in intensity until it reached a climax. While he was guilty of killing her, she herself unconsciously played a dominant role in her own death.

Contrary to the verdict—"an open and shut case"—from a psychological perspective the question of guilt was complex. He was sentenced to life imprisonment.

This case happened more than twenty years ago. I was instructed to keep to the "bare facts" in my testimony. Today the understanding and acceptance of psychiatry has gained a foothold, mainly in civil cases but not infrequently in criminal ones.

A relationship that is basically sexual gives a violent act in general, and murder in particular, a special quality which moves the killing from the conscious realm to that of the unconscious.

The relationship between criminal and victim is much more complicated than the law would care to acknowledge. The criminal and his victim work on each other unconsciously. We can say that as the criminal shapes the victim, the victim also shapes the criminal. While the law looks upon this relationship from an objective, nonemotional viewpoint, the psychological attitude of the participants is quite different. The law differentiates distinctly between the attacker and the victim. But their relationship may be, and often is, quite close, so that their roles are reversed and the victim becomes the determining person, while the victimizer in the end becomes his own victim.

The victim turns against his victimizer and kills. I remember the case of a fifty-seven-year-old unmarried woman who killed her ninety-five-year-old mother. When I examined her in the prison ward of the psychiatric hospital, I learned that she had lived with her parents all her life. After her father died she continued to support her aging mother, taking care of her every need in a masochistically sacrificing way. Her own life had been narrowly restricted—she had held the same job for thirty years. Always the same routine, the same habits, the same constant criticism by her mother. While on the surface the daughter gave in to her mother's every whim, deep down she had begun to resent and hate her. Fearful of expressing her anger toward her mother directly, she took it out on her coworkers, being critical and suspicious of their behavior.

Four months before the murder, her mother had broken her hip and become bedridden. The incident strained the daughter's emotions still more. She was expected to show more concern and to give her mother more attention. By now she had begun to hate her mother openly. The daughter was caught in an emotional crisis. Having given in almost all her life to her mother's ceaseless demands, she now became severely depressed because of her inability to stand up to the older woman. She began to think of a way to get out of her miserable life and contemplated suicide. For a short while she sought psychiatric help, felt better and stopped treatment. But then she became more and more depressed about her situation until early one morning, as she watched her sleeping mother, she was overcome by confusion. Using a hammer she had covered with cloth to soften the blows to the skull, she clubbed her mother, who died the next day.

In this case, which happened about eight years ago, the court took all the circumstances of the murder into full consideration. The defendant received a suspended sentence and was put on probation for five years on the condition that she undergo psychiatric treatment. While in treatment she related, among other dreams, a very important one. "I was in a big spiderweb which covered the length of the bed. I must have moved to get out, but I woke up."

In her free association she said, "I think of my mother, the good times we had, of Christmastime, what we would have been doing. . . . I have not gotten rid of Mother, which is not the way things should be. I was caught in a web. I must have felt I was in her web."

This dream was her first realization of being ensnared by a devouring mother and her own flylike insignificance and helplessness. The web covering a bed suggests feelings of being seduced into submission; a need for embryonic protection; a growing awareness of her dependency; and perhaps more important, a knowledge of having been forcibly prevented from having a sexual life of her own.

The fact is, she had remained a virgin and had had no romances because, in her own words, "I never had the time. There was always Mother." Yet the major part of her sessions revolved around remembrances of how good her mother was. This revealed her continued inability to recognize the hostile feelings that had resulted in her reactive overdependence, which eventually led to the murder. While her superego retained only the image of her overwhelmingly demanding mother, in a masochistic way she created another image of a good mother who deserved obedience and love.

After four years of treatment she was better able to understand her motivations for the killing of her mother. In spite of being depressed because of her guilt, she was able to secure for herself a good job which gave her gratification and restored some of the self-esteem she had lost.

Victim and Criminal: A Mutual Tie

Many a young girl without realizing it has wanted to have sex with a particular man, and has seduced him in order to be attacked, thereby becoming a victim of her seduction, in accordance with her unconscious self-destructive desires.

The great number of forcible rape victims reported in 1971— over 41,890 (40 out of every 100,000 women)[8]—would seem to indicate the presence of the woman's seductiveness in rape. Girls' complaints that they have been raped are true sometimes, but more often than not are rooted in their own uncomfortable guilt feelings about having been a willing partner. In order to prove their innocence, they accuse the man of raping them. Sometimes, however, they refuse to press their complaints, in a way condoning, forgiving the rapist, which indirectly attests to their own guilt.

This seductive interplay is also common in young, flirtatious and adventurous girls who are led by their unconscious wish to be taken by force. Not realizing their own motives, they place themselves in a situation in which they can be sexually assaulted. A case I will never forget is that of a young man who, in burglarizing an apartment, had entered the bedroom where a girl was sleeping. After taking her jewelry, he had reached the door when she suddenly awakened and, seeing a man in the shadows,

8. *Crime in the United States,* FBI Uniform Crime Reports, 1971 (Washington, D.C., August 1972), p. 9.

screamed, "Don't rape me, don't rape me." Surprised, the young man turned away from the doorway and attacked her. The jury found him guilty without realizing that the girl herself unconsciously had been an instigating partner in the sexual assault. The judge sentenced him to ten to twenty years in prison.

A case which perhaps even more vividly illustrates the seductive role of a potential victim was that of a young woman in her twenties, who was fortunate enough to avoid being killed. She had deliberately angered her lover by teasing him, and he had forced himself upon her, which she felt was a sexual assault. Feeling disturbed and guilty about the incident, she sought psychiatric help. She admitted she had a "technique" for seducing men. "Leading a man on gives me a feeling of power, and then I reject him. I cut him off. It gives me a feeling of satisfaction. I enjoy being able to seduce. I like to control people. I really don't know who I am, I'm so many different people. It confuses me, but I feel a sense of power when I seduce." Through psychiatric help, this patient gradually began to understand the provocative and highly dangerous situations which her seductive behavior created. Even more difficult for her to comprehend were the emotions underlying her self-destructive behavior. By gaining insight into her own unconscious search for power and conquest, she changed her attitude and was spared being a further victim of violence.

This intimate connection, the causative bond, between murderer and victim in sexual relationships, is more prevalent than we realize. Probing the nature of such an emotional relationship is always time-consuming, but psychiatry is a slow-moving and difficult process because the deeply buried feelings have to be brought to light in order to define the mosaics of emotions that determine an individual's patterns of behavior.

One more reason for the intimate closeness between murderer and victim is the intertwining of our murderous and self-murderous impulses. Since, as mentioned, every homicide is unconsciously a suicide, and every suicide is, in a sense, a psychological homicide, this oscillation between murder and self-murder influences the relationship between the aggressor and the victim. Typically, the killer is afraid of killing himself, afraid of dying, and therefore he murders someone else.

Since the strongest emotions, be they of attraction or of repulsion, are linked to family relationships, we should not be surprised to learn that murder within the family made up 25 percent of the total number of murders in the United States in 1971. The victims were husbands, wives, boy friends and girl friends, parents, children.[9] The main reason for the high murder rate in the family is the close affinity between attacker and victim, basically a sexual attraction. In arguments leading to murder, the wife becomes the victim more often than the husband.[10] It is closer to the truth than we realize that the victim herself unconsciously provokes her husband to murder.

As a matter of fact, our knowledge of victims in crime has been gained mainly through sexual crimes, such as rape or prostitution. The prostitute's lack of family ties and independent means of support, together with her psychological makeup stemming from the absence of a strong father image in childhood, make her particularly prone to becoming a murder victim. Having entered her profession because of her inadequate personality development, the prostitute deliberately, if unconsciously, exposes herself to a variety of men, often under dangerous conditions, thus making herself an easy prey.

The attitude of the victim varies from being unsuspecting, indifferent, submissive, to actively provoking attack. We often think of the victim as being passive, just as we usually associate, however incorrectly, the woman with being submissive, playing the passive role in sexual intercourse. But women, in the eyes of man, are, even when passive, playing a seductive role.

To say that women are naturally victims is true only to a certain extent, because their victimization depends upon the strength and proportion of their feminine and masculine traits. This balance is determined by early emotional development. The extreme points in the spectrum of femininity and masculinity are masochism (the desire to be hurt) and sadism (the desire to injure) respectively. Those who have suffered a lack of gratification of their instinctual needs in childhood will adhering to the pain principle cling to pain

9. *Ibid.*
10. *Ibid.*

and hurt. They are more susceptible to suffering from accidents or illnesses, and often expose themselves to dangerous situations whereby—and this is not always unconscious—they are hurt. Preferring pain and misery, they prolong the pain suffered in their childhood, and may sacrifice their life, as many do, by laying themselves open to murderous attacks. Deep unconscious guilt feelings are at play, leading to self-torture, self-punishment, masochism. Without being aware of it, these people for some reason feel a hostility which they try to make up for by punishing themselves. A person suffering from this condition of unrealized wishes for self-torture unconsciously seeks, and seduces, a sadistic lover, someone who will hurt her.

More than this element of seduction, there is a symbiotic relationship between the murderer and his victim, involving suggestibility and dependency and cooperation. This sexually tinged symbiosis characterizes most violent acts. The closeness between murder and sex has undoubtedly been intensified by, if it did not originate with, the child's curiosity about his parents' sexual intimacy. Children who have observed their parents making love or who have been brutalized by their parents' physical or mental cruelty, and who may have consciously forgotten it, are found to be more inclined toward violence later in life than those who did not.

The interaction between the violent murder act and the sexual act is striking. If we can think of the sexual act as an intensification of the equilibrium between tension and release, we can understand how murder, as it is experienced psychologically by the killer, can also be conceived as a vital expression of tension which explodes into release. There is truth to the old story about the couple who fight all day long and at night make up in bed. Sex is substituted for violence and violence for sex; the two are closer to each other than we realize. This is the reason why homicide often takes place between people who are acquainted with each other.

It is estimated that five of every ten killings come as a direct result of quarreling and arguing outside the family situation. However, the people who participate in these arguments most often have known each other before the killing. As random as most violent crime seems when we read about it in the press, chance is far from the main factor. Because of the strong, often sexually colored emotional relationship, in 1971 72 percent of *all* criminal homicides took place between people who knew each other, or who lived in the same neighborhood, or who were members of the same family.[11] This means that out of 17,630 murders committed in 1971—an increase of over 60 percent since 1966[12]—about 12,-700 murders occurred between people acquainted with each other. In an overwhelming majority of murders, assailant and victim were of the same race. Homicide is predominantly an intragroup, intraracial act.[13] In the light of the racial tension existing in our society, this pattern would be perplexing were one not aware that the overwhelming majority of homicides take place between people who know each other.

The victim-victimizer relationship is present in most types of murder, between lovers, be they heterosexual or homosexual, and between parents and children. Even in gangster murders we frequently find an emotional relationship, though at times only a tenuous one.

The fact that in most homicides the attacker knew his victim beforehand is also true in aggravated assault. Here, too, most of these assaults—all together 364,600 in 1971[14]—took place within the family, among neighbors or acquaintances. But to obtain convictions based on the original charge was difficult just because of the close family ties or other emotional or sexual relationship that existed between assailant and victim, with the result that the

11. *Ibid.,* p. 9.
12. The increase seems to continue. It has been reported that in New York City the murder rate for the first half of 1972 set a new record. During this time 810 homicides occurred, in contrast to the similar period in 1971, when 729 people were murdered, and in 1970, when 548 were slain (*The New York Times,* July 15, 1972). In the week ending July 22, 1972, there were 57 murders in New York City, in contrast to only 25 in the same seven days in 1971. The average number of weekly homicides last year was 31 (*The New York Times,* July 22, 1972).
13. See Marvin Wolfgang, *Crime and Race: Conceptions and Misconceptions* (New York: Institute of Human Relations Press, 1964), p. 38. This study indicates that in 516 murders, or 94 percent of the 550 identified relationships, victim and offender were members of the same race. Thirty-four, or 6 percent, of these homicides involved an offender crossing the race line: fourteen were black victims slain by white people, and twenty were whites slain by blacks.
14. *Crime in the United States.* FBI Uniform Crime Reports, 1971 (Washington, D.C.: August 1972), p. 10.

victim often was reluctant to press charges or testify for the prosecution. Four out of ten cases therefore had to be dismissed or acquitted.

Our knowledge that in 1971, of the 425,000 violent crimes in the form of murder, assault and forcible rape that took place, possibly at least 200,000 of them were instigated by the victim indicates the enormity of their unconscious self-destructiveness.

In passing, I would like to mention that preventing anyone from becoming a victim of violent crimes will, beside reducing their number, consist of making the public keenly aware of the role of the victim. That the victim, through provocation and seduction, plays a large part in the execution of a violent crime must be brought to the attention of the public. To avoid becoming a victim of murder, assault or rape will in the last analysis depend on how well the person is able to refrain from getting *emotionally involved* with someone who is potentially dangerous to one's life and welfare. Keeping one's distance from such a person requires much emotional insight about oneself as well as about others, and this is not easily obtained, since to a large extent we are governed by our unconscious feelings. Among these feelings are wishes for adventure, defiance, greed and competitive inclinations, sometimes masked by sexual desires, which serve as a means to expose oneself to dangerous situations.

There is little doubt that many such victims could have avoided their fate had they been able from the beginning to scrutinize carefully their own motivations. These motivations are clouded by or intensified by frustrations. And when frustration takes the upper hand it leads to acting out of feelings, on the part of both the victim and the criminal.

The often intimate bond between murderer and victim raises the question: Why, in the last analysis, does the murderer have to carry out his act of violence? One fundamental reason when he kills, or carries out another crime, such as rape, is—and this is quite unconscious—because he *must* show his mother that he is not *insignificant* and is able to take revenge upon her for *rejecting* him. He must show her that he is not helpless, that he has the power to strike back.

People have by now become used to the idea that when the

criminal revisits the scene of his crime, it is in order unconsciously to betray himself so that he can get caught and punished. Even more important for him is that he has an unconscious need to proclaim that he is not helpless, that he is able to strike back.

These feelings are centered around his Oedipal helplessness, the "Struggle against passivity," as Freud terms it.[15] The reason why he has to carry out his deed is that unconsciously he strongly desires to obtain power, to show the victim that he has the power to kill. In achieving power, he attempts to restore his narcissistic masculine self-esteem. We find a parallel in the rapist who, by showing that he is able to have sexual intercourse with a woman, denies his passive feminine feelings, defending himself against his homosexual desires. But in order for him to become sexually aroused, he has to use violence. Violence for him, as for anyone else, is an ego defense against intolerable anguish, in his case intimately related to the loss of his masculine self-esteem. This low self-regard is rooted in a lack or impairment of his sexual identity, leading to inadequate virility or impotence. Feeling intensely frustrated—regardless of whether his frustrations are real or fantasized—he has to act out his frustrated hate in an unconscious desperate attempt to show his power. When he does not succeed in finding a new outlet for his violent aggressive emotions, and some sort of gratification is not obtained, his locked-in feelings will explode. Frustration is the wet nurse of violence.

This kind of person is beset by intense inner conflicts. While emotional conflicts of this type are found in many people suffering from a mental disorder, they are, I repeat, present in *all* ego-disharmonious murderers. Although a great deal of psychiatric understanding has been brought into court, on those rare occasions when professionally trained psychoanalysts have been given equal time their psychiatric opinion quite often has not been considered.

Victimology—the role of the victim in murder—will be a new departure from the traditional practice of criminal law. This is not to say that the murderer is not guilty, or that the victim is not

15. Sigmund Freud, "Analysis Terminable and Interminable," *Collected Papers*, vol. 5 (London: Hogarth Press and Inst. Psychoanalysis, 1950), p. 355.

dead. It means only that emotional interaction leads to an act of violence.

Trapped and helpless, and beset by inner conflicts, the murderer encounters his victim, who also is full of conflicts. Through the foreplay—comparable to foreplay preceding sexual intercourse—and interplay between attacker and victim, intentions and motivations may be spelled out, because the protagonists do not understand themselves. Instead they act out what they harbor in their mind. There is a victimizer and a victim; and the border between them during the victimization is as blurred as their self-image. Intertwined with each other, they represent on every level of the conscious and unconscious mind a stream of fluid and transitory emotions that can hardly be deciphered.

I have chosen to examine what was for me the most revealing case study of a murderer and his victim. Tiger was extremely complex: entangled, yet analytical; single-minded, yet ambivalent. Even while in control, he displayed dangerous signs of violence and murder that extended to his victim, who became part of him even as he became part of her.

Faced with the complexity of feelings involved in homicide, I have tried here to go beyond the form of narrative used in news media. Instead I have depicted the *process of murder* as it moves on the unconscious level. This subtle psychological process moves through emotional torture from one end of the masochistic spectrum to the sadism at the other end; from normal to illogical behavior; from the land of suicide to the border of insanity.

PART TWO

Tiger and His Victim

It is life or death and in between somewhere, is the Bridge of Love.

— 1 —

The case of the man who called himself Tiger began for me late one night when I received a telephone call from Dr. Ben Foster, a colleague of mine. One of his patients, a man named Mellowbrook, was in serious trouble. He was being held in jail for the murder of a young woman named Teddy Gladstone. The patient allegedly had committed murder four days after leaving the doctor's office. Dr. Foster had seen Mellowbrook for only two sessions, but sensing his desperate situation, he had recommended hospitalization. The patient refused. The doctor then had been able, by changing around his crowded schedule, to arrange a third session with the patient, but Tiger never showed up. Dr. Foster became alarmed and repeatedly tried to reach him by phone, without any success.

The case bothered Dr. Foster. The idea that Mellowbrook might have been contemplating the murder even while he was sitting there in his office was too complex for him. He told me that he had strongly suspected that the patient was suicidal. Generally, psychiatrists consider suicide as murder of the self. A man obsessed with self-murder is less prone to commit homicide because his self-destructive tendencies are stronger. By the same token, the man afraid of killing himself is often more likely to murder.

This case of Mellowbrook seemed to be an exception to the rule. The pieces somehow did not fit the usual pattern. Dr. Foster needed my help. Could I, as a psychiatrist who had dealt with criminals for over thirty years, take on this case? He assured me it would challenge any stereotype I might have formed of the mind that murders. Mellowbrook had depth. He was intelligent, sensitive, dignified. Dr. Foster considered it a matter of such urgency that he wanted to come to my office as soon as possible. Mellowbrook had been referred to him by the patient's closest friend, Neil O'Brien, who had urged Dr. Foster to see Mellowbrook right away as he was in desperate need of psychiatric help. Apparently Mellowbrook had tried to harm himself, but Dr. Foster was not clear about this.

Realizing how late it was, Dr. Foster apologized, but he felt I was the only one who would understand his complex patient. Foster said laughingly that since it was after midnight we would at least be fairly free of interruptions and telephone calls. In any event, he promised to be as brief as possible, and tired though I was—I had attended a seemingly interminable psychiatric meeting that evening—I felt I could not refuse him.

I was intrigued by Dr. Foster's initial analysis and concern. Why was he so sure that this case was so different from a hundred other murder cases? What had got him so involved in the fate of this man, Mellowbrook? Foster's seeming lack of professional calm surprised me a bit, though our work is often anxiety-provoking for doctor as well as patient. Our inner concern is constant. How will our patients handle themselves in the interval between appointments? Will they be able to cope with their problems? Even seemingly stable people do unpredictable things, and our work involves unstable people. Although the psychiatrist's work is often a matter of life and death—brinkmanship—as a protective device one must keep it at some distance, even when, as invariably happens, one's emotions are deeply involved. In helping people to free themselves of their problems we must first probe into their unconscious wishes and fears until we find out what is really troubling them. Once the problem is revealed to the patient in all of its difficult and unattractive facets, he must try to come to terms with it through increased insight. It is like training someone who has been paralyzed to develop the use of his muscles. Sometimes, just before a session is over, the patient arrives at an insight which can give a painful twist to his emotions. Will he, after he leaves the office, act out his confusions, angers, anxieties upon his mother, wife, children, boss? We are never sure. We must rely to a great extent on the patient's confidence that he can confront us with his reactions. He must feel that he can throw all of his anxieties, resentments and frustrations on *us* and in so doing relieve himself of them. To cushion the shock we arrange extra sessions, or work to alleviate tensions when the patient calls us up between sessions.

But what if he doesn't come back for our help? Suppose, like Mellowbrook, he never shows up for his appointment but instead may commit murder? What is it that sets the mind to murder? This man was in flight from himself. Was this man incapable of accepting help? Had psychiatric help failed him? The case seemed more and more intriguing.

I was dozing in my chair when the doorbell rang. Dr. Foster entered and greeted me with an old joke. "You're fine, doctor, how am I?" He seemed himself again. We began to discuss a certain turbulent psychiatric meeting we had attended two weeks previously. Then we settled down in my office to talk about the case of Tiger. He began by saying that on the phone the patient, Tyros Mellowbrook—a difficult name to be saddled with—a young man in his thirties, had been soft-spoken, even dignified in bearing. He had displayed no distress or anger when he couldn't get an immediate appointment and was quite agreeable to postponing his first consultation for a few days. On the appointed day he arrived promptly and upon entering Dr. Foster's office stood for a moment looking attentively at the pictures on the walls and at the books on the shelves. Finally he sat down in the chair next to Foster's desk. He was tall, fair, good-looking; his mouth was thin and drawn, his brown eyes sensitive and penetrating.

He began by saying that he had been waking up at four o'clock in the morning, unable to go back to sleep. He was a writer, now temporarily working on a political campaign, which he hated. His age was thirty-two. His mother was alive; his father had deserted the family when Mellowbrook was five years old. He had no idea where his father was, or even if he was still living. No brothers or sisters. No mental illness in the family as far as Dr. Foster could ascertain.

What my colleague sensed about the patient was that his funereal reserve, his pleasant but guarded attitude, reflected a great deal of control in dealing with emotions that were turbulent. In contrast to his outward manner, his hands were tightly clenched, indicating the tension he felt inwardly. Those hands were a sign of his anxiety and suggested the fight within him to keep anger and agitation under control in a difficult situation. He was fighting against his self—and from outward appearances there was a refusal to give in to depression. Was this because of his ambition, his pride, or was there some more complex explanation?

Foster's third ear, intuition, told him that the patient might be suicidal. He advised hospitalization, but after initially going along with the recommendation, Mellowbrook changed his mind. He was writing a book, Foster said. "Actually it was still in manuscript. It was called *The Silent Man.* Somehow the title made me think of him. He was so reserved and difficult to reach."

Mellowbrook was quite knowledgeable about psychiatry, but he had the good taste not to bury his confused thoughts under a camouflage of psychiatric terminology. And he was so unassuming when he talked about his writing that Foster was inclined to believe he might be talented, perhaps even to the point of being brilliant.

"Mellowbrook didn't know in what direction his life was leading him. He was so proud but so unsure of himself. He seemed unable to let himself receive help from me."

"What did he say about the victim?"

"He was quite guarded in what he said. Teddy Gladstone was a young career woman who worked in the same firm. She was dynamic, aggressive, very talented. Mellowbrook was reluctant to tell me too much, and said very little about how he felt about her. It was only when I asked him about his relationships outside his family that he mentioned her. He said he was drawn to her. She was beautiful and intelligent—a go-getter—but very unpredictable. He never knew what to expect from her.

"As I have mentioned, Tiger was extremely reluctant to talk about her in a personal way. I remember his words: 'I have a girl and she loves me. But there are obstacles.' His choice of words was so odd. 'Obstacles' seemed like such an impersonal way of talking about the problems of being in love. It showed how guarded he was."

"You mean," I interrupted, "he resisted your *intruding* questions, particularly those about Teddy Gladstone." This was of particular interest to me. As a psychiatrist, I find I have become increasingly preoccupied with the personality and responses of the victim.

The court calls on us to submit our full analysis of the subject but then restricts our field of observation to two points: the state of mind of the murderer at the time of the crime, and his capacity to stand trial. And if they find it convenient they may find another psychiatrist, who disagrees with this analysis. In the newspapers, and in the mind of the public, there is a tendency to paint the victim in simplistic terms: so good or so beautiful that only a raving maniac could have murdered him or her—or so utterly bad that he is better off dead. Whoever it is who is killed, the sympathy is—and should be—on the side of the victim. Even somewhat evil victims take on redeeming features once dead.

I looked at my watch. It was now past one o'clock and both of us faced a heavy schedule, beginning at eight o'clock in the morning. I offered Foster a cigar and lit one myself. Suddenly I said, "How can we save the somewhat piteous survivor from utter destruction?" His eyes caught mine. He saw that I shared his concern about Tiger.

Instinctively, as professional men of psychiatry, we sensed that this case went far beyond the average in its complexity. I knew it would be a long night. I turned to Dr. Foster and said, "We may learn a great deal from this case. Perhaps we can even bring a new appreciation for the murderer's mind and find a new way to present this case that can bring a greater humanity to the court of law."

Dr. Foster agreed completely. He continued to explain one interesting part of Tiger's psyche. One of the first questions he had asked his patient was about his name. Was he called Tyros or did he have a nickname? Not a nickname, the patient had replied, correcting him politely, but rather a *nom de guerre*—Tiger. Dr. Foster was surprised that Tiger was so emphatic about his name and questioned him further. "What do you mean by *'nom de guerre'*?"

"Clemenceau, the French Tiger. He was one of my heroes. I believe in heroes."

"Of course," Dr. Foster continued, "all of us have the tendency to identify with prominent men. It was irresistible when he said Tiger; I began, 'Tiger, Tiger, burning bright,' and he continued it:

> 'Tiger! Tiger! burning bright
> In the forests of the night,
> What immortal hand or eye
> Could frame thy fearful symmetry?'

"He looked at me with a flash of a smile. It struck me that Tiger probably identified with Blake's poem more than he realized. What insight those lines had in psychiatric terms! They are strong. My mind began to wander. . . . 'Burning bright'—the passion of a special person. 'In the forests of the night'—in a world of forbidden desires. And then '*fear*ful symmetry.' It was incredible. It seemed like something from *The Interpretation of Dreams*.

"I asked him how he got the name Tiger. He said his mother had given it to him when he was a child. She kept telling him that someday he would be powerful and famous, just like Clemenceau. When his father left her Tiger was only five. She was now alone and wanted to bind him to her. Tiger would be the only man in her life. He could also be a man who left his mark. 'You can't blame her for that,' he said. I could detect a slightly hostile edge in his voice. It was as if he were saying, 'You doctors blame everything on mothers.' "

Dr. Foster laughed, then went on. "One of my first feelings about Tiger was that he didn't expect to get much help from me. He seemed rather cynical about psychiatry. He felt that he was the best judge of what was right for him. So I didn't press him. I suppose I was wrong."

Foster sighed. "I do hope that you will take on the case," he said, rising from his chair. Noting the lateness of the hour, he said he appreciated just being able to discuss the case. It is very difficult for a psychiatrist to be confronted with a new case, particularly one as involved as Tiger's. It puts great strain on one's mind. I was glad to share Dr. Foster's concern and to see how relieved he was as he left my office.

A faint breeze came through the office window; summer soon would be here, I thought. Such a case might drag on through July and August. What would happen to the trip to Norway my wife and I had been so eagerly planning? Dr. Foster may have sensed my uncertainty. "My patient is being held for murder right now without bail. I have asked Tiger's lawyer, Mr. Taylor, to phone you."

"Let me talk with him before I call you," I answered. "Let's try to sleep on it."

Late in the afternoon of the next day the lawyer called me. He had been in court trying to get Mellowbrook out on bail. He asked emphatically and anxiously, more as a statement than as a question, if I wanted to take on the case.

When asked to become a professional expert in a serious case such as murder, I am inclined to hesitate, to retreat behind the pages of my large and overburdened appointment book. It would be a hardship on my private practice to become involved. And yet, having contributed a major portion of my professional life to the study of violence in America, I felt I could clarify Mellowbrook's psychological situation, which at present seemed rather difficult to fathom. How could one avoid being concerned about a man who was in need of psychiatric help? Besides, I thought to myself, studying an educated violent defendant would deepen my insight into violent behavior. Would his violence—based on different background, experiences, learning—differ remarkably from that of others with less education? Are the human instincts in every man the same?

I told the defense attorney that before I answered his question, I wished to know why, in view of the murder charge, he thought he would be able to get Tiger out on bail.

Taylor replied that Tiger's confession to the police was invalid since, apparently, he made it without being advised of his constitutional rights in respect to his right to counsel, his right to silence, his right to assigned counsel, and the fact that anything he said could be used against him.

"You are referring to Miranda versus Arizona in 1966," I interrupted.

"Correct. You know the law." Taylor went on to say that because of certain circumstances in the case, it would be presented to the grand jury in a few days.

Asked whether I could testify before the grand jury as to whether or not Tiger was insane, I told him that I couldn't do it because I hadn't examined him. Moreover, if he was considered insane and not criminally responsible for his crime, the court would order him to undergo psychiatric observation at the city psychiatric hospital.

"When can you see me?" the lawyer asked. "This is an *emergency.*" He stressed the word.

"He is behind bars. He cannot run away, can he?" I asked jokingly.

"One never knows, doctor. This man needs help very badly, psychiatric help."

Al Taylor came to see me the next day. He was a tall, good-looking man in his early thirties, attired in a dark business suit, and with sideburns fashionably low on his cheeks. When I had spoken to him on the phone the previous day, I had thought he was somewhat overfriendly, and now as he approached my desk it was my impression that his smile was a little too affable. I soon realized why. He was young and inexperienced. His manner was a way of covering up his insecurity. Hadn't I seen him somewhere?

Ah, yes. I remembered his face from my observation of participants while I had been waiting to testify during a long-drawn-out trial a few years back. He was a law clerk then, assisting a prominent trial lawyer. He was one of those young men who frequent courtrooms as whisperers and paper gatherers, hoping someday to make their mark before the judge.

When I looked at the card he handed me, I realized he was now on his own, and that perhaps his exuberance meant that Mellowbrook was one of the early cases in his career. The thought ran through my mind: What legal experience could he bring to the case? Would I have to give him a concentrated course in psychiatric criminology, as I had done so many times before?

I was interested in Taylor's observations about Mellowbrook.

He said he was struck by his client's disorientation. He had the feeling that the man was insane, whether temporarily or . . . But such decisions he left up to an expert like myself. "Nevertheless," he reiterated, "it could be highly probable, doctor, couldn't it, that he was insane?"

I smiled. "Lawyers always try to tell me, right off, which way the chips are to fall. It isn't that easy. This disorientation you speak of may well indicate that the man is only too aware of his situation, of the meaning of his act—that is, if he really was guilty of it. In other words, his present disorientation, however extreme, paradoxically may prove him sane and put him in jeopardy. And I warn you, even if I am able to prove him insane, he may not allow you to plead him as such. I have had cases where the murderer preferred death to a verdict of insanity."

"I haven't been able to get to the district attorney yet," he answered. "I don't know what he plans to do. Strange case though. Tiger allegedly killed the girl he loved, and then panicked and ran off. It doesn't appear to be a premeditated murder, not as far as I can see. I think he was insane. Don't you agree, doctor?"

"I don't know. I haven't examined him in depth yet. You must remember that not all murderers are insane—psychotic." I answered Taylor sharply because, like most lawyers I have encountered, he wanted to place Tiger in a clear-cut legal category. He obviously wanted him to be insane, and as such not considered criminally responsible for the murder. Otherwise, at the least he would face a prison sentence. But to Taylor it sounded like a cut-and-dried case.

The lawyer repeated that Tiger must have been out of his mind. "Can you give me a better explanation?"

I told him that obviously this question could not be answered until I had examined Mellowbrook. If he wanted a psychiatrist who would testify unequivocally that his client was insane when he committed the murder, I was not his man. My testimony would be built upon the circumstances surrounding the homicide, and I would have to know many facts about Mellowbrook's childhood, youth and adulthood. Then, and only then, could I say with some certainty what type of person we were dealing with, and what kind of mental disturbance he may or may not have suffered from, which would have a bearing on his violent act.

"Obviously," Mr. Taylor stated, "you have to examine the defendant first. But remember I am his lawyer. I have to defend him. Frankly, doctor, I think—that is, I hope—that the strength of this man's defense will lie in the psychiatric testimony, although of course I can't rely on that alone; I've my own job to do. I had a professor at law school who told us that after reading a psychiatrist's report we might feel we knew the client far better than we knew our own fathers or brothers—but we would be forced to disregard most of it because of legal restrictions."

He began to recount the preliminary steps, the small legalisms that had led to Mellowbrook's arrest, and which could in all propriety point the way to his destruction. This case could become quite a sensational one. Not only was the murdered girl extremely photogenic, but she was quite well known in her field. On several occasions her name had been linked with those of men prominent in business or politics. Taylor pointed out that too much publicity about the case would make it difficult for us, and could help to sway the court.

This way of thinking, I told Taylor, emphasized the difference between a lawyer and a psychiatrist. "As a psychiatrist, I can only go on the facts in the case supplemented by my interpretations. In my profession the so-called facts include all of Tiger's unconscious feelings, his fantasies, wishes, hopes and hates, his aspirations and his fears, all elements that made him the human being he has become. And then comes the murder itself."

"If you ask me," the lawyer said, "Tiger's a product of our times, of the violence of our society. We always were a lawless people, perhaps more so now than earlier in our history."

"When we talk in generalities," I answered, "we must remember that the American past was filled with violence. For example, take the violence against the Indians and Spaniards in Florida, the violence of the Ku Klux Klan, the vigilantes on our frontiers, the race riots which have existed in cities throughout the country. Our murder rate is the highest of any civilized country in the world. If you think our social climate mobilizes our murderous impulses, you have a point, but as a lawyer, Al, you know that the law has to be upheld, whether or not we like it. At the same time we shouldn't be so tied to tradition that we don't change in accordance with new psychiatric or scientific discoveries about human behavior. A real sense of justice comes only when we explore the full range of our emotions for answers to our violent behavior which go far beyond the obvious. Not everything in a case is clear-cut; there are many shades of all colors."

"And you, doctor, have to sift all these colors," Taylor said smilingly.

"Exactly," I answered, "and it takes time and effort."

"Do you think the color will be green?"

"Either green or blue," I replied. "You like to be reassured. In that you are just like any other lawyer—or any other professional man, including the psychiatrist. Everyone wants to be assured of a successful result. Regarding Tiger, I cannot—nor can anyone else—guarantee you a favorable outcome. I can only hope to discover the prison of his mind."

"I understand, doctor, but so much is at stake here—a man's whole future, his well-being."

"And how about the woman whose life was so suddenly ended?" I interrupted. "The jury will think of the murderer, but they also will keep in mind the victim. What do you know about her?"

"Well, first let me tell you that the autopsy is being performed now to find the cause of her death and we should have the results in a few days. . . . She was in her early thirties, worked in public relations; was very successful. I've seen her picture and she had the look of a model—tall, brunette, good legs. Funny, I can't remember her face exactly, but she was intelligent-looking. I do remember she had large penetrating eyes and high cheekbones. She gave the impression of being very alert. Really attractive."

"Do you have a picture of her?"

"No, I don't, doctor, but Neil O'Brien—a friend of theirs—can get it for me. It appears to have been a love and hate thing."

"Homicide is always an act between the murderer and his victim," I replied. "It is essential for me to study Tiger, but also essential to find out as much as possible about the victim, the murderee. Her name was . . . Gladstone?"

"Yes, Teddy Gladstone."

"Teddy," I repeated, "and his name is Tiger. Both names have the same initial letter. How interesting."

"Neil told me that she was a very strong woman who was devoted to her career."

"In other words, she was a 'goal-directed person.' "

"Is that how you define people who have only their career in mind, doctor?"

I nodded. "How was the murder discovered?"

"The superintendent of her brownstone got suspicious after he hadn't seen Teddy for a few days. Newspapers were piled outside her door and no one answered her phone. Then, when one of the tenants complained about a peculiar odor, he entered her apartment with his passkey and found her body on the bed. The room was a mess. The sofa pillows were on the floor and there were empty glasses on the table. He called the police and the Homicide Squad. The superintendent was suspected and interrogated, but apparently he had an alibi. He was able to describe two men he had seen in her company. One of them had curly blond hair and wore glasses—not very good-looking, just a little taller than she. The detectives also called Teddy's employer, Petterson and Schatz, who gave them Mellowbrook's name. Since he fit the description of one of Teddy's friends, they picked him up for questioning. You would think that would be all, doctor, but it isn't. The police are smart. They watched Teddy's house, and when they saw a young man let himself into her apartment with a key, they arrested him. So now the police have two prime suspects. The other man—his name is Clark, I believe—could prove his whereabouts since Saturday, but they locked him up overnight anyway. That same evening Mellowbrook was interrogated. He was offered the usual coffee and sandwiches, and then afterward some cigarettes."

"No Danish pastry," I interrupted. "Apparently they had him over the barrel, so they didn't need more persuasive methods. But joking aside, did he admit to the crime?"

"Yes, so the district attorney told me. As you know, he was booked on a murder charge, Murder I."

"Did Tiger have a lawyer when he was being questioned? You

told me that he is very intelligent, and he certainly is aware of his constitutional rights. The police certainly should have told him of his rights and warned him that whatever he told them could be used against him."

"This is complicated," Taylor answered. "Almost unbelievable. The police got a lawyer for him, but during the interrogation this lawyer had to leave to attend another case, and it was then, according to the district attorney, that Mellowbrook admitted to the murder."

"Without the lawyer being there?"

"Right."

"The police didn't need a search warrant for Teddy's apartment?" I commented.

"No, the body was sufficient evidence." Taylor became silent. Then he said, "The case will be up before the grand jury for indictment."

"He can waive a grand jury investigation, can't he?" I inquired.

"That's right," Taylor replied. "He could be indicted if he admits to the murder upon the information of the police officer who files the charge, and also if after really careful questioning he gives responsive answers about the circumstances of the crime and understands what he has been doing. If that's the case, then he may waive the grand jury presentation."

After a pause he continued. "But in order for him to be held, he has to be indicted, particularly in view of the fact that he claims his admission was made under duress and coercion, and he was not represented by counsel. But in a case like this, where a person is being charged with murder in the first degree, the grand jury will go into action and indict him in order to hold him in prison."

"And you thought that because of some special circumstances you might be able to get him out on bail?"

"Yes, doctor, there's always a chance, although a slim one," the lawyer conceded. "In any event, from what I've seen of him, he's above average—a very interesting man. He seemed to understand my questions, despite his disorientation."

"Was he drunk or had he been using drugs at the time of the homicide?"

"No, I don't think so," Taylor replied slowly, "but Miss Gladstone's superintendent told me that Mellowbrook on one occasion had behaved in a way one could describe as 'insane violence.' He tried to break her door down, and made an awful racket. The superintendent came running up and asked him to leave, which he did, quietly enough. It occurred to me, doctor, that he might be subject to psychotic episodes or fits or something of the kind, don't you think?"

"That would depend on the medical report, and don't forget the possible provocation that perhaps resided behind that door. That is why I have to know more about the victim, almost as much as I would have to know about your client."

"You know, doctor," said Taylor, "Tiger claims he doesn't remember anything about what happened at the time of the girl's death that evening."

"You mean he had amnesia?"

"Yes, something like that," the lawyer replied. "Now," he continued, "as to your compensation, I should mention that Tiger has some money. Then, too, an aunt of his died a few months ago, and as soon as her estate is probated he will receive some more money. Though you are of course aware that if the defendant were indigent the state would pay a pittance."

I could not help smiling at his last remark. "So you mean that for the sake of humanity I should take on this case?"

"That's what it amounts to," he replied.

"Well," I said, "I *shall* take on the case."

"Thank you." The lawyer seemed relieved. "I knew that you'd do it."

I answered, "I didn't."

— 2 —

I had become preoccupied with the case of Tiger, no doubt about it. My second patient the following Friday morning was a disconsolate, talented young girl in her twenties who had just gone through a traumatic affair with a married man. As she was leaving my office she stopped abruptly and asked, "Can killing be justified, doctor?" Her question startled me for a moment, but I told her it might have to do with the ending of the session—separation anxiety. I added that there were better ways of settling an emotional conflict and advised her to take it up in the next session.

As she closed the door behind her I thought of Mellowbrook. I was confident that my patient wouldn't do anything so dramatic, so destructive as killing since she was in good contact with her surroundings. Whenever anything upset or depressed her greatly, she would call me, sometimes asking for extra sessions, and she slept well at night, which was an important sign.

My thoughts went back to Tiger and Teddy. What forces had been at work in determining the role each of them played—murderer or victim? My query, I realized, was at the moment purely academic, but nevertheless it occupied my mind and it led up to the obvious question: What factors decide who will be a victim, while so many others are spared?

Someone once remarked that murder is like a million-dollar lottery. But with the unending increase of homicide, I have begun to feel that is changing. It has been reported that the murder rate in our large cities is one out of every ten thousand of the population. So Teddy *could* be visualized as a mere statistic—as the one person out of ten thousand chosen to be killed.

My thoughts were interrupted when my secretary called me on the intercom. Al Taylor, the defense lawyer, wanted to talk with me. He had told the district attorney that since there was some question as to Tiger's sanity, I had been appointed as a psychiatric expert to examine him. He urged me to hurry because the prosecutor wanted the defendant sent to the city psychiatric hospital for observation. "I got him to delay the transfer so you could see him at once. I'm sending a messenger with a copy of my letter to the court appointing you as psychiatrist. It's urgent."

I told the lawyer that I would come down to the jail as soon as I had taken care of my patients.

Like any other human being, the psychiatrist reacts immediately in certain ways to the stranger he meets, the unknown encounter. First impressions are thought by many to be infallible. The way a person reacts to another is often instinctive and his responses are compounded by many factors—visual, auditory, even olfactory—that enter into his initial impression. Instinctively he takes in the stranger's expression of his total self, senses his responses to their meeting, to their situation. Dress too reveals a person, whether careful or careless, elegant or shabby; then there are clues found in a handshake, a facial expression, a voice.

And memory, comparisons with past encounters with people, come into this response too. Doesn't the stranger look a little like Uncle Ed? Uncle Ed was kind. Hence the stranger may be kind. Or he is reminiscent of that belligerent boy at school who beat up everyone, so he is perhaps to be mistrusted. Finally, usually unconsciously, all elements come into focus as a product of a special insight.

The psychiatrist must seek to retain this special acuity in every encounter with his patients. He must remain unusually sensitive to them, crystallizing all his innate or learned skill into two pivotal questions: What does he want from me, this stranger? And—far more pressing—what can I do for him?

The defense lawyer, who I gathered was a keen observer, had given me the impression that Mellowbrook was a single-minded person. Would he be rigid, somewhat idealistic and narrow in his pursuits? Would he, for instance, seek out one type of girl, and would only this particular type satisfy his ego? If this line of inquiry was correct, I felt I must first set out to discover the nature of that girl. Was she in her way as much in need of a certain type of man? The dynamics of an emotional relationship are subtle, often sadistic and masochistic. Was this going to be a well-defined case of victimology? If so, how could I present it in an official court of law, because the case seemed to go beyond the established precedent of criminal law? For the moment, however, this question seemed rather remote. Right now I had a greater worry on my mind—Tiger.

I have always hated prisons. The high, naked, brutal walls, the unending cellblocks fronted with thick, cold iron bars, have always made a terrifying impression upon me. Few people fully realize what it means to be deprived of one's freedom. Only those who have been incarcerated are truly able to understand the devastating effect it has upon the mind. Being locked in a cell and unable to leave, compelled to arise at a certain time in the morning, regimented as to mealtime and bedtime, becoming little more than a number, is to be less than a human being.

Of course, when we established our laws and built our prisons, we delineated what every citizen could or could not do. If a man had transgressed the law or committed a crime he had to be punished, and this was the reason for building prisons. We established conditions behind the brick walls as a precaution against dangerous criminals, and we thought that all those who transgressed the law were dangerous.

Although we have slowly, ever so slowly, begun to change our attitude toward the imprisonment of criminals, we still put people, whether dangerous or not, in prison, including those who have only been charged with a crime and not convicted. All we do when we incarcerate them is to suspend them. We discontinue all their usual activities. We defer their life to a time in the future, if there is a future left to them.

The city detention center is a massive gray building about twenty stories high, with long rows of barred windows. The fortress—as I had christened it long ago—looks forbidding and it becomes even more threatening when the sky darkens and envelops the building in a heavy fog, as it did that Friday afternoon as I approached it.

I rang the bell embedded in the massive concrete gate. A peephole opened and a thin-faced guard with a long chin looked me over. He reached for my identification, the letter of introduction from the lawyer's office and the court order. He checked them out and buzzed to unlock the door. I entered the vestibule, where the same man frisked me, looked into my briefcase and cast a suspicious glance at my tape recorder. He led me to a desk, where I signed the visitors' book.

"You are a psychiatrist, right?" he said, pointing his chin at me. "You ought to *see* some of the nuts around here. Some of them real, most of 'em phony, if you ask me. Think they can beat the rap that way." Then he picked up a phone and in a low voice told somebody to send down Tyros Mellowbrook, cellblock 11.

I waited until I heard a click and then I could see a man in the distance, moving forward slowly. He seemed taller than I had pictured him, yet his shirt looked too large for him. His cheeks were sunken and he seemed to walk as if he had no destination in mind. He turned into a cubicle out of my view. Another click. It was now my turn. I walked to the right and entered the little room that was divided from the interview cubicles by a window that extended halfway up the wall. The rooms were crowded except for the one I walked into.

As I watched Tiger walking around in the cubicle, he stopped and looked at me with penetrating eyes. From the first I couldn't help but think that there stood in front of me a man of dignity. I looked at him as unobtrusively as I could, while his dark brown eyes, framed by wire-rimmed glasses, did not let go of me. The combination of brown eyes and light hair was striking. His mouth was full, determined. He didn't seem depressed. His expression seemed almost fixed, as if he were wearing a mask. I sensed that he was deliberately holding himself together in order to confront me with dignity. Behind his façade I sensed defiance born of loneliness.

Each of us waited for the other to begin. He had hooked his arm across the back of his chair. I wondered if this was a significant gesture indicating the tension he felt in being trapped. His expression changed. His hands, well shaped, with long artistic fingers, seemed to hang lifelessly. Had his fateful act obliterated all his emotional power? Did he feel free at last from the corrosions of the anger he had repressed from childhood? Looking at him, I thought of a wise, sick child who manifests eerie wisdom when he awakens in the night and wants to talk to a parent. He was curious to see what I would do.

I introduced myself and told him that I would have to ask him some simple questions in order to get myself oriented. He would of course know the answers. He did not reply but stared defensively at the wall. I told him it would be difficult for him to talk about what had happened, but the more he could tell me about himself, his life, his childhood, the more I—and others—could help him. I tried to avoid giving him the impression that I was putting pressure on him.

I began my questions. Did he remember seeing a psychiatrist— Dr. Ben Foster? He nodded almost imperceptibly. I told him that Dr. Foster had suggested I take over his case because of my considerable experience with the courts, particularly in murder cases. I deliberately used the word "murder," spoke it clearly to gauge his reaction. There was no noticeable response.

Did he have any suggestions? Speaking more to himself than to me, he said without inflection, "What good can come out of it?"

"You can help yourself and the court to find out what has occurred; I understand your reluctance, but this is your only chance."

No answer.

"Without communication between us, there is little if anything I can do. There must be a reason for your silence. Are you a fatalist?"

"I bet that lawyer would like me to say I'm insane," he blurted out. And then his voice steadied and became distant again, as though he were speaking from afar. "I think Taylor's waiting for me to foam at the mouth, knock my head against the wall, or something like that, but I don't intend to. Long ago I decided I wouldn't become insane; I would not permit myself to become insane. People can control their insanity."

"How can they do that?" I asked softly.

No answer.

It surprised me that Mellowbrook thought man had such control over his feelings and that he seemed to have a high regard for his ability to dominate his emotions. This was evidence that he lacked insight into himself.

A long pause followed during which nothing was said. I lit a cigar, saying I hoped he wouldn't mind my smoking. Tiger only looked at me.

"You and Freud with your cigars," he said suddenly. "He had to pretend his potency—and you imitate him."

I chose not to respond.

Tiger retreated into his thoughts. There was nothing for me to do but wait. It was important for me, and for him, that we reconstruct all the events leading up to the homicide, as well as what took place at the time of the murder and what happened afterward. Had he been psychotic, under the influence of drugs, intoxicated? How had he behaved *after* the murder? Had anyone seen him in the interval shortly before or after Teddy's death? I would have to be both detective and psychiatrist: inner reality of emotions, outer reality of events, acts, sequence in time. It was essential to find out all I could about what had happened to Tiger between Saturday—the night of the murder—and Tuesday, the day he was arrested. The success of a psychiatrist or a lawyer in court depends to a great extent on how well he knows the case. If I have had some measure of success it is chiefly because I have always made it a point to learn even seemingly inconsequential facts.

I studied Tiger's face. He seemed tired. His eyes were closed and his mouth half open. Let him sleep, I thought. Let him escape. But suddenly he opened his eyes. They were deep, dark; unfathomable. He mumbled, "I can't control the course of events. Shouldn't one have a reasonable control over one's actions?" He raised his head, looked around and apparently discovered me. And it occurred to me to ask him to take off his eyeglasses. Were his eyes unequal in size? The right eye certainly looked larger than the left. The right eye was calm, the left, inquiring. What Ibsen called "the terrain of the face" struck me. His was uneven, the left cheekbone higher than the right, raising the left eyebrow and making the forehead seem less curved on that side. His mouth drew imperceptibly over to the left. As a doctor I was acutely aware of his physical configuration. The thought of slight brain damage crossed my mind. I would check this point later. He noticed that I was observing him, but he still seemed preoccupied.

"They tell me I've been intimidating people. . . ." Then, as an afterthought, "I fear the loss of freedom the most."

"Have you been intimidating someone?" I asked.

"I don't like to discuss things of little value. I hate those who talk on about nothing. People think I'm aloof. I'm no good at small talk. Of course I scare people sometimes by being so reserved. They resent me. If you call that intimidation, I agree."

Tiger fell back on his chair toward the wall. With eyes closed, he said, "Men like to see women cry although they say they don't. It makes them feel superior."

"Why?"

"When an individual puts another person down, he is trying to make himself bigger and more important than the other guy."

Tiger apparently was talking about himself. I suspected that getting to him would be an arduous task.

My method of examination was that which I always use when a patient or defendant is watchful and reluctant to reveal himself. It is called free-associative anamnesis and it encourages the interviewee to talk freely, saying whatever comes to mind—thoughts about himself, his family, whatever experiences he has had, his aspirations, his wishes, fears, or fantasies—anything he can recall.

With this method, the patient is asked to describe his experiences without the examiner telling him what he wants to know. Whenever a point that touches his feelings is brought up, he is told to elaborate on it. By stimulating him to talk about matters related to his feelings or attitudes that were not previously disclosed in the interview, the psychiatrist may succeed in uncovering the conscious or unconscious basis for his behavior. I used this strategy of free-associative anamnesis because I felt Tiger was not the kind of person who would divulge his thoughts to a stranger. He didn't ask for my sympathy; I felt he was reluctant to trust me—or anyone else. I admired him for maintaining a sense of dignity despite his desperate situation. He did not complain, yet he invited pity, for he had little or no understanding of his own difficult situation.

A psychiatrist can see a patient far better than the patient can see himself. Sometimes this awareness is painful for the psychiatrist.

There is one drawback in the use of free-associative anamnesis. The patient must have a positive attitude toward the doctor, so that the emotional relationship between them—the transference—is positive. I suspected that Tiger's attitude toward me was ambivalent, though it was too soon to be sure.

Tiger, obviously alluding to himself, had asserted that when a person belittles someone, he tries to make himself bigger than he is. At that point I felt I had to wait for him. There was no other way. So we just sat there, Tiger with his eyes closed and I looking out into space.

Then he said almost inadvertently, "I haven't said much yet, and I know that I shall have to talk. But there is no beginning—only an end."

"Why don't we try to get some order into things?" I said, thinking it didn't sound convincing. "We do not have all the time in the world to wait for you to communicate with me. Of course nobody can force you to talk. But I think when you express yourself verbally it lessens the burden you are carrying. Why don't you open your eyes? We need an eye-opener," I said, testing his sense of humor.

Tiger looked up at me then, quizzically, and said, "Doctor, am I schizoid?"

"That term is meaningless," I said. "The question is to what degree is one schizoid? What do you yourself mean by the term 'schizoid'?"

"I question my own opinions, I constantly do that. I realize that violence is immoral. But I believe in violent revolution. I could call it hostility and aggression, but why I should feel that way I don't know. Facts can be verified through others. If not, what can we believe?

"My attempt at being rational is a defense against going mad. Being rational is my way of eliminating doubt about myself. You know, sometimes I feel so mixed up inside. I protest against myself, against the world. I'm not really aggressive. I never show real anger, but I certainly feel it sometimes. I guess I suppress aggression, maybe without even knowing I'm doing it."

As Tiger talked about himself, he became eager and enlivened. I was growing to like him. His incisive opinions, but more the way he expressed them, surprised me. I knew now why Dr. Foster's reaction to Mellowbrook had fascinated me. Psychiatrists are supposed to be objective about their patients, but we are after all very human and in addition are extremely sensitive to people, particularly those who are complex and talented.

Though Tiger was impressing me as being a highly intelligent person, his views about himself were distorted. Despite his desperate personal situation, he spoke about aggression and revolution as if he were a free man. He denied the reality of being in jail. But his concern about what was going on in society was not entirely an escape from his own personal problem.

Sensing what might happen to him in his disturbed frame of mind, I had to bring the examination down to a personal level.

"Are you afraid of going mad?"

Tiger only looked at me. "You heard me," he answered curtly.

"Tiger," I began, "you seem to know quite a bit about psychiatry. Tell me, please, about the treatment you have had."

"I saw my last analyst only a few times. Then it stopped."

His last words trailed off into silence.

"Why did you stop seeing him?"

"Teddy didn't want me to see him. Yes, it sounds strange, damn it! She didn't want me to see him."

"Why?"

"Everything is so absurd. For a second I was blaming her. I'd seen somebody else before—two, as a matter of fact."

"Who?" I asked.

"Some women psychiatrists. I didn't get along with them. They were telling me things, just like my mother. Do this, do that. When you do this you will do right. If not, you are wrong." He was intimating that psychiatrists thought they knew all the answers—at least for other people. He looked at me, smiling faintly. I caught his sarcasm and smiled back.

After a pause he continued. "I'm taking out my aggressions against all those people who want to control me. They didn't do me any good. No, I'd like to correct that. The second woman was better than the first one. She didn't talk too much. You don't talk either, but then you don't seem to have many questions. Are you leaving the questions to me, doctor?"

"Yes, for the most part. I'll have the tape recorder with me again tomorrow. Would you mind if I used it?"

"It doesn't make any difference."

"What happened in your treatment with the psychiatrists?"

"Not much. I talk to myself, a sort of interior monologue. That is much better than talking to psychiatrists."

"What do you talk to yourself about?"

"About being trapped, overwhelmed, held down . . ."

"When did you see these psychiatrists?"

"Four or five years ago."

Tiger became preoccupied again. Finally, I interrupted his meditation. "Why did you want to see a psychiatrist?"

"I came to New York. The city is a dynamo, but it devoured my energy. You would call it my libido, doctor. The city ground me down, sucked out my strength, and all my ambitions seemed to dry up. I became a nonentity, a zero, a nobody. I was ignored. New York was like a woman—at first it seemed to blow hot for me, and then it turned cold. I had come to conquer this city—this woman—and I couldn't do it. It was too powerful for me. I got caught, trapped. I lost out."

Tiger's description of New York was interesting, especially his weaving together of the images of the city and a woman. But he seemed completely unaware that he was describing New York as a castrating woman. This was significant to the murder, so I asked what he meant when he said, "I lost out."

But Tiger had become suspicious of me. I was probing too deeply. He became defensive, as happens at one time or another with most patients. He stopped talking.

"I'll be back tomorrow morning. Try to put up with your situation as best you can."

As we shook hands his palm was wet with perspiration. From our talk I could see how turbulent his emotions were, even though he tried to deny them. And he didn't seem to realize that he was in fact trapped.

Being aware of his unrealistic thinking and of his tendency toward impulsiveness which made him a potential suicidal risk, I told the guard that Mellowbrook ought to be watched carefully.

"Is he psycho?"

I merely replied, "He needs watching, careful watching."

When I returned to my office I felt tired. My first interview with Tiger had been more of an encounter than anything else. His case was risky, complex. Much was buried in his mind. The first thing was to get Mellowbrook acquainted with me, and I hoped that in time, perhaps, he would transfer to me some of the feelings he must have repressed for many years about his father, who had been missing since he was a child. In my long experience in psychiatry I have observed how the father who has deserted his son before he is four or five will yet remain in the son's conscious and unconscious mind. The father image remains not only as an enigma, but as a symbol of desertion, abandonment—and hence of disapproval of the child's very being (or so it seems to the child). Even more, the father symbol remains as a phantom friend with whom the child converses in his loneliness as a youth, while in his maturity he hopes to find a substitute in other males. His feelings for his father will fluctuate between love and hate, but they must find expression somehow, somewhere. If Mellowbrook would begin to invest me with some attributes of a father figure, then in his desperation he might open up somewhat when I returned the next morning, or so I hoped.

I started out the following morning, Saturday, at 8 A.M. At the jail I identified myself again and showed the guard my letter and the court order. Again he checked my briefcase and my tape recorder. I was struck this time by his resemblance to a bulldog, with his protruding underlip and chin, his humped nose. He went over to the desk and I heard him say, "Send down Tyros Mellowbrook, block 11."

Still holding the telephone receiver, he riffled through the pages of a record book.

"Like I thought," he said loudly. "Mellowbrook has been transferred to the city hospital."

"How can he have been sent to the hospital? I saw him here yesterday, late in the afternoon."

The guard didn't seem to hear my question.

"If he hasn't been sent, he will be," the guard remarked coldly.

"Is he here or isn't he?" I asked somewhat impatiently. "Has there been an emergency?"

The guard evidently didn't hear what I said. Suddenly he said into the phone without any urgency, "The doctor is waiting for him here." He evidently had no intention of hurrying his fellow officers. The round black-rimmed clock on the wall showed nine, the hands at a right angle.

I remembered how overcrowded the partially separated interview rooms had been the previous day. The confusing din of voices from the overzealous, gesticulating lawyers, talking assertively and authoritatively, and the anxious, sometimes tearful interruptions of the perspiring transgressors or their relatives, had made listening to my own patient somewhat difficult. Under such conditions it was almost impossible to discover all those subtleties so necessary for a well-constructed psychiatric examination.

In view of these difficulties in interviewing Mellowbrook at the detention center, I had come as early in the morning as possible so there would be few, if any, people around. Standing in the corner room farthest away from the other interview rooms, I beckoned to Tiger as he shuffled into the cubicle. No shoelaces, no belt. He appeared emaciated. He must have lost five pounds overnight, I thought.

"Good morning, Mr. Mellowbrook. Do you remember me?"

He nodded. His beard was heavy, his skin had a dark yellowish tinge, his brown eyes were sunken. He had changed dramatically since my visit the day before. He looked pitiful. Yet there was still something attractive and self-contained about him. I could see he was tormented. His mouth was tight with pain. His high cheekbones seemed more prominent, his cheeks hollow, and his face drawn and fatigued. I always pay special attention to a patient's

features, his hands, the expression of his mouth, subtle manner-
isms. To a psychiatrist the visible traits and features of a person
go far in helping him understand the invisible. He must constantly
exercise diagnostic skill in discerning the mental framework and
temper of the patient. While to some extent it is possible to predict
what a patient's reaction or answer may be in the treatment situation, the psychiatrist's diagnostic ability is always spurred by curiosity as to what will be discovered next about the patient's hidden
self.

"I know very little about you," I said to Tiger.

His right eye was wider, as before, but now his left eye was
without animation. He slumped forward as if held down by an
invisible weight.

A long pause. Then out of nowhere, from far, far away, he said,
"I don't want to die. I don't know why I want to live, but I don't
want to die."

"What makes you think you're going to die?" I asked.

Talking as if to himself, he said without inflection, "I don't
know how I got here. I'm in a nightmare filled with all the elements of a crime story. I don't know how I got here and yet I
cooperate in everything, a part of my own nightmare. The cops,
the questions. I answer the cops and I smoke the cigarettes they
offer me. When they let me go, I walk with the guard into a cell
he unlocks for me. I watch him as he locks me up. He goes down
the corridor, and now the corridor is empty. I turn around. I am
in a cage filled with a glaring light. A man old enough to be my
father is sitting on a cot. He looks me up and down, and says,
'Make yourself at home. My home is your home.' He laughs but
the nightmare doesn't end there. This world is so unreal. It op-
presses me. I want to leave, to get out. Sooner or later the nightmare must have an end. I know I'm here and I don't know why.
Why are you sitting there? What are you trying to do? What is
this all about?"

His words came slowly. He looked dazed, too preoccupied with
himself to be cognizant of his predicament.

"Have you received any medication—sedatives—since I saw
you yesterday afternoon?"

"What difference does that make?"

"A great deal. Isn't it obvious?"

"If it's so obvious, why the hell do you ask?"

"I must have it from the horse's—or Tiger's—mouth," I said. He seemed to become more alert. He looked up, caught my smile and smiled back.

"What has happened?"

"I was transferred to another place. The light was on all night long. These idiots—" He stopped suddenly.

"Continue, please."

Tiger looked down at the floor.

"I—I'm in a limbo—dead or alive. . . . There was a man in my cell, in the upper bunk. All evening long he was calling for his wife. Then he began to snore, and then to scream. The guard woke him up, and then the same thing happened again. The same thing all over again. The doctor came and gave him an injection. The man was quiet. Too damned quiet. Then the guard came again. He said that I had screamed. I denied it, and he called me a nut."

"Why did you scream?" I asked.

"They said the man in the other bunk was in jail because he had threatened to kill his wife. He had assaulted her, so I thought he wanted to kill me too. When the guard said I was nuts, I told him that I didn't want to be killed. I could kill myself.

"But then the guard called out, 'Now we have two nuts here,' and pulled the cell door shut."

Tiger's face was red with anger. Then, slowly, he began to calm down. For a while he was silent. Finally, he spoke again.

"I decided," he said in measured tones, "that I couldn't become insane. People who are physiologically insane can control their insanity. It means you give up your will to live. Insanity is an alternative to suicide."

To make a choice between insanity and suicide was an idea he undoubtedly had gained from his own unhappy experiences. If he was to become insane, he had the option to kill himself. This balancing between psychosis and self-destruction had in all probability been going on in him for a long time and was a definite clue to his inner turmoil.

Tiger was in a precarious situation. As far as I could make out, although the prison guard had sensed his frantic status, nobody here was aware of the extent of his suicidal condition, or that his depressed state of mind had existed for years. I shifted my examination to what had happened to him after the guard had left his cell.

"He returned and transferred me to another cell. They took my shoes and pants and gave me a sleeping pill."

"How do you feel now?"

"Trapped. Life is a punishment. And don't tell me that Dostoyevsky said it. *I* said it."

"But why do you say this now, Tiger?" I hoped that he would elaborate.

"Why do you need to be so personal? Can't I say anything without getting myself into it?"

"Yes, of course you can, but don't you think that your statement that 'life is a punishment' is something to ponder? There must be experiences in your life that make you feel there is some basis for your idea. Don't you agree?"

Tiger seemed amazed. "It just came to me and I wrote it. It was that simple." He seemed to speak with an air of superiority. I could see that his somber mood had lifted somewhat. But I was troubled because he didn't understand that his statement had something very real to do with him. It surprised me that he knew so little about himself, and that he was so intolerant of his emotions. It is a symptom of severe mental illness if a person cannot recognize his own feelings, even superficially.

Concealing my concern, I told him that it was time for him to come down to earth. There would be other times when he could discuss philosophy. Now I needed facts. Now he would have to try to get back to the real world. Carefully omitting reference to Teddy's murder, and hoping that Tiger would understand, I asked if he could tell me about Teddy, the details of his activities in those crucial few days, their last encounter, and the circumstances that led up to his arrest.

Tiger's expression changed immediately. The wall was down again.

No answer.

"Do you want to defend yourself?" I went on.

"What difference does it make?" Then, "They say I killed her."

"Did you?"

"Maybe. I don't remember."

"What *do* you remember?"

"I went there for a drink. I don't remember."

"Tell me what you can recall."

"She didn't believe the truth."

"Truth? What was the truth?"

"She had a dinner date—that's what she said."

"With whom?" He seemed to be half asleep. "Are you listening, Tiger?"

"My mother used to say that. 'Are you listening?' "

"Tiger," I said slowly, changing the subject, "your attorney wishes you to plead not guilty by reason of insanity. Is that what you want?"

"I don't remember."

"Don't remember what? What don't you remember?" It was a tense moment. Tiger had opened up a little. His guard was beginning to falter. It was important now to widen the psychological wedge. "What comes to your mind?" I asked.

"I don't know, doctor. I took these 'ups' Saturday morning. I had to have something."

"Why?"

"Why?" Tiger had become annoyed.

"What were they?"

"Dexedrine, speed."

"Did you know they can be dangerous?"

"You're old-fashioned, doctor. Times have changed. Everybody—" He stopped.

"What do you remember about the evening Teddy died?"

"It's all a blur. I went there. I know I went there to her apartment. We had a fight."

"What kind of fight?"

"She made me so mad. She's like a volcano. She erupts. I just can't take it—the way she always tries to put me down. Do you understand?"

Tiger spoke here about Teddy in the present tense as though she were still alive. His slip in speech expressed his denial of her death and his wish to have her restored to life. He continued:

"I loved her. Do you understand?"

"What do you mean by love? Were you engaged?"

"Not officially. But I loved her. I wanted her to marry me."

"Suppose you start at the beginning and tell me everything you did Saturday, everything you can remember."

"I got up early—seven-thirty—as always. I made the usual breakfast—coffee, orange juice and toast."

"Did you take a pill—Dexedrine?"

"Maybe, maybe not."

"Do you usually work on Saturday?"

"No, not usually, but this Saturday I had to because I was going to research some new data for the election campaign of Senator Callahan. Then Teddy called me at the office at about eleven o'clock and was curious about rumors that the senator had been going out with a young girl, Dottie. I thought this question was strange, but then it occurred to me that Teddy must be interested in the senator. Before I had a chance to mull this over, Teddy said rather offhandedly, 'Oh, by the way, I don't know if I can have dinner with you tonight, but do come up for drinks in the afternoon anyhow.' I was angry. When I asked Teddy to come with me to meet the senator, she had been really enthusiastic. I'd made the reservations ten days ago. And now she was standing me up. What the hell was going on? Why did she think she could do this to me? Trying to figure out her game was not easy. She was always making me do things for her, so I had little time to work on my book."

"You were writing a book?" I asked.

"Yes. I had to pin down something but it was hard going."

"Why?"

"My first book was about a mass murder in Washingtonville. It was all facts. But this one is more difficult. It's a novel of ideas, impressions, my philosophy. I want to write but I'm not interested in fame. I want my ideas to be heard but not for my sake."

"Has writing the book been a relief to you?"

"Yes, doctor. I wanted to be a writer. As a kid, whenever I read a book I was always conscious that a person had written it, and I marveled at what an author could do. I was a bookworm, just as my mother said. My ambition to write someday was my secret;

my book was my dream. Perhaps the reason for my depression is that I could never pursue my dream. There was never enough time to spend on my own book. And Teddy was a big obstacle. She was like my mother, always asking me to help her with things when I wanted to be left alone to do things my way—my own things. She thought I was a child, inferior to her, and made fun of my book.

"Even in bed she wanted to control everything. She always tried to put me down. 'A man *never* asks, he takes.' 'What man?' I shouted.

"Teddy made me feel that I was wrong. She made me feel guilty about loving her. I knew she wasn't the kind of girl one could bring home to one's mother."

"Why?"

"I really don't know, but I was defiant to her."

"You wanted to shock your mother?"

"No; why?"

"You resented her," I answered. Behind his wish to shock his mother was a sadistic desire to hurt her, though he was unaware of it. . . . Tiger had become preoccupied with Teddy again.

"One evening in my apartment, she happened to see the manuscript of *The Silent Man,* which I had been working on before she came. 'What the hell is that?' she asked. I told her that it was my book—my first novel. She laughed and I had a terrible feeling of self-betrayal. First she had made fun of me in bed, and now she was trying to make fun of my book. I couldn't stand it. It never seemed to occur to her that I was really a writer. She just dismissed the whole thing with a glib remark: 'Am I in it?' I said, 'No, Teddy, this is a book about ideas. You wouldn't understand.' 'How can you write a novel? You don't know anything about life, Tiger, and I don't think you ever will.' She still thought the whole thing was a joke.

"Does this give you a pretty good picture of the woman, doctor? She was so damned self-centered, a shrew. But in public Teddy could be charming. She could turn on the charm when she wanted something. She was very successful in the business world. She was . . . I don't know. I suppose in private she had to be herself and let out her frustrations and that's why she was so hard on me.

"She knew how to take care of herself. She made the world come to her. She never accepted me as I was. A friend of mine had a girl who took him just as he was. This impressed me. But not Teddy. There was something powerful about her. Basically, you like to be loved. A dog is loved for what he is. He eats and plays and runs around. He is liked for what he is. But not me."

Tiger sat back in his chair, eyes closed. Then, "I don't think I should talk about Teddy. It sounds petty—but I was angry at myself."

I could see that Tiger was beginning to reconstruct his emotions about Teddy. It was essential to find out what his feelings were on that Saturday—the day of the murder—so I pressed him a bit. "What else did you feel?"

"I was angry at her. A sense of futility. I had to get out of the office. I was upset, mad. Teddy was on my mind. I walked up to Central Park. There were other people around but I didn't see them. I was beside myself. I don't remember if I dropped any speed. I was upset and I don't remember faces or places. I smoked my pipe."

"You were beside yourself. Why?"

Tiger didn't know. Was he depressed? Yes. Anything else? No. Was he tired of life? No answer. Was he lonely? My question aroused him. He was lonely, wasn't he? Yes. What came to his mind in connection with his loneliness? Tiger only looked at me. I repeated my question and added, had he been in despair? That he didn't answer my question about loneliness didn't surprise me too much because in general, loneliness is a significant symptom in those suffering from a severe maladjustment, most often connected with hatred of the self, which gives rise to suicidal thoughts and serious suicidal acting-out. But he wasn't ready to give himself up that easily. I knew that I couldn't confront him with this primary question, so I asked him an obvious one.

"When did you get on speed?"

"About a year after I met Teddy, on and off, now and then. It didn't have anything to do with my situation."

Did he hope to be more aggressive by taking speed? He didn't know.

What did he do that Saturday afternoon?

"I don't remember much about the afternoon. I went back to the office. I felt strange and tired, afraid to dictate my notes for Callahan—afraid they would sound crazy. I was angry at Teddy. I didn't want to call her. We'd had it all planned. We would have drinks, then dinner. Now she had the nerve to say that she couldn't see me because something big had come up. Come over for cocktails, she had said. I thought I could persuade her to have dinner with me. I don't remember much after that—just flashes." Tiger cringed. I could see his defenses mounting, so I told him we would stop there. But before I left I mentioned to him that this was no time to give in to self-destructive tendencies—by that I meant feeling sorry for himself—because it was time for him, notwithstanding his desperate situation, to defend himself.

"I'll see you tomorrow, Sunday," I told him as I shook his hand.

When I returned to my office, Al Taylor called. Tiger's apartment had been searched and the police had found certain things that were pertinent to the homicide.

"It's important for your examination of Tiger," the lawyer explained. "May I leave the search warrant with your office, doctor?"

"By all means. I'm sure that you are curious about how I found Tiger. A complex case. He has been, and perhaps still is suicidal. Extremely interesting and sad—more sad really."

Tiger was suicidal and secretive about it—two aspects of his psyche which disturbed me. He had given me more information about Teddy than about himself, probably because it is easy to blame someone else for one's own actions.

If he had been free it might have been easier for Tiger to stand up to his suicidal tendencies. His loss of self-esteem, of which he was unaware, had taken a central place in his self-destructive inclinations. These emotions had been intensified by his incarceration. In his cell Tiger had to overcome his isolation and his loss of freedom, which could only deepen his depression and augment his suicidal thoughts. I called Dr. Foster and brought up the question of Tiger's self-destructiveness.

"As I told you, he wasn't very communicative when he came

to my office," Foster said. "What he didn't say was more important to me than what he did say. He was agitated and depressed, almost incoherent, but nevertheless managed to be in control of himself. He appeared to be going through some sort of deeply personal crisis, and I had a feeling of foreboding. I prescribed two sleeping pills and made him promise to come back to my office the next day. On the second visit he looked taut, frightened, like a wounded deer, hunted and hurt. His eyes flickered. In his present condition he was no candidate for psychoanalysis, only for supportive psychotherapy. I urged him to go into a hospital. He consented, but then reneged. He hadn't filled the prescription, so I advised him to do so, take a pill and see me again the following day. As you know, he didn't show up. Have you seen him?"

I said I had interviewed Tiger twice in jail, but that I hadn't made much headway in my examination of his personality problems because he was defensive and secretive. He was angry at himself and Teddy; he was depressed, preoccupied, bitter and suicidal.

"I'll see him tomorrow," I added, "and I'll be in touch with you when I have more to report."

By now I could fathom that Tiger was not a murderer in the normative sense. The act had certainly not been committed for personal gain. And, although jealous and revengeful feelings go into the making of the homicidal process, one could guess from the information at hand in this case that there was a great deal more to it than that. One overriding factor was his suicidal inclinations, which had not come to the fore until he was put in jail. Although he had been unaware of them, I felt, these tendencies had been buried in his mind for a long time. It is well known that every man who kills, first wanted to kill himself. To the psychiatrist *murder is suicide of the self, however unconscious it may be.* Tiger's case, though, offered many other conjectures. Already the case loomed as one containing overwhelming psychopathology, more so than I had foreseen or bargained for. I had a strong notion that here both victim and murderer were more involved in the murder than was apparent on the surface.

I began to read the search warrant the lawyer had sent me.

COUNTY COURT: NEW YORK

In the Matter of the Application of

DETECTIVE JOHN MCGEE OF
THE CITY POLICE
DEPARTMENT, HOMICIDE
SQUAD

for the Warrant authorizing the search of one apartment occupied and utilized by TYROS MELLOWBROOK, located at 778 East 69th Street, New York, N.Y., for the following enumerated personal property belonging to the late TEDDY GLADSTONE: A lady's ring, wedding-type band with letter T engraved on the face; a gold braided chain necklace, a square man's wristwatch, and a sharp instrument, all of which being evidence of the commission of a crime and evidence that a particular person or persons committed a crime, to wit, Murder.

STATE OF NEW YORK   )
)   ss.
COUNTY OF NEW YORK   )

JOHN MCGEE, being duly sworn, deposes and says:

That he is a detective in the City Police Department attached to the Homicide Squad thereof.

That he is one of the detectives assigned to investigate the homicidal death of TEDDY GLADSTONE, whose body was found in her apartment.

That according to Police Department records at Police Headquarters, the autopsy of this deceased victim indicates her cause of death was due to asphyxiation around the neck, bleeding from the throat and chest.

That on or about May 15, 19____, TYROS Y. MELLOWBROOK, after having been advised of his Constitutional rights by your deponent with respect to his right to counsel, his right to silence, his right to assigned counsel if he could not afford same, and anything he said could be used against him, and after indicating that he understood these rights and warnings, stated that he wished to make a statement. He stated, in effect, to your deponent that on May 12, 19___ while in TEDDY GLADSTONE's apartment at 226 East 55th Street, he did kill the said TEDDY GLADSTONE.

That TYROS MELLOWBROOK also indicated to your deponent that on the night of the crime, he rode in a taxicab around 42nd Street, that the name of the cabdriver was Max Golden.

That your deponent, this date, spoke with Milton Bridges, office manager of Petterson & Schatz, a public relations firm, located at Broadway and 42nd Street, New York, who advised your deponent that TYROS MELLOWBROOK was under special contract and that he had been absent from the office on Monday, which was the location where TYROS MELLOWBROOK was initially confronted by the police on May 15, 19___.

That your deponent has checked with the State Motor Vehicle Bureau and ascertained that taxicab driver Max Golden, residing at 41 Sedgwick Avenue, the Bronx, drove said TYROS MELLOWBROOK from and around East 55th Street, and that after driving him to East 42nd Street, he left the taxi without paying the fare.

That your deponent interviewed a long-time friend of the deceased by the name of Neil O'Brien, who saw the victim the day prior to her death. According to Neil O'Brien, the victim at that time was wearing a chain necklace and a small square man's wristwatch. He thinks she may have worn on right hand a lady's ring, wedding-band type, with the letter T engraved on it.

That TYROS MELLOWBROOK's family is unaware that he has been arrested this date, and they might attempt to dispose of the items listed in the Warrant since some of the property sought to be seized is small and can be easily disposed of. It is requested that an immediate search be authorized for nighttime execution in view of the lateness of the hour herein, and that no notice of authority or purpose need be given in the execution of the Search Warrant.

That when the victim's body was found, the above-mentioned jewelry upon her person was missing.

That no other application for this relief has been made to any Court, Judge, or Magistrate.

WHEREFORE, it is respectfully requested that this Court issue a warrant in the form annexed hereto authorizing the search of the prem-

ises and places above captioned for the property above listed and captioned.

Sworn to before me this
16th day of May, 19_____

John McGee
_____

I was curious about several points in the search warrant. Why
did Teddy wear a wedding band? Did she feel so insecure that she
needed it? And why a man's watch? Did she have difficulty in
acknowledging her femininity?

The next point of interest in the warrant was the matter of "a
sharp instrument." Could it be that Teddy had been both stabbed
and strangled? It sounded formidable. I had to see the autopsy
report, so I called Taylor and asked him to send me a copy as soon
as he received it from the district attorney.

"I suspect this was not premeditated murder, at least not on the
conscious level," I said, "so you may have a pretty good chance
of reducing the charge to assault first degree or manslaughter, but
this you know better than I. In the meantime, I'll see Tiger tomorrow morning."

"Any opinion about his condition at the time of the crime?" the
lawyer inquired.

"I haven't come to first base yet," I confessed uneasily.

I was seated with Mellowbrook in the narrow interview room
at the detention center. It was Sunday morning and he looked
remarkably relaxed. He even smiled when I shook his hand.

I told him that I had brought my tape recorder. Would he
permit me to use it? He agreed readily, which impressed me. I told
him he could talk about anything he liked—"Anything that comes
into your mind."

"Free association, you mean."

"Yes, if you please. From your present life or childhood, or
anything you would like to talk about."

These are some of Tiger's thoughts about himself that I recorded that morning:

"I don't like to be embarrassed. If you ask me why, I couldn't
answer for sure, though I have a suspicion about it. And it took

me a long time to figure it out, if you understand what I mean. But Teddy, whenever she could, made me embarrassed, damned embarrassed. Even when we were in bed together she tried her old game on me. . . .

"Where did it begin? Everything has a beginning. I know I sound like an old man, even though I'm only thirty-two. But sometimes I feel as if I was born old. Even when I was a kid I was old. I never played much with the other kids. Mother used to say, 'Go out and play with the boys, don't be a bookworm.' Hide 'n' seek—they never could find me. I hated hopscotch because it was a girls' game, not for boys, but I liked to wrestle. Most of all I liked to play by myself, climbing rocks or trees, or fishing. I used to think how boring it must be to be a grownup. They couldn't play. Yes, why didn't the adults play? Why?

" 'Adults don't have time to play,' Mother said. It embarrassed me. 'They have to work,' she continued. 'And you'll have to learn that too, Tiger.' You see, Tiger is my first name. If you ask me why I got the name Tiger, I really do not know. Mother used to tell me that Tyros or Tiger was the name of a Confederate colonel in her family who fought in the Civil War—an outstanding soldier who fought bravely but was defeated in battle.

"A long time before I was born, our family had lived in New York, and then one of my great-grandfathers moved to South Carolina. Mother told me he was some sort of an inventor—an engineer—something to do with the cotton gin, and he made a fortune on it, built himself one of those large plantation homes with big white columns in front. It was high up on a hill—Tiger Hill, it was called. It had an enormous ballroom, and on the wall was the head of a tiger, which they said the colonel had shot. It sounds incredible but I believed it. Today, though, I am not quite sure what I believe. But one thing is sure: My name is Tiger. I know that well.

"And that name is me, as if bred in the bone. I like it, my name. It says something. It has substance, damn it, it means something. It's subtle. It's not just a wild animal prowling around, wanting to kill something. No, to me Tiger means power and pride. The tiger looks you straight in the face, as if to say, 'Who the hell are you?' and if you cannot answer, he will entreat you. He won't leave you until he has the answer. I know it because the tiger in my head has been asking every day as long as I can remember. I have seen his regal head, his majestic neck, his powerful body and muscular limbs covered with his velvet yellow dark-striped skin. His strong body, coordinated, powerful—always alert, ready to spring. And I see his bottomless, lamplit eyes staring at me in soft fury, waking me up from a bad dream. But his eyes remain with me, day and night. They follow me, seeing everything I am doing, always questioning me. I know the tiger in my mind would never hurt me because I am too fast for him. I'm not afraid of him. I feel as if this tiger has always been trying to say something to me, repeating over and over again the question: 'Who are you?'

"This question embarrasses me. Of course, I know I am a man, that my name is Tiger Y.—standing for Yarnell—Mellowbrook. My name fits me. I am mellow, but I am restless too. You might say I am like a brook which is fast-flowing and perpetually changing its course. It must flow around pebbles and rocks, but the basic course remains constant. A brook keeps flowing; it is constant, like me. 'Find your own groove,' Mother used to say. I didn't need to find it. I had it—and I knew it—but my course was a secret. Mother didn't know, and I didn't tell her. But if you ask me about the specific nature of my groove, I couldn't tell you, although somehow I felt it was there, somewhere. . . ."

Tiger had stopped talking. It was evident that his thinking went around and around. Being intellectually oriented, he had little appreciation of his feelings. When he compared himself to a brook, as being constant, his constancy was intellectual in nature. But how about his actions, or his feelings? Was there any constancy there? From his almost euphoric state of mind he had slipped into silence. He was now preoccupied, doubtless fantasizing.

"Anything else you would like to say—about your mother maybe?"

"Mother had large brown eyes. They seemed to follow me everywhere. 'What are you up to now, Tiger?' she would ask. 'Nothing, just thinking,' and then I would run out of the room. She would never let me alone. I was mischievous. One time, when I was five or six years old, the house next door had been burglarized. The policemen came around and asked if anyone had seen the burglar. Nobody answered, and the policemen looked straight at me. Suddenly, out of nowhere, I said, 'I saw them.' 'You saw them,' the policemen repeated. 'Yeah,' I answered, and started to run. 'Hey, come back here,' he hollered, but I ran. I was scared."

This incident revealed a behavior pattern. Wanting to be the center of attention, Tiger had used his fantasises to help him along until he realized that he had gone too far. Then he sought escape.

"I hate to have decisions forced on me. It makes me unhappy. It makes me feel that I want to be left alone. That's it. I like to be left alone. When I was four years old I played Tarzan. I pulled a rope between two trees and pretended that I was in the jungle swinging on vines. I remember a girl who helped me swing. Once I fell, hitting my head against a sharp piece of rock, and started to bleed quite profusely. She came over and helped to wipe away the blood. I was afraid to go home."

"Why?"

"Mother would be angry. She always wanted me to behave like a perfect little gentleman. She was always thinking of her aristocratic southern background and wanted me to follow along in that tradition. I was not allowed to fail. She set impossible goals for me which I could never live up to."

Tiger became silent again. "Stop the tape recorder," he suddenly ordered.

"Why?"

"Because it's noisy."

"Is that the reason? Are you angry? Would you please let me use the tape recorder? It's important."

He acceded reluctantly.

I continued, "You don't like yourself, do you? Hate has to do with self-hate. When you hate yourself you hate others."

Apparently Tiger wasn't listening. Suddenly he raised his eyes and looked alert.

"She was wearing a flame-colored, well-tailored pants suit. She looked great. She had made a pitcher of martinis. I like bourbon. I told her she should have let me fix the martinis. After all, the man is supposed to mix the drinks. She looked so darned attractive. I wanted to go to bed with her, but she said she had another date." He shook his head helplessly. "I can't remember any more —except that she laughed at me and said, 'What good would it do me if you did go to bed with me?' She laughed. That's all."

"What do you remember next?"

"The detectives came. They said I killed her. They brought me to the police station. A judge. And now here."

I waited for Tiger to go on. Since apparently he wasn't going to talk about his sex life, I asked. He said it was a personal matter. How personal? Women had come into his life late. How late? Twenty, twenty-five, thirty? Well, somewhere in the middle. Then Mellowbrook became tongue-tied. But after a while he spoke again. "Life is punishment."

"I think you have already told me this once before. What is really on your mind?"

"What I mean is that when you want to kill someone, you punish yourself. Can you kill without pain?"

"Can you answer this question yourself?" I asked.

"My question is my answer."

While this was an answer I could very well expect, what did surprise me was the sudden shift in the tone and temper of the interview. From an almost relaxed, euphoric mood, he was now in the grip of somber thoughts, in agony. His eyes were closed, his cheeks sunken, his shoulders bowed. His face invited pity.

In order to alleviate his tenseness, I asked him how long he had been in New York. Where did he come from?

"I'm from South Carolina, a small town—Washingtonville. I went back about six months ago. But Teddy needed me. She kept telling me that she needed me. They don't believe it, but I swear to you that it's true."

"Did you want someone to need you?"

"No. But it's natural."

"Did you need her?"

"I've always wanted to write, as far back as I can remember. As a boy I wrote stories and poetry. Later I kept a journal in which I jotted down my impressions of things that happened to me and to people I knew—the sudden death of one of my teachers, who died quite young, leaving behind a widow and three small children. When I was in my twenties I wrote my first book. I have been trying to write another book, but it has been hard to find time to work on it. Teddy needed me. I kept thinking that maybe I should go away, not to Washingtonville, but somewhere. Teddy wouldn't go with me. She was very successful and earned a big salary, but I think she was afraid that, given the chance, I might surpass her. She really was threatened. I wanted her to go with me. New York consumes you. It is not a place for creative people. I had to get away."

Apparently Tiger didn't understand how wedded Teddy was to her success and her career. Even if she did love him, it is indeed doubtful that she would leave New York. His remarks indicated how little insight Tiger had into Teddy's personality and her drive for success and recognition.

"When I was fifteen years old," Tiger continued, "one of my poems was published in the *Washingtonville Gazette.* I wanted to come to New York when I finished college. I could have become famous. But Mother was alone and she needed me. So I stayed in Washingtonville and worked as a reporter on the *Gazette.* But then I did something really important, so I came to New York."

"What was the important thing you did?" I interrupted.

"It was a story about a mass murder."

"In Washingtonville?"

"Yes. Four people were killed. I was the only reporter there and I was able to view all the bodies. The *Gazette* was glad to buy my story. They asked me to write a series of articles about it and I expanded them into a book, which sold quite well. So the *Gazette* gave me a job writing a column on a regional basis. I had some success, but it was hard going. Teddy didn't have to worry. She was successful, always." He stopped. It was revealing to observe how absorbed he was with Teddy—as if she were still alive.

He continued, "I'm in public relations temporarily. Public relations—ridiculous. It's worse than advertising. At least in advertising they're frank about going all out to sell their client's product. In public relations they are more interested in giving their firm a good image. Oh, no, they never sell. It's a deceitful game—and I hate it. I was able to do Teddy a lot of business favors in my present spot. But I don't like Petterson. He doesn't like me either. He's after Teddy, that's why. I got more from her than he ever did. But sometimes she deliberately put me down, and then I felt like hitting her. No, I don't mean that. I've never hit anybody."

His voice betrayed him. It had become just a trifle higher-pitched. I attributed this to the presence of intensive anxiety and hostility.

Behind his hostility I sensed his fear. I put the question to him: "Are you afraid of anything?"

"I'm afraid because I don't know why I'm here. I can usually explain things—I make my living explaining things." There was another long pause.

After an interval, "When did you become afraid?" I asked.

"As long as I can remember I was afraid."

"Was that the reason you sought psychiatric help?"

"Yes."

"And when you saw the last psychoanalyst, were you afraid then too?"

"It was getting worse. I was afraid. . . . It was Teddy."

He stopped again. He looked tired. This confrontation with his past and the rolling up of events that plagued his mind had worn Tiger down emotionally. He had begun to feel the impact of the interview.

"We will take a break. Can we continue after luncheon, Tiger?"

He looked up sullenly. "Do I have any choice?"

"Hardly," I admitted. "I'll be back in about an hour."

I too was exhausted by the morning session. I needed my favorite drink—coffee—and I went straight to the first coffee shop I saw. I must have been immensely absorbed with Tiger's case because it was not until I had swallowed the last few drops that I discovered that it tasted abominable.

During the interview I had been strongly aware of Tiger's humanity and his need for Teddy. Despite his almost professional flair with words and obvious keen intelligence, he had, all morning, talked in circles without understanding his central problem. Tiger had spoken of Teddy as if destiny had brought them together. From the hints he had given me—evasiveness is customary in initial interviews—I could surmise the invisible tie between them. Fate does play an important role in the molding of lives from separate entities to a single unit. But in this case it wasn't only fate that had drawn them together. More importantly, for the murder to take place Teddy's attitude and Tiger's reaction had to be interlocking forces.

— 3 —

I was deep in thought when I returned to the detention center. As I had hoped, Mellowbrook had opened up to me; he had gone beyond the laconic remark he had made to Dr. Foster: "I have a girl and she loves me. But there are obstacles." He had given me a picture of this alliance but had not yet told me anything about the events leading up to his fatal outburst. And he had not acknowledged his participation in what looked like a murder. The protective censor that shields our conscious mind from unbearable memory might be blocking any reconstruction of that fateful evening. We had, however, made progress, Tiger and I.

Even though Tiger had no understanding of what had caused his temporary flight from his usual control during that disastrous night, I felt that I still would have to ask him about what had happened. When we were seated in the cubicle—so cagelike and dehumanizing—I came right out with it.

He thought for a while. At last said, "I don't remember. It's vague."

"Yes, I understand, but we must try. Why did you go there?" My questioning was gentle.

"The whole thing is chaotic," Tiger answered. "When I arrived at Teddy's apartment I was confused, angry, upset—not myself. I remember things looked different—the bright yellow sofa, the white rug on the floor, the black and white chairs, the Miró picture, and the glass and stainless steel bookshelves. I wasn't on drugs, but things looked different. It was striking. Like her. Fire and ice. She looked dazzling. Her flame-colored pants suit seemed to set her on fire. She looked wildly passionate. I tried to kiss her, but she looked disconcerted and turned away. I thought that somehow she had changed. I asked her if she had missed me, but she didn't seem to hear my question. Instead she offered me a drink. I felt uncomfortable, far apart, but then she reached for my hand and caressed it gently. The next thing I knew she was leaning against me and kissing me softly. She had tears in her eyes. At that moment I felt very superior and said to her that she shouldn't cry, that I was going to make her part of my life, and she could be sure about this. She didn't stop crying. I remembered Mother always telling me that she liked to have a cry once in a while—so I sat there wondering why she was crying. I was confused, even embarrassed. I didn't think I had done anything wrong, so what could I do?

"It's funny," Tiger reflected. "Now it's becoming clear to me. She hugged me so tightly that I felt her heart beating against mine. I must have said something comforting, something to the effect that I wanted her with me forever. Then suddenly she asked, 'You really do love me?' I told her that I did. 'I believed you once,' she answered, 'but now I'm not so sure.' I can't remember what she said next, but then she began asking me a lot of personal questions. Had I ever been in love before? How many girls had I known? What the hell did this have to do with us? She knew very well that I had to take care of my mother. She became more and more inquisitive and assertive. Her mood changed. Teddy was being sarcastic, trying to embarrass me. I told her—like a fool—that I was trying to do my best, but she cut in, 'Your best is not good enough.' Can you imagine saying such a thing to someone you love? She accused me of being tied to my mother, saying that I wasn't weaned from her and probably never would be. 'Don't get me wrong,' she said. 'I know you're trapped but you let her dominate you inside. You're not really a man. You would do anything for her, but what about me?' "

It was clear to me that Teddy wanted Tiger's complete devotion. But Tiger couldn't understand that he used his mother's dependence on him as a constant excuse for not developing into an emancipated individual. As we shall see, this reaction was typical of him.

"I was stunned at Teddy's outburst. What did she mean? I yelled back at her, 'I wanted you to marry me, you bitch.' She looked at me strangely and said, 'This is the first time you have ever mentioned marriage,' and gave me a little kiss, but then, God damn it, she told me that she would only marry me if I loved her the way she loved me—I really didn't know the meaning of love between a man and a woman. Doctor, the situation was ludicrous. What can you do when a woman gets belligerent?"

I understood that Tiger's relationship with Teddy existed more in his fantasy than in reality.

"I tried to calm her down and said I was afraid. She looked surprised and asked whether I was afraid of her or afraid that my mother wouldn't think that she was the right girl for me. 'Your name—Tiger,' she said mockingly. I knew she didn't understand. How could she know about my family? I heard her say under her breath, 'You and the Chinese paper tiger!' Although she said it very quietly, it was like an explosion in my head. Aren't the most devastating lies told in silence?

"Teddy went on, 'I loved you once.' I couldn't understand what she meant. She didn't make sense. Then she became aggressive. 'You're thick. So thick,' she screamed. 'You always came running to me. You talked and you were silent, you talked and you were silent. Oh, yes, I respected your mind. You have good taste. You know about music and paintings, but what else did you give me?'

"I got mad. 'I showed you my book, but you made fun of it. I gave you gifts—that necklace you're wearing.' She replied, 'Didn't you also give your mother a necklace?' Hell, what could I say? You see, doctor, I can't show aggression. But I like to be aggressive inside—in my own mind—without anyone knowing it."

"Why?" I asked.

"It's more intelligent than brute force. Brute force leads to trouble."

"What about the time you broke her door in?"

"Ah, that. How did you know?"

"The superintendent told the police."

"I might have known. In the end everyone will know, or think they know, everything about me. . . . Yes, I broke the door down some time ago. I think Teddy secretly liked what I had done. I was trying to show her how forceful I could be. That particular night she had told me—no, she had asked me the day before to come by her place for a drink. And then when I rang the bell, she ran to open the door and said, 'I'm exhausted, utterly exhausted. Call me tomorrow night, darling,' and slammed the door in my face. I was halfway down the stairs when it occurred to me that if I let her get away with it she would drop me, because she would lose whatever respect she had for me. So I went back and broke the door in. She was shocked, and I saw a mischievous gleam in her eye. I had to show her who was boss."

"The superintendent said that Teddy had apologized for you, Tiger. She told him that you had been frustrated in your job, which was beneath your talent, and you were worried about your mother's health and—"

His face darkened. "I never thought she cared enough to say all that."

There was a long silence.

"What happened between you and Teddy later on that last evening?"

"She told me she could never feel close to me. She couldn't understand me. And then the doorbell rang. Damn it, so many things happened. I don't remember the exact sequence. She brought in a telegram and tossed it on the table.

" 'Aren't you going to read it?' I asked. She answered in a cutting way. 'No. No one sends good news in telegrams, and bad news can wait.'

"Sometimes when she really was being difficult, I would think, 'You're a real bitch,' and thinking of her that way calmed me down. I would feel a rush of blood to my face, and I would break into a smile. When I smiled at her she would suddenly fling herself into my arms, or caress my neck, or nuzzle my ear. She was the Teddy I loved, tender, docile, affectionate—and so it went, hot and cold, never on an even keel.

"It's very difficult to understand a woman. Her psyche was complex. Teddy was strong—castrating—but of course I didn't say that to her. She would have been furious and made me leave, so I kept quiet. She hated criticism. Anyway, that evening I became quite upset when she finally admitted that she had another date. She tried to be very coy about the whole thing. When I told her we had a dinner date with the senator, she answered, 'Who said anything about the three of us going out to dinner? I merely asked you over for a drink.' I was confused. Then Teddy said, 'You don't own me, Tiger. I don't have to go out with you if I don't want to.' She was being petulant. She was belittling me. I could feel my anger rising. The room had become very warm. I was breathing heavily. I think she really enjoyed tantalizing me. I was the one who had done all the research she used in the senator's campaign. Didn't she owe me something? I wanted to interview the senator because it would be important for my book —for my career. I wanted Teddy to be there too. She would make me look more important.

"I don't think I've made myself clear, doctor. I had made reservations for the three of us to have dinner at the hotel. She had told me the week before she thought it was a good idea. She always had to play it her way. The more I talked about the interview, the more Teddy seemed to turn off. She looked preoccupied, as if she wasn't listening. She had other plans.

"She turned on me and said, 'Why do you think you own me? You don't own me. You've never done anything with your life. Why do you think you can control me? I don't want to have dinner with you.' I was stunned. What was she saying? What the hell did she mean? She didn't make any sense. I was furious. I felt my cheeks grow hot. Suddenly the room became blurry. I was filled with rage. I felt I was going to explode. Teddy said, 'Oh, Tiger, get another drink. Come on, I'll fix it for you. I have to leave pretty soon.' Suddenly the phone rang. Teddy jumped up. Her voice as she answered the phone suddenly became soft and seductive, the way I remembered it. She seemed to purr. 'Oh, yes, I'll be there,' she said. 'Oh, don't worry about that. I have no plans for dinner.' After a pause, Teddy said, 'Good-bye, Senator.' So that was it. Incredible. I suddenly began to see what Teddy was doing.

"I was shaking with anger. I couldn't talk. I was overwhelmed. Teddy was trying to be coy. She said, 'See you later, Tiger. I've got things to do. Why don't we meet back here at ten? Okay? Have a good evening.' She laughed as she said this. I stood silent, stunned, unable to comprehend the situation. Suddenly I remembered my plan for the interview, the dinner reservations. As I fixed myself another drink, I thought to myself, 'God damn it, at least I can have the interview.' I remember leaving somehow and going to the Plaza Hotel, where I waited for the senator five, ten, fifteen minutes, but he didn't come. The lobby was full of people. I began to wonder if I would even get my interview. Suddenly I heard a familiar laugh. I just couldn't believe it. There was Teddy, laughing, throwing her head back, acting like a child, facetious, playing games, smiling as she held onto the arm of the senator. It was too much. It was beyond anything I had ever thought possible. I went over to the bar and began to order drinks—doubles. I lost all track of time. All I remembered was that Teddy had said to meet her back at the apartment at ten. Somehow I *had* to be there. I would get even with her for this. Who did she think she was, doing this to me? I was the one who had made the dinner reservation. It was my interview. What the hell was she doing, ruining me? I would pull her down a peg or two.

"As I rode back to her apartment I began to suspect that she didn't really care much about me. She was jealous of me. But then I remembered the first night two years ago. We were in bed together. I had this marvelous sense of achievement. She had gone to a great deal of trouble to seduce me. No woman had ever tried so hard. Now I realize that it had nothing to do with me really. It was her ego—a way of expressing the self she loved so much —not a reflection of how she felt about me. I soon began to feel this. Teddy was a selfish person. After a while I became disenchanted with the role I was playing in her life, and with the role she was making me assume in my own. But I was grateful that she'd seduced me. Sometimes I flattered myself by thinking that by belittling me she was trying to keep me from expressing my prowess with other women. No matter how she teased me, she still went to bed with me, I tried to reassure myself.

"And then she would turn on me. She would get all dressed up. 'I have a date,' she would say. 'Don't wait up for me. I'm not coming home tonight at all.' It was like being betrayed right before your eyes. She was so deliberate about it all. I would go back to

my apartment and work on my book. I learned to laugh myself
out of my anger by telling myself that women are impossible.

"When I returned to her apartment that Saturday evening I
tried to rationalize my anger. But I couldn't. I loved her and I
wanted her to love me just as much. There *must* be a reason why
Teddy did this to me, I thought. So I said to myself, 'Take it easy,
Tiger.' When she returned to the apartment I was out of sorts and
didn't want to hear her account of the evening. I told her that I
would like to hear some music, and she said, 'Go ahead.' I put on
Mozart's Symphony Number 40 in G Minor. I sat there somberly.
Teddy was quiet. Music always had a terrific influence on me. This
symphony is my favorite. Music puts me in a special mood. Mozart was saying something very meaningful; it was the hidden
world of a romantic artist.

"I must have said something like this aloud because Teddy
looked at me, tilted her head and said, 'I'm a romantic, Tiger.'

"I felt the ice was thawing.

" 'Did you know,' she said, 'that you have fenced yourself in?
You're afraid of something, and always holding back. You wrap
yourself in a shell.'

" 'Maybe you're right,' I said, 'but I have always had to struggle
for myself. That is the way I was brought up. I had to learn it and
to learn it the hard way. I grew up without a father. Nobody stood
up for me except Mother.'

" 'Yes, you thought you were a big shot, but you hid your
thoughts from me. Maybe also from yourself.' She looked unhappy.

"I started to think, If marriage is like this, the hell with it. I
don't need it. Whenever she complained that she wasn't lucky, I
simply couldn't understand her. What the hell did she mean? She
had lots of friends, and she was doing the work she enjoyed. She
was better off than I was. At least she didn't have to slave away
on a political campaign which she hated. I told her she was
spoiled.

"After that I felt good about the way I handled her, and I
poured myself another drink. I offered her one, but she shook her
head, went over to the window and stood there looking out. It was
quiet and then she came over to me and said softly, 'I don't know

how to say it, but you may as well know it. I am going to have a baby.'

"Slowly the words took shape in my brain. 'Impossible!' I exclaimed. 'What kind of joke is that?' Then Teddy said, 'I need you, I need you.' The floor fell under me."

"It was a surprise to you?" I asked. "She disappointed you then?"

For a long time there was no answer.

"Disappointed isn't the word. I wept inside. This was the girl I wanted to marry. She was to be the center of my life, and now this was the way it had turned out. We didn't speak for a long time. I wanted to leave, but I didn't think that I could leave her at this moment. She mentioned a horrible dream she had had the night before. In it her face was ugly and distorted. She was terrified and ran to the mirror, then she realized that it had only been a dream. But I could see that she still was very upset.

" 'I looked so ugly in the dream,' she said. 'My face was flushed and swollen and it looked bluish. I had a birthmark in the middle of my forehead. I looked old and ugly.

" 'I knew I looked ugly because I was pregnant. I was distorted. I hated the sight of other women. I imagined that they were pregnant too. Pregnant women have no figure. They wear dresses like sacks, and now I was one of them. Soon I would look swollen and shapeless. I would be as ugly as I was in the dream.'

"Teddy looked so sad. I felt sorry for her. It was awful. She said, 'I have lived in a nightmare. I still do. I'm afraid of the day, and I'm afraid of the night. I dream of all kinds of animals coming to get me and I try to escape from them, but they drag me back. I'm so afraid. I hate everything I'm afraid of. I didn't want it to happen.'

"You see, doctor, when a woman is that upset, you shouldn't interrupt her. Then Teddy began to talk about her sister, that her father loved her sister much more than he loved her, that she quarreled with her sister, and then she said something which I think I will never forget. 'Father always loved my sister more, and you love your mother more. Everyone I love loves someone else more.'

"I didn't know what to do. I poured myself another drink to

calm me down. Then I became furious. Why should I want her anymore? I was angry at myself and at her. I began to freeze. It was chilly, so I closed the window. Then for a second I looked at her face. I thought it was yellow.

"It surprised me. You see, doctor, when people's faces look yellow to me it means that I hate them. I asked myself, 'Do I hate Teddy?' But I was glad that her face didn't look red, because red means evil, and I don't think that she is evil." Again Tiger was using the present tense as if Teddy were still alive.

He continued, "I looked around. It was dark outside. Teddy's face was partly in shadow. It looked jaundiced. I shivered."

Seeing a person's face change suddenly to another color indicates a high degree of disturbance. Although it is not a common phenomenon, we observe it in patients who are psychotic or who have been under the influence of certain drugs, such as mescaline. Sometimes this type of patient may perceive that a face is distorted, which also reflects mental disturbance. Tiger's significant description of Teddy's face was an indication of his psychotic condition.

"I tell you, doctor, I just couldn't sit there. I had to do something. I wanted to leave, but something—damn it—held me back. I wanted to say something, but I couldn't. I asked her why she had told me about her pregnancy. She answered that of course she didn't have to tell me about it, but she thought, or she imagined, that we were close and that I would understand. Hadn't she threatened to abandon me? What was I to understand? I could understand that her life was painful and torturous, and I felt sorry, sorry indeed. 'When life is this way it isn't worth living,' she remarked, and I answered that she could have an abortion. 'No, I can't,' she screamed. She became furious. I tried to calm her down. 'Why are you so afraid of an abortion? You can have the child,' I said, and I meant it. I wasn't going to stand in her way if she wanted to marry somebody else. Then she said, 'My mother died when she had me and my sister; we were twins.' 'I'm sorry,' I said. 'I didn't know. Now I understand.' I realized Teddy was horribly afraid of dying.

"I probably shouldn't have said it, but I told her that she had been looking for trouble. You know, doctor, I am also a psychoanalyst in a way. Then the real trouble began. She said, 'This whole thing isn't my fault. It's yours too.' I yelled at her, 'Mine! What the hell did I have to do with it?' Then she answered quickly —you know, she was always quick on the trigger—that my doing nothing was as bad as doing something."

Faced with such a critical situation, it is strange that Tiger didn't ask her a realistic question about her condition. Was she sure she was pregnant? Had she consulted a doctor? If she was pregnant, how many months? True to his nature, he retreated from reality by asking her questions unrelated to her physical condition.

"I asked, 'Why do you want to have a baby?' 'Well,' she said, 'my sister had a baby, and I would like to have one too. She's married. I am not. I am alone, so desperately alone, and I wanted to have something that belonged to me, something I could call my own, and still share it with someone. You, I mean,' she said, and looked at me intently. Of course it made me feel worse than ever. And you know, doctor, this was one of the few times she had spoken to me so openly. I had nothing to say, but then Teddy told me that when she was growing up her father used to say, 'Watch out for the boys,' and when I think of it now I think that he loved her, and he also gave her all the attention she wanted."

Tiger's clear recollection of the events that took place between them surprised me, particularly because her actual death was a blank to him. Not wanting to distract him, I asked, "What happened then, Tiger?"

"I really don't know," he answered. "I wondered who was the father of the child, but I didn't have to wonder about it long, because she told me herself. I can't remember, but she said he was a business friend. She mentioned that he had a scar on his face, and then added that very often she was attracted to people who were not good-looking.

"I don't understand women," Tiger continued. "This intelligent girl, with all her troubles, began to tell me what a good dancer this man was, and she accused me of never dancing with her, and this simply was not true. I did dance with her. She contradicted herself. I was angry as hell. She didn't need to use my dancing as an excuse. I accused her of being in love with him. She wanted him, and now she really had him. 'But,' I added, 'this is your business.' Then I thought to myself, 'Why should I be sitting here? I should have left long ago.' But I didn't want to give up, so I asked her, 'Were you close to him?' 'Yes, in a way,' she answered. 'At least more than with you. You were so far away, lost in another world —heaven knows where.' I was furious. I couldn't take any more. I had to get out. I slipped my pipe in my pocket, picked up my pocket knife from the table, rose and said, 'I'm leaving.'

"But Teddy didn't give in—she never did—and do you know what she said? That I couldn't love her anyhow, that I was too wrapped up in myself, or with my mother or someone else. God knows what. . . . Yes, doctor, love is body, and I don't think I had her body."

"Go on, Tiger, what happened then?" I asked.

"I don't know. I simply don't know. I remember that I looked at her, and I saw the necklace. It happened then. I don't know. Yes, I remember. Now she wanted money for an abortion. Well, I didn't have too much money, but certainly I could lend it to her, and then she changed her mind again and said that she didn't want to have an abortion. She wasn't even sure that she wanted to marry. After all, she could even support two children, by herself, quite well.

"I was confused. I asked her if she had forgotten how she had felt about marriage before I left to visit my mother. I told her that she had said she wanted to marry and taunted me because I was always running back to my mother. I told her that when I had come back I was ready to marry her. Wasn't that what she really wanted?

"She burst out, 'To hell with marriage, and to hell with men.' I was shocked, and in a way felt a moment of triumph. At last I understood why she had called me a paper tiger, looking at me as if I were someone contemptible, not really a man. She had always accused me of unconsciously despising women because I never stood up to her, so what in hell should I do? She was in a rage and I was choking with anger."

He stopped. His hands were clenched.

I encouraged him to continue.

After a while he said, "The next thing I knew, I was out on the street."

"But didn't something happen before you found yourself out on the street? What happened to Teddy? Don't you remember?"

"No, nothing."

"Tiger," I asked quietly, "did you do anything to her, did you hit her?"

"Maybe I did, maybe I didn't."

"Did you choke her?"

"I don't remember."

"Did you stab her?"

"No, I didn't stab her. Why should I stab her? I was out on the street."

At this moment I only asked, "You were on the street?"

"Yes, yes, I was on the street. It was so quiet, so terribly quiet. My head was spinning. The street lights looked like white globes of burning light."

"What did you do then?"

"I don't know. I think I walked—or I ran—and then there was something on my mind, like: I didn't mean to do it, it was all her fault." He was agitated, so I tried to calm him down. He needed a tranquilizer, which I couldn't give him, since it was against the rules for an outside physician to give medication to a prisoner. After telling the guard that the inmate needed a tranquilizer, I returned to Tiger. After a while he continued:

"I walked, and stared at the street lights, and I passed them, and then they passed me. They hung in midair—big yellow eyes, staring at me. Then I noticed people passing me. Their arms were dangling back and forth as if they didn't belong to them. I remember looking at my hands and my arms and I began to run. Run away from them, I thought. But they followed me. I ran faster, but the yellow lamps were still there staring at my hands. That's funny, I think I put my hands in my pockets. My hands couldn't do it. They couldn't. They had no reason. I then began to think of hands, how good they were, or how useless, and I thought that hands are always in the way. Anyone could walk without hands, just as I was doing."

Tiger stopped talking. His forehead was perspiring, his face looked pale and lined. He evidently was reliving his psychotic episode. I let him sit there a few minutes, and then I tried to tell him to go on. "I am not crazy. A taxicab driver stopped me that night and said I was crazy. I didn't watch out for myself. Later I found myself in the subway, and then I was upstairs and there were lights, hundreds of lights, staring at me and following me. Then I was in a dark hall; it must have been a movie theater. I don't know. I was in a daze."

Tiger stopped again. He had closed his eyes. He appeared deep in thought. Then he said, "A melody went through my mind, over and over. I couldn't recall what it was. Then I remembered that I used to hum it when I walked along the street, or when I was writing. I couldn't get the melody out of my head. It was slow and it was soft. Another tune had emerged from the darkness of my mind. The melody grew insistent, it became more distinct, loud, and then became wild, faster and faster, until it escaped and disappeared. Then it began again, slow, fast, escaping, disappearing. And then I realized what it meant: *Slow, fast, escape, disappear.*"

"Tiger," I asked, "why did you want to disappear? You must have had a reason for it. Why?"

"What do you want from me? Are you a friend, doctor? What do you want from me? Who are you?"

"Do you think I am against you?"

Apparently he didn't hear me. He said, "I'm a criminal. I have done something."

"Look here, Tiger. Why do you suddenly say that you are a criminal?"

"I don't know."

"Why don't you try to go on and tell me what happened?"

"That night," Tiger said slowly, "a policeman stood in front of me. I was at a bar and I tried to hide my face. I looked in the mirror behind the bar. The reflection blurred. I could not recognize my own face. I knew that the policeman was still there.

"There was a lot of noise in the bar. A jukebox blared, and a sailor and a girl were dancing. Then I remembered what Teddy had said to me. I didn't dance. Then there was a fight and I found myself on the floor, and I think a policeman came over and asked me what I was doing, was I looking for something? The policeman got angry. 'Too much to drink,' he said to me, and I remember he used the word 'mister.' 'You'd better go home and behave.' 'Tell you what,' I said. 'Would you like to hear a good story? Get the morning paper and there'll be one.' And do you know, doctor, the policeman laughed at me. He called me a crackpot—I went around making up stories. 'Don't try to run my beat, mac. You're lucky I'm off duty now.'

" 'You don't believe me?' I said. At that moment I sensed some disappointment, and then I became aware of the policeman's stare. I felt the alcohol burn in my body and I was so dizzy that I went over to the bar and ordered another drink. Then I felt a hand on my shoulder. I was so terrified that I didn't even turn my head. I just sat there quietly. I heard a voice say, 'I'm sorry I slugged you.' It was the sailor. It wasn't the policeman at all. 'That's all right,' I said."

Tiger was staring at the tape recorder as if he didn't realize what it was.

"What else happened?" I asked.

"I don't remember anything from that night, only bits and pieces, and there was so much talking and so much drinking. They talked about killing and about murder, and I remember someone saying that twelve people were killed, but I couldn't follow it. And then somebody else said that anyone who could do that must have been nuts. The two old ladies who committed the murders were psychos, and the guy who buried them was another, and some woman mentioned a wife who killed her husband and then went to a movie with her lover, and she asked how can people do things like that? First kill and then go out and have a good time. So cruel. Then another man said he guessed the trouble in our age is that we are too easy on murderers. I said that a murder takes place almost every hour. Even at this second a man or a woman is being killed. Then a girl shrieked and said, 'Stop it.' "

Tiger's reaction that a man or woman is being killed at this second reflects his own experience with Teddy.

"Do you remember what happened then, Tiger?"

"I found myself on the street again. I was walking faster and faster. Couldn't even hear my own footsteps. It was like a dream. The melody came again. *Slow, fast, escape, disappear.* I said it aloud. Then I saw a man walking on the street. I couldn't make out his face. I thought it was my father. I remember that as a boy I often imagined that I saw my father coming along the street, although I knew that he wouldn't return. Yet I kept watching for him. Waiting and hoping. Mother didn't know how I suffered, but I didn't hold it against her. She didn't mean it. It wasn't her fault. It was his. Then I remembered that I used to stand in front of the mirror and look at my face so that I could study my features. If I knew how I looked, it would help me to remember my father. But every time I went down the street I forgot how I looked. That was funny—I couldn't remember myself. I only had an impression of my face; imagination, nothing more."

"What did you do on the street then, Tiger?" I asked.

"I don't know," he replied. "I went into a bar and a girl invited me over to her table. She asked me if I lived at the hotel. I couldn't understand what she said. 'What hotel?' I asked. I looked at the bottles behind the bar. They were green, red and yellow, in all odd shapes. The girl said to me, 'Look at the painting over there. Isn't it really something? A nude in the raw.' I peered up but I couldn't see anything. At least, it wasn't clear. Then she said, 'You ought to wear glasses, you squint so much.' 'No,' I answered, 'I don't need glasses.' Then I thought, where were my glasses? I hadn't had them all evening. I began to go through my pockets. I panicked. I might have left them at home, or somewhere else, but I didn't know. I said to myself, 'I don't need them anyway. I only need glasses for reading, nothing more.' Then the girl said that she was getting married and I asked her what the hell she was doing at the bar. She wanted to have fun, she said. I began to leave, and she yelled, 'Come back, come back. Where are you going?' I came back, and she said, 'I'm going to marry a man, but I don't know whether I'll go through with it or not. He's much older than I am, but I kind of like him, and he's nuts about me.'

" 'Where do I come in?' I asked. 'Don't you understand?' she replied. 'I like to have a good time. I'm not going to marry you. I want to have a good time, to have some fun.' Then I said, 'Yes, you must have fun.' The girl was strange. While we were sitting at the bar, she suddenly said to me, 'I touched your arm, and I knew you. Why do I have to tell you all these things? Why should you care?'

"The girl astounded me. She was right, she had her feelings all right. She had her life figured out, just like Teddy. She knew what she was after, and she was going to get it all right."

Tiger had stopped talking. He looked sleepy, and when I asked if he was he admitted it.

"Could you tell me more?"

"The girl had something around her neck. But then I dozed off. I don't know whether I was dreaming or sleeping. Then I woke up suddenly and I asked myself, where were my eyeglasses? Where could they be? In my office? I had been at so many bars. My apartment? Maybe they had fallen out of my pocket. I asked the bartender if he had seen a pair of eyeglasses. I was relieved when he said that he did have a pair, and he shoved them to me across the bar. 'No,' I said, 'these are not mine.'

"I walked over to a table thinking about the glasses. I could get along without them. Then I looked up and I moved toward the bar and I saw a sign I could read: 'Occupancy by more than 85 persons is dangerous and unlawful.' I looked at the girl and then I remembered where the glasses were. They were in Teddy's apartment. They could trace the glasses to me. Just as they did to Nathan Leopold in the Chicago case in '24. It was always a little thing that gave one away. Damn it! The glasses were there. Doctor, it was like a revelation. My glasses were in her apartment. I couldn't understand it."

"What did you do then?" I asked.

"I don't know but I think I was on the street again and it was dark. I was lonely, it was night. I began to walk, and I walked and walked. I thought of taking a taxi but there was none in sight, so I kept on walking. Then I stopped at a corner and looked at a clock there."

"Tiger," I asked, "did you take a taxi earlier that night?"

"No," he said. "I don't know. Maybe."

"What time was that?"

"I don't know."

"Didn't you take a taxi before that?"

"I don't know. Maybe."

"It will come back to you. All right. Let's see what happened later."

For a long time Tiger didn't say anything. His eyes were half closed.

"Maybe we should stop here today?" I asked, while I looked at him intently. I could feel he was wavering.

"What's going to happen to me?"

"Nobody knows for sure, but there is one thing you can be sure about, Tiger, and that is that the more you can tell me about yourself and what happened between you and Teddy, the more I will understand; and the better I can explain it in court, the better they will understand you and your predicament. . . . I think that we will have some tests made on you, Tiger—psychological, neurological, and electroencephalogram. All this is painless, I assure you."

"So the more I tell about myself, the fewer tests you will make on me—is that the case?"

"No, not exactly," I replied. "Furthermore, no tests will be made upon you without your consent."

"Something comes back to me," Tiger volunteered slowly, "something that didn't make sense at all."

He paused. I waited—and waited. Almost in a whisper, I asked him what he was thinking about.

"That evening," Tiger answered, "Teddy told me, 'I am scared of you in a way. There isn't anything really to be scared of. You are nice. But I am scared of you!' That is what she said: 'scared' and 'nice.' It was a big contradiction. Why did she say it? She was always a contradiction. I believe she said she loved me, and I think she did, but I had a feeling that she wanted to get rid of me— particularly that night—and I got damned angry about it. What the hell did she mean? I just couldn't talk sense to Teddy. She was always trying to confuse me. She could be insulting too and never explain what she meant."

At this point I felt it was important for me to try to establish a closer relationship with Tiger. Although I would have preferred that he continue to talk about what happened after the murder, I thought I should wait for that. The tie between us was brittle, so I had to nurture a sense of trust which would help him open up parts of his mind that seemed blocked out. I had noticed that below his rather formal demeanor there were some soft spots that could be probed. Most important though, as in any psychiatric relationship he had to gain some satisfaction from talking with me. As long as he felt satisfied, which meant that he was achieving some gratification, the transference between us would grow.

I asked him to tell me more of what he thought of Teddy.

"She was selfish," he answered, "but she may have had her reasons. There are always reasons why people behave the way they do. But she told me that she didn't want to be used as an object to please men. She didn't want to play a role. She wanted to dominate, to do things *her* way. I was mad."

"Have you been thinking about her after her death?" I ventured. "Are you sorry she is dead—killed?" I took a chance with that question, trying to stop the flow of his thoughts and to divert him. Tiger had still refused to acknowledge the fact that Teddy was dead. His mind had blocked out this reality. He went on in a distant, matter-of-fact tone.

"How could I have had anything to do with that, doctor? I needed her, really needed her. And I was able to discount all the unpleasant things. Sometimes I would think about the words in the marriage ceremony—'for richer, for poorer, in sickness, in health'—and I knew she was sick inside. She told me things. She was aggressive, contradictory, traumatized, full of guilt—the kind you doctors label 'sick.' She had been hurt, pushed down. I could always work on my book but she had nothing. Instead she threw tantrums. I understood. She was the way she was, that's all. When she put me down, I would sometimes come back at her, sometimes tease her, or be condescending. 'No other man would put up with your nonsense,' I would tell her. But she had to have the upper hand, to be the dominant one. I was jealous of her, and she of me because I could control events. She told me—it's true—that once when she was in an apartment with a young man, she went through his drawers and found some contraceptives. She took a needle and pierced them. Whoever he was going to have sex with might become pregnant." Tiger stopped suddenly. The tape had come to an end, so I changed it quickly. I looked at him. He was pondering something.

"*He* must have been the one who made her pregnant. Damn it. She fell right into the trap she had set for some other girl. What irony!"

"You think, then," I interrupted, "that Teddy unconsciously wanted to be pregnant? That goes well with what you told me earlier, that she wanted to have something that belonged to her —didn't she, Tiger?"

"Yes, yes," he answered emphatically.

"Was she possessive?" I asked.

"Yes."

"How about you? Are you possessive?"

Tiger looked surprised. "That hasn't occurred to me."

"What do you think?"

He didn't answer. His thoughts evidently were elsewhere. His facial expression seemed like that of a much older man, and it was without any trace of emotion.

"Do *you* think I am possessive?" Tiger finally said, in a somber voice. There was a pause. "That night I was walking . . . I stopped at the corner and I saw a clock. Four-thirty. I didn't have my watch, but I wasn't worried because it was on the dresser in my apartment.

"I don't know how long I was walking, but then I looked up. I think I saw the windows of Teddy's apartment.

"I had no idea what I was doing there, although it seemed rather natural. Should I call the police? But I had told the policeman that something had happened and he didn't believe me. I tried not to worry about my eyeglasses. You see, doctor, I worry too much. I always worry about losing my glasses. In school the kids teased me for worrying about little things. One day I lost the glasses and I was sorry—sorry because Mother had to pay for new ones. But I wanted my glasses now, and I had to have them because I could not work on my book without them."

Noticing how he had diverted his thoughts, I interrupted him.

"What did you do then, Tiger?"

"I went back into the house. I thought I was crazy. What was I doing there?"

"How did you get into the house?"

"Through the cellar kitchen door. It was pitch black, but I fumbled to find my way. I remember opening the door, and I walked up to her apartment."

Tiger stopped for a second. "I was in front of her door." He became silent.

"What happened then?" I asked.

"I began turning the knob."

"And then?"

"The door opened," he answered. A long pause.

"I walked in and sat down." Tiger was perspiring.

Leaning forward in my chair, I asked, "What happened?"

"I don't remember. I sat down. It was dark. Then I fumbled with my hands to find my glasses. I knocked over something, but I found them. I couldn't see anything. It was dark—my glasses."

I waited for him to continue, then asked if he hadn't been afraid that someone in the house might awaken. He answered. "No, I had no thoughts. I only wanted my glasses."

"Why?"

"I couldn't see without them."

"But you had been walking all over town. You had been in several bars, in the subway, a movie theater. So somehow you *did* see. Were you afraid, Tiger?" I asked. "Were you perhaps afraid that if you had left your eyeglasses in Teddy's apartment they might be traced to you?"

"Yes."

"How long were you in the apartment?"

"I don't know."

"And what happened then?"

"Nothing," he answered. "Tomorrow, I thought, all will be lost. I had a terrible headache."

"What you have told me, Tiger, sounds rather incredible. What you have described to me is almost a Dostoevskian scene. Couldn't this be a figment of your imagination, Tiger? Did it really happen? Or did you dream it?"

"I don't know. There it is."

Throughout my thirty years in the practice of psychiatry, I of course have heard many events described by my patients that seemed totally unreal, unbelievable. Not long ago I had a patient who, after spending the night at his girl friend's apartment, discovered that he had left his briefcase there. Instead of calling her, he took a cab to her house, came upstairs, unlocked the door, tiptoed in without awakening her, and picked up his briefcase, without being discovered by her. She was never to know that he had returned.

"Did you go home then?" I asked Tiger.

"Yes, I came home. The only thing I could think of was sleep. I thought what I had gone through was a nightmare."

"What happened during the following days?"

"I slept. I think I took a sleeping pill that the doctor had given me, and I slept for one or maybe two days. I was depressed, confused. Nothing seemed real."

Again I asked, more boldly than the first time, whether he knew what had happened—that Teddy was dead, and that "you might have something to do with it."

"I was involved in something but I didn't know what. I remember looking in the newspaper one morning, but I couldn't find anything."

"What were you looking for?" I asked.

No answer. He looked down at the floor. I could see an expression of pain on his face. He was silent. I wanted to relieve his suffering. I told him that despite his good mind, he needed professional help in learning how to cope with his long-standing frustrations. No answer. Attempting to communicate:

"You must read a great deal, don't you, Tiger?"

"Yes, doctor, even as a little boy, and as I grew older I had a real drive to learn things, to know all I could. It was almost like an intoxication—to be filled with knowledge, understanding, insight. I wanted to be able to analyze and to understand everything. Learning became almost an obsession: to know about everything —our social structure, the political system, technology, our culture, the American Dream. I tried to remember everything that I had read. I used to test my memory, but some things I just couldn't remember. I finally had to admit that not everything is worth remembering. Memory is important, but forgetting is just as important."

By now Tiger was speaking quite fluently again. Apparently he had overcome some of his agony about the night of the murder, and was diverting his thoughts. There seemed to be a growing sense of trust; he was anxious to tell me about himself.

"Have you been aware that you have been depressed, Tiger?"

"No, not exactly. I believed I was depressed, but I think I was also experiencing a sense of frustration, as you said."

I knew from this remark that Tiger wanted full control over his mind. It was as if his mind was a machine which could be turned on and off. What again surprised me was how little he recognized his emotional forces. I knew it would be difficult to break through this rigid control and learn what really had happened between Teddy and Tiger.

"Have you had any dreams?"

"I had one," Tiger answered. "It had to do with Mother's death. I went to her funeral. It was so strange. I had no one to talk to. It was sad, really sad. . . . Doctor, I know how you are interpreting my dream. You don't need to spell it out."

"I understand, Tiger. Just by looking at your face I could see that you understood some of the meaning of what you have said. But you *have* been depressed," I asserted. "When did it begin? How long has it lasted, do you think?"

"I don't know."

"Can you remember being seriously depressed at some earlier time—during your childhood or youth?"

"I was never lighthearted," Tiger replied. "Sometimes I was accused of not smiling, of not communicating. When people told me that I wasn't communicating it would make me mad inside. That word is so unreal. Opening one's mouth doesn't mean that we are communicating."

"You spent a great deal of time by yourself, didn't you, Tiger?"

"Yes," he answered in a noncommittal way.

"But you had a family though, didn't you?"

"Only a mother. I wouldn't call that a family. I never thought I had a family. So when I came to New York I created my own family—that is, me. I became my family."

"Were you depressed when you were alone, without a family? Did you feel sorry for yourself?"

"No, I don't know whether I felt sorry for myself. I never knew what it was like to have a family. I was always alone. But I think I *was* depressed."

"When, for instance?"

"When things went bad, when I couldn't write, when thoughts came very hard for me, when I couldn't make a go of it with girls. That upset me. I started out with a girl, and I felt alone, and you know, doctor, it isn't normal to be alone, but I don't think it's easy to build a serious relationship in our society. Too many pressures. To be alone is like a substitute for life—at least for me."

Tiger, in contrast to what he had said earlier, had admitted that loneliness was his way of life. But he couldn't see the relationship between his loneliness and his suicidal ideas.

"Doctor, there is something else I want to tell you," Tiger said suddenly. "Loneliness is something that comes when you cannot communicate with someone. I had no one to communicate with."

"Do you mean in your childhood?" I asked. "You had your mother."

"Yes, I had my mother, but I had no father."

"Let us talk about this the next time I see you." It was time for me to leave.

Before I walked out of the cubicle I looked at his face again. There was something proud about Tiger. His face was strong, reflecting a kind of dignity that seemed to remove him from the drabness of prison. I felt I was on the verge of reaching that closed inner sanctum of Tiger's mind.

When I returned to the office late in the afternoon I was exhausted. I kept thinking about Teddy and Tiger.

Why did this aggressive, dynamic girl seek out a man so insecure about himself, I thought, one who did not match her in strength? To find the answer I would have to probe far back into Teddy's childhood. From the time Teddy learned that her mother had died when she was born, she had come to feel it was her fault, and with that feeling came guilt. How could she wash off the guilt she assumed for her mother's death? Teddy could not erase the guilt from her conscience, so she had to placate it, ingratiating herself with her superego, or conscience, in order to come to terms with it. Unable to overcome her debt to her conscience, she began to feel worthless. But her intelligence and beauty rebelled against such a surrender. Nevertheless, her guilt was the stronger force and her sense of worthlessness dominated her self-image. She began to feel more secure with men who appeared unattractive, because she felt she could dominate them more easily. It gave her a sense of power which she needed emotionally. But whatever relationship she would establish was bound to fail because it was based totally on her own selfish need to assure herself of her worth.

By the time Teddy was past thirty, she had had several affairs, all of which ended abruptly. Faced with her failure to love, she remained superficially cold and stoical, while inwardly she cried. In time she seemingly was able to cover over her inability to establish a close relationship by saying to herself, "Men are so shallow; they are not worthy of my love." Yet the pattern of love and rejection repeated itself with every man she met. By now she had adopted what in psychiatry is called the repetition compulsion —a compelling, blind, unconscious impulse to repeat, to redramatize her earlier painful experiences with men, always blaming them for not recognizing the true woman she was. Driven by her hidden guilt about her mother's death, she unwittingly punished herself by in effect saying, "I mean nothing to any man." She unconsciously sought those seemingly normal, self-contained men whom she attracted, but who could humiliate her, while at the same time she could control them by tantalizing them through her beauty.

Tiger's story had been sometimes incoherent, at other times full of insight. I could not free myself from the impression that his vivid imagination might have distorted and exaggerated some of what really had happened on the night of Teddy's death. It was my intuition speaking to me; I had no proof. More important to me as a psychiatrist were his self-destructive tendencies and his relationship to the girl. The one could not be explained without the other. From my interviews with Tiger it seemed that Teddy responded to his weaknesses, to what he lacked, rather than to his strengths and assets as a man. Likewise, Tiger responded to what Teddy lacked rather than to what she had. It would seem then, at least on the surface, that each one fitted the other as a key fits a lock. Each played upon the weakness of the other. Tiger was moralistic but naïve. He had idealized her and thought he had found in her a mother, something Teddy herself lacked. On her side, she had tried to find a man in Tiger, a father, which he had missed in his own life. The result was to be compensatory, a symbiotic relationship, in which the invisible tie between them became as inevitable as the murder itself. Tiger considered Teddy a challenge, while she on her side felt challenged by him. She felt threatened by his ambition to be a man of power. They played on each other in a destructive way, not only on their "nerves" but, so to speak, on their whole being, on all their emotions. For now I would have to assume that Tiger's self-destructive tendencies had been turned away from himself toward Teddy. Somehow, although she was not aware of it, she had wanted him to attack. Feeling guilt, she had unconsciously wanted to become a victim of his aggression. It was almost a pure form of victimology.

One finding which for the time being I could not reconcile was the assumption that Tiger had been taking drugs, a matter he had denied or minimized. When I examined him there were no withdrawal symptoms, such as unusual perspiration, dry mouth, loss of appetite, shakiness or extreme fatigue. Such signs can sometimes be misleading. Tiger's individuality, however, was of such a type that even if he had been taking drugs—Dexedrine or amphetamines—he could not try to protect himself. His ego did not permit him to hide behind excuses because he wanted to take the responsibility for any act as far as this was possible for him; nor did I think that he denied using these drugs because he was ashamed to admit it. True to his character, he wanted to stand on his own.

Nevertheless, the aspect of drug use would have to be explored and one source would be his friend, Neil O'Brien. Judging from Tiger's story and from his experiences with Teddy, he was a man who had permitted himself to be abused. Without being aware of it, he loved misery, but in his relationship with Teddy this self-indulgence lasted only up to a point. Assuming that Tiger had stabbed or strangled her—the latter being the most probable—he might have felt unconsciously that this act was a symbolic way of saying, "You killed me—my self-esteem, my virility—and I am going to retaliate and kill you—more." One of the first things Dr.

Foster had said to me was that Tiger appeared to be hurt or wounded, or hunted like an animal. He felt Tiger had been exposed to a kind of hidden violence, which had hurt and wounded him. Even though it didn't kill him—that is, it didn't kill his body —this subtle kind of violence was killing his senses, his spirit, his soul. So far throughout my interviews Tiger had not made any exceedingly cutting remarks, or told of any experiences in which he had tried to humiliate someone through abuse. The reason for it possibly may have been that he himself had been hurt, for which reason on the unconscious level he could not hurt anyone else. He himself had asked me the question "Am I schizoid?" Not wanting to attach a label to him, I did not answer. This question, nevertheless, was revealing. Tiger was hypersensitive, yet in his contradictory mind he let himself be exposed to abuse.

One may well say that Tiger suffered from a sadism that had been strongly repressed from his earliest childhood. This sadism he turned into self-torture and, on the other side, overkindness and overgoodness, as shown in his behavior toward his mother and at times toward Teddy.

One thread that ran through his entire life was his depressive mood, which seemed deep-seated, ingrained in him, and could be considered a main factor in his difficulty in coping with life in his present difficult legal situation.

The most astonishing fact about my interview with Tiger, which covered almost two and a half days, was that he had never once used the words "killing," "murder," or "death." He never mentioned that Teddy had died. It was as though this thought was alien to him. The idea of having killed her was to him agonizing, painful. Since he was unable to remember anything of what took place during those last hours, it would be important, for him and for the case, to find out what really happened the night of the murder. To unravel this tangle of events and passions would be a task of the first order.

— 4 —

I returned to the case of Tiger a few days later when his friend Neil O'Brien came to my office. From the start he was more than willing to do whatever he could to help Tiger. He was quite disturbed that Tiger had been accused of killing Teddy, since both of them were his friends, and as a matter of fact Neil had introduced them to each other. Tiger and Neil had been friends from early schooldays. They had grown up together and visited each other's homes frequently. When asked what he knew in particular about Tiger, Neil answered that at times he was quite secretive about himself.

"Tiger was always a strange one. He didn't warm up to people easily. You could sense that he was standing off to see whether the other person was worth his trust, or whether he would be betrayed and ridiculed. Even though we were friends throughout elementary and high school, there were times when I caught him looking at me in that funny quizzical way of his, as if he were questioning if I was taking him seriously or making fun of him."

"Tell me, please—and it may be difficult to answer—if you can recall the first time you saw him."

"I do remember the first day I saw Tiger. It was in the fall and school had already started. My family had just moved to Washingtonville that summer so this was my first year at the school. I was in fifth grade. My first impression was of a tall woman who walked into the classroom, holding firmly by the hand a pale, thin boy. She seemed very big and spoke with authority. I remember her giving the teacher detailed instructions in a voice loud enough to be heard by those sitting toward the front of the classroom. She was Mrs. Mellowbrook and her son Tyros had been ill. He could go outdoors to play during recess only if the day was warm and sunny, and even then he was not allowed to run around and get overheated or tired. While this monologue was going on, the boy, Tyros, looked furtively around the room. He had on round glasses that seemed too large for his face. I later learned that Tiger had had rheumatic fever a year or so previously, and although it was not severe enough to cause damage to the heart his mother had become overprotective and kept Tiger out of school on the slightest pretext.

"That day happened to be quite nice so Tiger went out to the playground with the rest of us. He stood over to the side watching the other children—boys playing handball, girls skipping rope. He looked so lonely and defenseless, the perfect target for the school bullies, and we had our share. There was one in particular—Jack, I think his name was. He was husky and tough, the son of a millworker. I saw him walk over to Tiger, and could see that he was talking to him, trying to get Tiger into a fight. I could also see that Tiger did not want to fight but he was talking right back to Jack, and I could sense a certain dignity and pride in the way Tiger was handling himself, although by now he was close to tears, and looked so weak by comparison. Well, four or five of my friends and I went over and told Jack to stop picking on this kid. After that Tiger followed me around like a puppy. Although I became his best friend and remained so for many years, I never felt that I knew the real Tiger. There was an elusive quality about him. I didn't pry and just let him tell me what he wanted to about himself. During those long months when he was recuperating from his illness, he had turned to reading, devouring every book he could find. He was extremely bright, but not the type who tried to show off in class by keeping his hand up to answer the teacher's question. He was deeper than that. Later on in school he would discuss things like evolution, life, death, destiny—large, abstract ideas. I was terribly impressed, but often I didn't understand what he was talking about, so I went along with what he was saying. It was like talking to a grownup, not like someone your own age."

Neil stopped to light a cigarette.

"Tiger was close to his mother, particularly since his father had left home. She took in roomers to support them. One of his mother's roomers was a musician who gave Tiger violin lessons. I think that he could have done something with that if he had wanted to. Tiger was quite attached to this man, whom he called Uncle Roger, and they spent many weekends together, hiking, fishing, or just talking. Tiger became alive when he was with him. It's funny; the first time I went over to Tiger's house I met this man who acted as though he owned the place and was very friendly with Tiger's mother. Of course I thought he was Tiger's father, and addressed him as Mr. Mellowbrook. I remember Tiger's face getting red and the two grownups looking uncomfortable.

"As I remember it now, Tiger became embarrassed easily. One time, one of the fellows in our class found a full pack of cigarettes and we thought it would be quite a lark to go someplace and smoke them. There was an old deserted summer house all covered over with vines, and this seemed like an ideal place. At first Tiger didn't want to come along with us, but someone started to tease him and he finally joined us.

"We sat around smoking and talking and feeling very grown up. Someone told the rest of us about the time he had gone into the bathroom in his house and seen his older sister naked, just about to step into the bathtub. She had forgotten to lock the door. Well, that started things rolling, each of us trying to impress the others with how much he knew about sex. All except Tiger. He just sat there with a pained expression on his face. Finally, he ran out and when he didn't come back I went to see if he was all right. I found him sitting on the fence and I called out his name, but he didn't seem to hear me. Somehow sensing my presence, he turned around, startled. When Tiger was in this kind of daydreaming mood it was difficult to communicate with him. When I was sure that he was all right, I went back and joined the others. Tiger would come out of it. Better to leave him alone."

"How was Tiger in school?"

"He was smart, but sometimes he got himself in trouble with the teacher. One time I remember she hit him—I don't know what the reason was—but he hit her back. He was president of the student government, and once he told me that he was going into politics.

"I really think that if Tiger had daydreamed less in class he would have got much better grades, and I'm sure that he could have attended college on scholarship. He sat looking out of the window as if he was bored. Of course his schoolwork also suffered because he was so absorbed with his own writing."

"Do you remember anything peculiar about Tiger?"

Neil thought for a while, putting his hand to his face with three fingers on the cheek, thumb on chin and little finger in his mouth as though regressing to his own childhood.

"I remember that he used to play with animals, but that of course isn't peculiar. He had a cat and he would play with her in the attic. Once she bit him and he threw her out the window. The cat landed on all fours, unharmed, but Tiger was very upset and ran downstairs. I remember it very well because he tried to catch the cat, but she ran away. Tiger brooded about it a great deal, and swore never again. I think his rash action really surprised him. He was embarrassed about it. He had lost control."

"Anything else you would like to say about Tiger?"

"He didn't like to argue. He always thought that arguing was petty, and he didn't want to be involved in pettiness. He used to go to Sunday school, but one day he just stopped. Later on he told me that he had stopped believing in God. He said reason was his God."

Neil thought that Tiger got along quite well, on the whole, with his mother, but also he was afraid of her. She was always after him, nagging him. She expected a great deal from him because he was all she had. He was moody and resisted her attempts to control him.

"Moody, you said. Tell me more."

"He was often disgruntled. He had to be cajoled out of his—whatever he had. He wasn't easy to be with—he wasn't exactly sunshine. But he was straightforward—except for his secrecy about his personal life. Whenever he had a date with a girl, he never volunteered any information. But then he didn't have many girl friends."

"What more can you tell me about him?"

"I mentioned that Tiger read a greal deal. One day he came and told me about Darwin. I had never heard of him, and Tiger told me about evolution, which I misunderstood as revolution. He laughed at me. *E*volution, he repeated—the development of the species. I didn't dare ask him what he meant by 'species.' "

"Outside of the time when he threw the cat out of the window, did you ever see him get angry?"

Neil didn't think that he had seen Tiger get angry; he thought rather that he was disappointed and frustrated, and so kept to himself. He wasn't much of an athlete. He felt that sports were an inferior activity. "They were for the birds," he used to say. Instead he read books.

"After graduation from high school," Neil recalled, "we drifted away from each other. He went to college and I took some courses. I became a public relations man—a promoter. We would see each other during the summer, but then I left Washingtonville for good and came to New York, and one day Tiger showed up here too. He had been working very hard on a book, he told me."

"Do you know what kind of a book?"

"I'm not sure. I know that it was different from the first one he had written, which was all about a multiple murder in our home town."

"You said he told you about his present book?"

"Yes, but nothing really specific. At times I had the feeling that he worked on it feverishly for days at a stretch, without stopping to eat. I would call him up to invite him to dinner, but he would politely refuse. 'Sorry, no time,' he would say. Sometimes I invited him to a party, and occasionally he did come, and it was at one of those parties that he met Teddy—about two, three years ago —and they saw quite a lot of each other, I think. One never knew what was going on between them. They seemed like such an odd couple. Teddy was intelligent and very attractive. She could be quite impulsive. The one thing I know about her is what he wrote down and gave to me, apparently something to be included in his book. I took it with me. I have it here. In the manuscript he doesn't call her the girl Teddy, but I think it was she. Here it is, doctor." He handed me a faded paper.

Her face wrinkled unexpectedly. I tried to analyze her limpid expression, which changed quickly back to a glamorous impassivity. I didn't really know whether that way she looked very young and about to cry, or very old and trying to be pleasant. I decided that for a moment she had looked lonely, or maybe lovely. I was trying to learn about a woman's face—concentrating on it carefully, as if I were trying to describe her for someone. I wanted her to be my girl, that is why I watched her face to find out how she felt about me, what she thought. But I was too embarrassed to look directly into her eyes; I was afraid to appear like an innocent country boy in love—which was how I felt. Was there something disagreeable, dominating buried behind that beautiful face— as if she was capable of looking at me the same way Mother had when I first fell in love?

"I have something else here," Neil said, as he handed me two typewritten sheets. "This is about him."

He may end up alone. He is not able to settle for the type of arrangements other people make, I don't think anyone should seek out a relationship just because he is lonely. . . .

He didn't like being a nonperson. He had his job and his apartment, but what else did he have? His identity did not depend upon his surroundings. His life was part of being an object. He always thought of himself as a child. He found conversation empty, void of any meaning. It was meaningless. When he had something to say he would like to talk, but to say something in order to keep up the conversation was abominable to him.

He was in most situations conventional, but in his mind he was different, really unconventional. He was a contradiction.

At one time he dreamed about fame, but who doesn't? It was all empty. He fantasized about writing a book, a novel, and then refusing publication to prove that it had no meaning. Fame is without meaning.

"What do you think of this, Neil?" I asked.

"What Tiger meant was that fame could only have meaning when there was something behind it, something substantial. He used to compare himself to Georges Clemenceau, who also had the nickname 'Tiger.' He was famous, and Tiger identified with him. When I think of it now, I believe that Tiger wanted to be a physician, but he felt that it was too narrow for him because he wanted to be out in the world, to go into politics. And then Tiger told me that Georges Clemenceau originally was a physician and then became a statesman. I don't know whether this is true or not, but it's what he told me."

"Do you think your friend was unusually ambitious?"

"Yes," Neil said, "very ambitious, but he had a reason to be ambitious. He was so intelligent. But now everything is lost. You *must* help him, doctor. I think this whole thing is very unfair. I've talked on the phone with Tiger's mother and she's coming up here to see him. I also talked with Teddy's father and sister, and that was extremely painful."

"What was the real relationship between Tiger and Teddy?" I asked.

Neil somehow thought that they were a good match, but they argued a great deal. "I thought they were more lovers' quarrels than anything else, and I didn't pay too much attention. He always gave in because he didn't like to argue. I remember he wrote down some words, like the more compelling the ties were between people, the sharper the arguments would be. Then he said something which I think had to do with his close relationship with his mother, or maybe also with Teddy. It was something to the effect that"—Neil hesitated a second—" 'the more extreme dependency there is between people, the more prone they are to dislike each other.' Frankly, doctor, I didn't understand it, but then I'm not a psychologist. Tiger was heads above me."

Asked about Mellowbrook's dislike of his mother, Neil said Tiger felt that she had been kind to him and had helped him, and he thought that he should do the same for her. He admired her for much of what she had done for him, but he did resent her. "I think she controlled him, which he hated."

"Do you think Tiger was violent?"

"No, not really. He wanted to avoid violence. That also was the reason why he couldn't stand any argument. Tiger became a pillar of strength to his mother, too much so. He was angry at himself for it. But he had no choice in the matter."

"What about that cat?" I interrupted. "The one he threw from the attic."

"Oh, but that only lasted for a moment."

Yes, I thought, but in that moment he became violent and threw the cat out of the window.

"Was Tiger attracted to his mother?" I asked.

"When he was in the mood. Then I think he liked her very much and was happy with her."

"Neil, you told me before that Tiger was not an athlete. Didn't he participate in any sports at all?"

"Yes," Neil replied. "He was a very good swimmer, and during our high school years we often went to the ocean to swim. He particularly liked high waves, and enjoyed himself tremendously. He enjoyed the waves as if he became a part of them, part of their violence. I found it very strange because I wouldn't think of staying as far out in the ocean as he did. It was as if he was trying to defy the force of the waves. He always came to the shore by himself. And then I saw that he was quite exhausted, but also proud of himself because he had been able to get out from the waves."

"Do you think then, Neil, that Tiger was playing with the waves?"

"It didn't look like that. I rather think that the waves were playing with him."

I was intrigued with Neil's commentary. This last information was important to me. It seemed that by defying the waves Tiger was trying to prove that he wasn't afraid of them—which of course would mean that he really was afraid. He was struggling to prove himself, to assert his will, his supremacy. But this fight was filled with personal risk to the point of self-destruction.

"Was Tiger afraid?"

"Not to my knowledge," Neil answered, "but he was afraid of hurting himself. He had had some bad accidents. I remember that he always climbed high up in the trees, and sometimes he would lose his balance and fall. Once he fell and hurt his leg quite badly. Another time he cut himself with a knife, and the doctor had to stitch the wound. There were other minor things."

Neil's information confirmed that Tiger seemed to be accident prone and to display psychosomatic symptoms and self-destructive tendencies. He courted danger, defying it, but still he was

afraid of hurting himself. Where there is a fear, there is an unconscious wish. Unwittingly, or even wittingly, he was playing with
death.

"Is there anything else you can tell me about Tiger and Teddy?"

"I remember seeing them at parties, close together, but suddenly out of nowhere she began to argue about something. What
it was I never knew. You would almost think they were enemies.
But then in the next moment they made up and were friends again.
It puzzled me, but of course I never asked."

"Do you mean to say that they were both friends and enemies?"

"Something like that. Teddy's blood was hot. She had a temper
and was impatient, and Tiger had to calm her down. She was very
gifted. Practically everything she touched turned to gold. She had
money—she liked to earn it and to spend it. She was hard-working, doctor. I was pleased to see Teddy and Tiger together because
I thought that he might calm her down. I was dead wrong. I feel
awful about it because it really is my fault. I should never have
introduced Tiger to Teddy—it was such a mistake!"

Trying to reassure Neil, I said that he had tried to do his best
for them both. It was not his fault that their relationship ended
so tragically.

Neil looked at me in a quizzical way and said, "I could never
understand Tiger. Sometimes he became completely tongue-tied,
and I told him he wasn't making much sense. I couldn't understand how he could write so well and yet not find words when he
was speaking."

"May I ask you a frank question, Neil? What made him keep
up his friendship with you?"

"That's an interesting question, doctor. I'm not sure I know. He
thought I was outgoing, that I had a good sense of humor, and
that I wasn't afraid to speak out. But of course, I think it went
deeper than that. Probably it was nostalgia for his hometown and
we'd had quite a few experiences together."

"Anything in particular?"

"Oh, you know, boys play with each other, innocent stuff."

I made a mental note of his last remark.

"Did Tiger use any drugs?"

"Once in a while, but not very much. He used Dexedrine to perk him up, sometimes amphetamines, but not very much. He was afraid of drugs. He didn't like to take anything."

"Did he drink?" I asked.

"No, he didn't drink much. Very little. In fact he would walk around with a glass of ice water in his hand, and people thought that it was gin or vodka. But he drank very little. Except, of course, when he was very upset."

I asked Neil if he knew of any excessive drinking in Tiger's home. He couldn't say for sure. I decided to ask Tiger's mother when I spoke to her.

"Well," I said to Neil, "you will have to be a witness when this case comes to trial. I am sure that Tiger's lawyer, Mr. Taylor, will be in touch with you and will talk to you about the case. In the meantime, let what we have talked about here be strictly between you and me. Don't, under any circumstances, say anything to anyone about the case. You might get telephone calls from newspaper reporters. . . . Oh, one final question, Neil. Do you think that Teddy was jealous?"

"Yes, I think so. Sometimes she told me that jealousy expressed self-anger. I argued with her about it. I couldn't understand how one could be jealous and angry at one's self. But then she had her hang-ups—like all of us." Neil smiled. "Teddy was attracted to him, there is no doubt about it, but then, she really could argue."

"Possibly about sex?"

"Can't say. Tiger never said anything to me. He kept it a secret. One time I heard them argue about some plans they had. It was my impression that he was wrong, but she wasn't right either. What a strange couple, I thought. But I wasn't going to say anything."

"Do you think that Teddy led him into arguments deliberately?"

"She was impatient," Neil said, "and fast on the trigger. It was easy for her to get involved in arguments."

"Thank you for coming to my office, Neil," I said. "If you have anything more to tell me, I would be much obliged to you. Further details, as many as possible about Tiger and Teddy, particularly about their relationship. I would like to know about this because it all may have had a bearing upon her death. Try to remember and write down any incident that may throw some more light upon their life together—any incident from his childhood or youth. The more we know, the better we will understand what happened between them that led to the killing."

I had an uneasy feeling as I pondered Neil's comments, and as I prepared to see my next patient that afternoon, I thought about his remark that Teddy easily got herself into arguments. It made me think that without her knowing it, she formed, or shaped, or created some sort of intrigue with Tiger. Perhaps she liked intrigue because she was then really able to create advantageous situations where she became an important, if not *the* important part. To her intrigue was necessary; possibly it was an essential part of her life on which she built her feminine fascination. She enjoyed it, for it enhanced her ego. It might very well be that this tendency to plot, innocent though it might have been, was the most effective weapon she had in drawing men to her. Apparently she had learned this art of manipulation at an early age and had perfected it with time. She was rebelling against Tiger's attempt at authority, while he in his quiet and indirect way was rebelling against her domination.

Teddy's ability to engage in intrigue with sadistic delight put a surprising dimension into the case. Her intrigue-making, one could say, made her a partner of the murder that later took place. Without her being aware of it, she goaded Tiger and played with him, so to speak, challenged him to attack her, and thereby mobilized his violent desires—another manifestation of victimology.

Another aspect of my interview with Neil which surprised me was his sophisticated use of language. With only a high school education, he certainly had learned a great deal about personality analysis, possibly through psychoanalysis. Perhaps he had adopted some of the words and ideas that Tiger used, and even if he did not understand completely what they meant, he had incorporated them into his vocabulary. That he was extremely concerned about Tiger was later corroborated by his calling me whenever he thought of something about Tiger which might be of interest to me.

Following the first interview, Neil gave me some of Tiger's

manuscript, which was hand printed in large letters. It was rather disjointed, epigrammatic:

What is mortal seeks to be immortal. Death is the seperation of the mind, the spirit, from the body.

Some people wait to be slauhgtered. They wait to die.

Who that can conquer life will be a man.

Man is the most ferocious of all animals, more than a tiger, more than a shark.

A man kills his own species, not for pleasure but because he wants to.

Who can conquer his own desires can or will be a man.

There is a time to despair, and a time to enjoy.

Emotional infidelity is worse than sexual infidelity.

To step on one's soul is criminal.

Do I love you? Do you love me? You cannot love what you don't know.

A sense of honor must be present. It has to be defended.

Dread is the pit of hell. Overcoming it is heaven.

Beauty was never born, it never dies. A man in constant touch with beauty, he will become immortal.

While reading Tiger's notes, I noticed that "slaughtered" had been misspelled; the *g* and *h* had been transposed. The word "separation" had been spelled "seperation." This misspelling was due to his desire to spell the words as his imagination directed him. Even if there are many intelligent people who can't spell and do not become violent, and even if the sample here is small, it may be another factor of circumstantial evidence confirming Tiger's violent act. Neil didn't know anything about Tiger's misspellings. He said jokingly, "I'm a poor speller myself, but I don't go around killing people."

Remembering that he had told me that Tiger rarely drank, I felt I had to ask him about it again. Neil said that he had been thinking about it, and had remembered an occasion just before high school graduation when they had gone out together on a drinking spree, had become drunk and the next morning woke up in a field. "I remember that Tiger asked me whether he had killed someone. I had a hangover and didn't quite understand what he meant. It seemed so out of place. I think he forgot about it later on, but now as I think of all that has happened I doubt very much that he forgot it."

I was extremely interested in this last insight about Tiger. To fantasize about killing someone is not unusual. People may not notice this trait in themselves because they are unaware of their murderous impulses, even though they may have guilt feelings. We all know that the child or the adolescent (or even the adult) has death wishes toward his parents, or his brothers or sisters, or anyone who may serve as a symbol of authority. For the child in particular, when the unconscious part of his mind wants to kill someone, it may be only a temporary, fleeting wish, not final, fatal. He also has the desire to bring the dead back to life. "I want to kill him" therefore means that the unconscious wishes to get the person out of the way and then recall him to life when it is necessary or desirable. The normal child therefore does not feel guilt about his death wishes. But Tiger most certainly had felt guilty about his death wishes against his father, or his mother, which to some extent could explain the brooding resentment and hate which were buried beneath these death wishes.

"Neil," I asked, "did Tiger think seriously of entering politics?"

"It's hard to say. He talked about it but never gave any details. It was more of a daydream. He was interested in society and read all kinds of newspapers and books."

I recalled what a murderer had told me once about what he thought of himself as a criminal. He said, "From society's standpoint I am a criminal. But I am really a rebel against modern times." Asked whether he felt guilty about his deed, he answered only, "To me authority means nothing. It doesn't bother me to kill. It doesn't result in emotions. It is like an animal instinct."

In some way Tiger was like this man. He too didn't fit into the structure of our present society. But the source of his own moral system, his own standards of justice, was his emotions, which, in contrast to the criminal, made him feel guilty.

Another criminal, in trying to justify his murder, said, "When society kills another human being, they don't think it is wrong. They wanted to kill me. They look upon killing as if they enjoyed it. Even the taxpayers enjoy the killing of other people, and the ministers enjoy it—they watch the execution. If the majority thinks it is right to kill, why couldn't I do it?"

Most murderers think that they can commit an act of aggression or violence and get away with it. This is far from the truth, because so many of them get caught. Tiger's depressive attitude and his Hamlet-like brooding had shown his guilt about his behavior. He felt that he had done or wished to do something wrong which he didn't want to express, and which he therefore tried to keep as far as possible from his mind.

That Tiger himself had in a way tried to rebel against society, or that his rebelliousness had been stimulated by Teddy, could very well have been the case. To him she represented the dynamism and the oppressiveness of New York City, the bustling society which he abhorred but which he nevertheless had tried to accept and dominate—the society which he felt had rejected him.

Reviewing briefly the relationship between Neil and Tiger, I found that Neil was quick and aggressive. He liked to accomplish things and had chosen to work in publicity and promotion. He felt that essentially Tiger was a dreamer who talked about evolution. This just didn't fit in with the real world. Who needed that anyway? Neil dressed modishly and when he dated a girl he liked to take her to a good restaurant, to get the best tickets for a show.

I liked Neil because he was direct: he knew what he was and what he wanted. Perhaps that is why Tiger was attracted to him. The relationship between them was built upon contrast. Neil had the body of an athlete, tall, muscular, lithe. His features were strong, and there was an open spontaneous quality about him. He showed candor. Even when quiet he seemed to radiate suppressed activity. His views were strong and simple. His dark eyes met my gaze directly, reflecting sincerity and concern about his friend. Neil was attractive and forceful as a man; he liked girls and was popular. Perhaps that is why he was anxious to introduce Tiger to Teddy, for Tiger, being introspective and shy, had never been able to socialize easily with women.

Though Neil and Tiger were total opposites, the ties of loyalty from childhood were strong and kept them together in New York. It made Neil feel important when he introduced Tiger to Teddy, a girl he himself had tried to date. Neil, though, was not sophisticated enough for Teddy.

It crossed my mind that Neil and Tiger were drawn together *because* of their complementary personalities. When I questioned Tiger about this a few weeks later, he seemed surprised and indignant. Once again I realized that he was a person who believed that behavior should conform to respectability, or what society or he himself thought was right. Whatever unconscious emotional or physical attraction he might have felt toward Neil he repressed, which is what one would expect from him. This was in contrast to Neil, who apparently had few repressions. He was quick to comprehend, and did not work against a rigid frame of mind.

In a way I would say that their relationship was gratifying, but there was probably some strain between them at times, particularly when Tiger was jealous of Neil's easy behavior. While Neil was the master on the bodily level, Tiger surpassed at the intellectual level. This strain in their relationship might occasionally mount to something like the psychological torture we often see between highly intelligent people. Their life, so it seemed, was intertwined to quite a degree.

Slowly one point began to play at my mind: Neil's information that at one time Tiger had dreamed or fantasized that he had killed someone, which, coupled with his particular personality makeup, could mean he had wanted to kill his mother or father but never did. This same thought, however, made me wonder whether Tiger *had* killed Teddy at all. Against such an assumption there spoke the fact that he had not, or could not, or did not want to remember anything at all of that particular event. But the reason for this might very well have been that his fears of wanting to kill her were so strong that they gave rise to an idea that he really had killed her. Where there is a fear there is a wish, and while this wish had been submerged, the fear of it had come to the surface and made it look as if he had killed her. Not surprisingly, I found myself thinking like a detective.

A psychiatrist *is* a kind of detective. He tries to find in his patients hidden emotions, hidden motivations, which he attempts to bring to the surface so that they can see clearly the feelings that drive them. The factors that make or don't make a person function, the reasons why he doesn't get along with people, why he is sexually impotent, a failure, or too successful—these are lodged deeply in the mind, their roots buried in the past. The task of the psychoanalyst is to unravel these emotional forces and clarify them so that the patient can understand them and cope with them. This is not an easy matter since the analyst is forced to delve deeply into the unconscious in order to find the unconscious sources of his patient's behavior. And this is one fundamental reason why psychoanalysis takes such a long time. It is a time-consuming process, often prolonged due to the patient's resistance to divulging details of his life which have been painful to him and which he has repressed.

There was no doubt that Tiger had repressed many experiences, not only about his own life but also about his relationship to Teddy. Some of the things about himself he did perceive he distorted by refusing to recognize the full range of his emotions. And he was reluctant to divulge whatever he saw. What went on between Tiger and Teddy was greatly a mystery. This is not very surprising since, in general, we know very little about what the real relations are between a couple. How a couple appears to other people is often a distortion, a false picture of the real link that binds them.

Neil had described Teddy and Tiger as an odd couple. Odd couples do strange things to each other. They challenge each other, they are at odds to the point of being at each other's throats; they also love each other in a certain way. But there is tension between them, the one uncertain of or insecure about the other. From what I had learned, however, Tiger's case seemed on the surface to be an impossible crime, which raised an interesting question—the possibility that there never was a murder, only many coincidences ending with an event that looked like murder.

The search warrant had implied that Teddy was stabbed and strangled. It was hard to understand how Tiger had stabbed her. Where was the murder weapon? Tiger himself was a man who lived more in books than in the real activity of life. For all practical purposes, books were almost his whole life. It was strange that I had not yet received the autopsy report which the district attorney had promised to send to Taylor.

In my work as an expert witness, I have always found it essential to ascertain all available facts in the case, from the defendant, the police, the medical examiner, the court and the defense lawyer, as well as any other sources. Psychiatrists are inclined to limit their examination to the accused himself, neglecting to probe into what has been going on around him. I have been consulted in too many cases where the psychiatrists have paid scant, if any, attention to the circumstances surrounding the crime. While it is good to rely on the lawyer, they should try to make up their own mind about how and why the crime was committed.

Tiger had the cards stacked against him. There was the confession, which he had not signed; it was possible that it might not even be admitted into evidence because he was questioned at the time of his arrest without a lawyer present. Perhaps more important was the fact that nobody had really seen him in Teddy's apartment. When a person confesses to a crime, it does not always mean that he has committed it. Many people accuse themselves of imagined deeds for which they feel guilty.

For many reasons Tiger was guilt-ridden. He was fundamentally hostile, and fearful, and where there is hostility there must be guilt, conscious or unconscious. He claimed to have revisited Teddy's apartment, but how much credence could one attach to that? If he had revisited the scene of his alleged crime, it could be because he had an unconscious need to be punished, to betray himself by hoping that he could be caught. But, in addition, it could also very well be that since he had been dominated by his mother from early childhood on, and had felt rather helpless toward her, his returning to Teddy's apartment could express an unconscious need to proclaim that he was not helpless; to show his mother, apparently indirectly, that he was strong and virile, able to strike back.

As I had expected, my interview with Tiger's mother didn't reveal much information about his inner life. She was in her early fifties, neatly dressed. She held a pair of white gloves in her hand, a sign of southern gentility. She was highly emotional. At first she wept and sobbed almost uncontrollably. Slowly, as she regained composure, she spoke about Tiger's infancy and early childhood. Her pregnancy had been normal, although she was very disturbed about her husband, whom she described as a drifter. He was not home as the time approached for her to give birth, and she had to ask a friend to drive her to the hospital. The delivery was prolonged, but as far as she knew, forceps were not used. She couldn't remember anything unusual about Tiger during the first few months. He talked clearly before he was one year old, was toilet trained, and he began to read by himself when he was four and one half years old. (Obviously no brain damage, I thought.) He fussed about his food, but on the whole he was a "good boy." When her husband left her, Tiger slept in her bedroom until he was nine or ten years old. He was fond of climbing trees and even fell down on one occasion and hurt himself, but one couldn't keep him away from trees. He did very well in school, that is, in math and reading, but he was a poor speller.

"A poor speller?" I repeated.

"Yes, he couldn't spell. Either he didn't know how or he didn't want to, but I think later on he improved."

She wanted Tiger to continue his education after he graduated from college—perhaps he would become a doctor—but he wanted to take a year or so off. "I remember how horrified I was, and I told him that everyone has to have a profession in order to support oneself. I was afraid that Tiger might become a drifter, just like his father had been. But then he got a job on the newspaper and he began to write."

"Did he ever get angry at you?"

"Sometimes," she answered, "but he was a good boy. Whatever he earned he brought home and gave to me, and then I gave him an allowance, and we kept this up for many, many years until he came to New York, some four or five years ago. He would write to me from New York at least twice a week, and of course I wrote back to him, and he called me every Sunday—collect, of course. Or I called him. Sometimes I came to visit him, but only for a few days because I had to go back and take care of my roomers. I have talked with Neil and with Tiger's lawyer, Mr. Taylor, who seemed to be an awfully nice man. I don't understand anything. . . ."

"Did Tiger tell you anything about Teddy?"

"Once in a while, but nothing important. Of course I was eager for him to get married, because as you know everybody should get married, and Tiger is now past thirty. I wanted so much to have a grandchild." She began to sob again.

"Did you ever meet Teddy?"

"No," she said. "Tiger always explained that she was busy or that she didn't have time to meet me. It seemed very strange because I thought they were going to get married."

"Were they ever engaged?" I asked.

"No."

"Did Tiger have any girl friends when he was home?"

"No, he didn't. But he met a very nice girl, quiet, and she was so nice. She would have been so good for him. They went out together a few times, and he even had dinner at her home, and I was there too, but nothing came of it."

While it seemed that Mrs. Mellowbrook was eager to talk about her son, what was uppermost in her mind was that he had to be saved. "You must help him, doctor," she said. "I don't know whether there is anything wrong with him, but I cannot think that he did something to Teddy. That isn't in his nature."

I asked her whether Tiger had had any temper tantrums, but she denied it.

"Did he have any nightmares?"

She couldn't remember any.

"Try to think," I urged her.

"Yes, I remember," she answered. "It was just one time, just before I moved him to his own room. He had a nightmare. He couldn't explain it, but he said that he was looking for something. It must have been that he was looking for his father and found him. You know, doctor, he grew up without a father."

Her interpretation of his dream surprised me at first, but then I realized that feeling guilty about Tiger's father, she projected her own thoughts onto Tiger. "Did he ever mention that he wanted to see his father?" I inquired.

"No, he didn't. Never."

"Did you find this strange?"

"No, I didn't."

Did she have anything more to tell me about her family?

She hesitated, smoothed imaginary wrinkles in her dress with her small, well-shaped hands, bit her lip, and said in a weak voice that she had belonged to a wealthy family but they had disowned her when she married Tiger's father. "He was so attractive, but he was no good—a drifter, a heavy drinker. But what else could I do? I was pregnant. I should have known better. After we were married he forced me to drink with him. I was so afraid of him." Her attempted smile turned into a grimace. "Oh, I was ashamed of myself, so ashamed." She stopped and began to weep quietly.

Mrs. Mellowbrook looked tormented. Under such circumstances it is always difficult to ask further questions. Why open old wounds? But still it might be good for her to unburden her heart. I sat quietly, looking at her darkened, grief-stricken face, her tear-filled eyes. I thought to myself, What have *you* done to deserve this fate—to have to come here and find your only son accused of murder? As every mother, you too had dreams for your child, of excellence, of fame—of all the things which you yourself had longed for in your youth but had never captured. . . .

After a while she looked up. "Everything is lost," she muttered. I remembered that Tiger had used the same words.

By now she began to regain her composure, and I attempted to resume my examination. I asked her about her husband. No, she didn't know where he was. As far as she knew he had left Washingtonville and never returned. "The less I talk about him the better." Observing her eagerness to steer away from the topic of her former husband, I asked her about Tiger. Had he been unwanted? No, she had loved her husband, but she had hoped and prayed that she would have a little girl. She had been disappointed when Tiger came along instead. This was important information which went a long way in explaining why she had tied him to her so closely. That she had wanted a girl undoubtedly aroused in her feelings of guilt toward him for which she tried to compensate by smothering him with love.

Turning away from my own thoughts, I asked her about her life after her husband had deserted her. It was lonely, hard. "The only thing I had to live for was Tiger." But didn't she see any friends? Once in a while, not often. Taking care of her boardinghouse and making her roomers comfortable took up her time. She really didn't care for her roomers, but it was her livelihood.

I asked, "Did you only have Tiger around you?"

"No, there was one boarder of whom Tiger was very fond, and he stayed around a lot. I was lonely. You can't spend all your time going to church. What do you do after church?"

"What did you do, if I may ask? Of course you don't have to answer if you don't want to," I added hurriedly.

"What does a lonely woman do? Can't you guess?" Not waiting for my answer, she continued, "I drank myself to sleep. When I awoke I was ashamed for Tiger. I found myself half naked. I was embarrassed. I tried to hide my nudity. I was ashamed, doctor, so ashamed. *Please* believe me." Her voice rose to a crescendo.

"I do believe you," I answered instantly. But *she* didn't believe *me*. She burst into convulsive crying. Her guilt seemed excessive, I thought. When she had quieted down, I asked her if she had any questions. She only wanted me to help Tiger. She had been at the hospital—Tiger had been transferred there for psychiatric examination—and he looked awful. All the people around him—drug addicts, all kinds of strange ones. She had never seen such a bunch in her whole life. Couldn't Tiger be transferred to a private hospital? she pleaded. He was, I reminded her, under the jurisdiction of the court, the only authority about to make such a decision. To transfer him to a private hospital would be against all regulations, and at the present status of the case, I doubted very much that a transfer would be permitted. On the whole, I said, the outcome of the case was in the lap of the gods, or more correctly, in the lap of the law. I tried to reassure her that the doctors and nurses at the city psychiatric hospital were doing their best.

She didn't think there was anything wrong with Tiger; she certainly never thought that he had ever been insane, although she admitted that at times he had been quite moody. Yes, now that she thought of it, he had had temper tantrums, but even if he did become angry at times, he tried to control his anger. His moodiness stemmed from the fact that she could not always give him everything he wanted. It had been a great disappointment to him that he couldn't apply to Harvard or Yale, but instead had to go to the state college, where the tuition was low. But—as any mother would like to believe—she thought that her son was never frustrated. She didn't bring up Teddy in the interview unless I did. As she said, she was trying to save her son from the disgrace of murder. If necessary, she would be willing to testify in court about his good morals. At the end of the interview Mrs. Mellowbrook tried bravely to control her desperation. Although she had wept several times, I could see on her face traces of the great dignity I had noted, though there it was more pronounced, in Tiger.

In the interviews with Neil and Mrs. Mellowbrook I had learned several important elements about Tiger's emotional development. From the earliest time his mother had been a dominant force, in both his conscious and his unconscious mind. He exaggerated her power, and felt dwarfed by her. I could readily see how Tiger had developed such an attitude because my own impression was of a strong woman who had tried to do more than her duty. Since her husband had deserted her and her child, she felt she had to compensate, becoming both mother and father.

The fact that Tiger had slept in the same bedroom with his mother until he was nine or ten years old—even though she denied that they had slept in the same bed—must have resulted in a great deal of intimacy between them. When she drank to excess, as she had admitted doing, it is quite reasonable to assume that she appeared before Tiger in her nightgown or underwear. On such occasions she might have seemed particularly seductive to him. It may very well be that he was also exposed to sexual intimacies between his mother and the roomer he called Uncle Roger. This may have stimulated his anger and increased his already severe frustration.

Feelings of sexual overstimulation and constant frustration may have mobilized in Tiger a tendency to try to find out what was going on with his mother or around the house. Now I could better understand Tiger's interest in observing things. He was able, in part, to satisfy these needs to look and to observe—scopophilic inclinations—by incessant study and reading, through which he might obtain universal knowledge. His sexual overstimulation brought about a disturbed psychosexual development, resulting in feelings of guilt and of fear.

5

The following days were hectic. I had arranged to see Tiger at the hospital on Tuesday and wanted to speak to his lawyer first. But Taylor was busy too, so we made an appointment for a working luncheon together Wednesday at a quiet place where we could talk freely. He was eager to hear my findings and I gave him a thumbnail sketch of Tiger's personality makeup, and his story of what had happened at Teddy's apartment. I also told him that Tiger had no memory of the actual event during which he allegedly strangled or stabbed her.

"What else can you tell me?" Taylor asked.

"You mean what do I want to tell you?"

"Well, have it your way."

"I wish I could," I said facetiously. "You know a psychiatrist should always be right, apparently because he is on the side of the angels. But to be serious," I continued, "Tiger's personality makeup is rather unusual. He certainly represses a great deal of reality, particularly about what took place on the night of Teddy's death. And not once did he directly ask me for help."

I reviewed my interview with Tiger's mother, particularly the significant point that they had shared a bedroom until he was nine or ten years old, which undoubtedly created a great deal of closeness between them, though not necessarily sexual intimacy. I began to muse aloud. "She said Tiger's father had an unsettling influence on him, even though Tiger was very young when his father left. It is strange, though, that Tiger never told her how he felt about growing up without a father.

"You know," I continued, "lack of information about the father might have suggested that he was weak and powerless in the family. Whenever there is little or no reference to any family member, especially a father, even if he has abandoned his home, we must start to suspect that this particular person had significantly *more* influence than suggested, though in a negative way. In our case, Tiger was angry at his mother and he berated her even though he didn't say one disparaging word about his father. His silence was telling."

Taylor then told me about the autopsy report. The only finding was an uneven, somewhat rough line around the neck. There were no stab wounds. Apparently the cause of death was strangulation. The murderer must have ripped off the necklace, thus strangling her. The amount of bleeding in the larynx and pharynx might indicate that some force had been exerted.

Next I brought Taylor up to date by reporting on my examination of Tiger the previous day at the city psychiatric hospital. It had been a short interview—only an hour. I had asked him again about the events on the night Teddy died, but Tiger's response had been completely negative. Talking to him at the hospital was difficult since no examining room was available, and I had to interview him in an open room which served as a kind of corridor where patients and police guards kept going back and forth. It was noisy and confusing, just the kind of atmosphere that would make Tiger tense because he would feel he was on exhibition, and deprived of the privacy his personality demanded.

He had sat in front of me in faded gray pajamas. I questioned him from all angles about the night Teddy had died. He was emphatic about having no memory of what happened. His denial was so strong that I began to think that maybe he hadn't been in her apartment at all, and that he had not strangled her. I wondered whether the police in searching Tiger's apartment had found the necklace with which presumably he had strangled her.

It was curious that when Tiger finally left Teddy's apartment that night he apparently returned home as if nothing had happened. There were times, he said, when he tried to remind himself of what he possibly might have done, but at other times he tried to deny with every part of his body that anything had taken place. He said he was incapable of violence. I had to remind him about the cat he had thrown out of the window when he was younger, and that he was at times angry without expressing that anger.

I told Taylor that during the night Tiger had gone back to Teddy's apartment to find his glasses. But I couldn't say whether this really happened, or if it was a dream or a wish. There was much psychopathology and many contradictory elements in his account so that it was hard to distinguish between what really took place that night and what existed in his fantasy.

Then I raised a new question that had been bothering me. I had asked Tiger's mother for a description of her husband and she told me that he was dark-haired, tall. She, too, was dark. I sensed that there might have been some doubt about paternity, that the man who Tiger thought was his father possibly may not have been his real father. As we knew, Tiger had very light hair. Of course it could very well be that some of his grandparents were light-haired and that he had inherited the genes. These were only speculations on my part. But if that was the case, then he might have felt, given his sensitive mind, that he didn't resemble either his mother or his father, and possibly that was the reason why he would gaze into the mirror, searching for some echo of his parents. I had not asked Tiger about any of these questions because I didn't want to disturb him with more problems. But this issue of paternity, I thought, may have been crucial to his emotional development.

The lawyer asked me what I thought the results of the psychiatric examination at the hospital would reveal. I answered almost without hesitation that because of Tiger's reluctance to reveal information about himself, he would be found able to stand trial. Taylor felt, however, that a sanity hearing was necessary. He said he would speak to the judge and request that it be held before the trial.

For the next fourteen days I found myself in a quandary about a case which was far from clear-cut from either the psychological or the legal point of view. Even if Tiger was not found insane by the court, there were many psychological elements that put him in the twilight zone between sanity and insanity. Whether or not he had really killed was within the province of the court, but this legal question was intimately involved with Tiger's mental condition.

Some five weeks later I received from the defense attorney a psychiatric report on Tiger which he had obtained from the city psychiatric hospital.

Tyros Mellowbrook, 32 years old, white, male, was sent for observation by the Criminal Court on June 1, 19____, after being charged with homicide. During the psychiatric examinations, the examiners found patient to be well oriented as to time and person. He was tense and pale. Sometimes he did not answer questions put to him, particularly those related to the charge against him. His answers were rather guarded, and he showed some hostility. Most prominent in his demeanor was his state of depression. The patient appeared preoccupied, and talked slowly. He had no complaints except that the place was noisy and he was unable to sleep. For some time he had been sleepless, but had not taken any sleeping medication. He denied using drugs although he admitted to have taken Dexedrine and amphetamines at times. He considered himself to be a writer, but now he was a failure. He did not want to go into the events during which he allegedly had killed a girl. No delusions or hallucinations could be ascertained. There seemed to be some paranoid ideas in that he is afraid of people. The psychological examination obtained through the Wechsler Adult Intelligence Scale showed a verbal IQ of 132, a performance IQ of 120, a full-scale IQ of 127. He may be classified as having a superior intelligence, with some occasional disturbance of his thinking. His Rorschach tests indicate a great deal of hostile and aggressive tendencies, which at times seemed to reach paranoid proportions. He seemed self-controlled. There was no evidence of the presence of a formal thinking disturbance. This may well be because we are dealing with a highly intelligent person who knows how to guard his answers.

Because of his depressive moods, the patient has been given medication to counteract it. Diagnosis: Mental depression of a reactive nature, stress and strain reaction in a highly intelligent individual. Conclusion: At the time of the alleged crime, Tyros Mellowbrook (as the result of mental disease or defect) did not lack substantial capacity to know or appreciate the wrongfulness of his conduct, or to conform his conduct to the requirements of law.

Tyros Mellowbrook is able to understand the charges against him, he is able to confer with his lawyer, to aid in his own defense, and to stand trial.

It was apparent to me that the two psychiatrists who had examined him at the hospital were unable to probe fully enough the depths of the defendant's emotional condition. This was due in part to the great number of patients they had to examine. More noteworthy was the fact that no mention of Tiger's intense relationship with Teddy had been made. Possibly the heavy caseload was also a reason why no electroencephalogram or sodium amytal interview had been done. The latter procedure might have brought out some of the strong emotions that Tiger had repressed.

Although the psychiatric report contained only an outline of Mellowbrook's mental condition, I knew from earlier experiences that court- or lawyer-retained psychiatrists usually make more complete observations than are contained in their reports. There was little reference to his emotions, his childhood, or his youth, but all this information would be presented at the sanity hearing. The psychiatrists' report nevertheless indicated that there might be difficulty in deciding whether or not he was "legally sane." If he was the person who had killed, then most definitely unconscious elements played an overwhelming part. Should I succeed in uncovering those decisive unconscious elements, I would be able to establish the psychodynamic relationship between his mind and his alleged murderous act. The importance of establishing such a connection can be seen from the fact that the very pattern of behavior by which a person manifests his actual and potential traits is also expressed in the homicide he has committed. Although circumstances may give the murder a certain color, the motivation stamps upon it a character that makes it possible to identify the killer.

The most famous case I have studied in this connection was that of Lee Harvey Oswald. The pattern of his personality makeup was sharply defined: his disturbed early childhood emotional development; his distorted character, resulting in the lack of superego; his inability to withstand frustration and his acting out of hostility; his withdrawal and lack of masculine identification; his feeling of being insignificant and powerless; his excessive feelings of revenge

and fantasies of grandiose accomplishment; and his previous delinquent acts and violent actions representing strong wishes to
harm a person seriously. All of these traits showed an intimate
connection between his personality structure and his psychological capability of murder.[1]

The configuration of traits naturally varies with each murderer.
In Tiger Mellowbrook's case I had found the following: paternal
deprivation, maternal sexual overstimulation, lack of male identification, accident-proneness, sudden anger, impulsiveness, violent acting out (throwing the cat out of the attic window). His
spelling had been poor in comparison to his superior intelligence.
He was fearful, shy and lonely and felt threatened by the environment. He had a strong tendency toward fantasizing, his fantasies
being anxiety-provoking rather than gratifying. The evidence of
his fascination with suicide and death indicated his self-destructiveness—all revealing his psychotic-like condition. In general,
findings of this nature indicate the importance of a psychiatric
examination of anyone charged with a serious crime such as assault or murder.

I had some work ahead of me, I thought. Although I had a great
deal of knowledge about Tiger's unconscious motivations, I still
would have liked to know more, particularly about what happened the night when Teddy died. One method to obtain further
information, especially concerning the question of insanity and
legal responsibility, would be to employ sodium amytal during the
psychiatric interview (narcoanalysis), which could reduce resistance by loosening up material that had been suppressed. The
drawback with such a test, as I had learned from previous experiences, is that the patient or defendant can withhold the truth and
that therefore the sodium amytal interview is not infallible. If he
is a psychopath, or if he is suspicious as was the case with Tiger,
he could possibly resist this type of interrogation also because he
was against using any medication. Then, too, such a method could

1. David Abrahamsen, *Our Violent Society*, "Lee Harvey Oswald: Psychological
Capability for Violence and Murder" (New York: Funk & Wagnalls, 1970), pp.
129–60. David Abrahamsen, "A Study of Lee Harvey Oswald: Psychological
Capability of Murder," *Bulletin of the New York Academy of Medicine*, Second
Series, vol. 43, no. 10 (October 1967), pp. 861–88.

only be used with his consent and only after he had been informed that the findings from this research method might be used against him. Furthermore, there was the question whether or not the court would recognize and accept the findings obtained in narcoanalysis and permit them to be admitted as evidence. While the courts sometimes have accepted the results of the sodium amytal interview, the defense's request for a sodium amytal interview with Tiger was later refused because the court considered it a hospital procedure and Mellowbrook could not during the sanity hearing be transferred from the prison, to which he had been returned after his psychiatric testing.

Some weeks later, Taylor tried to get Mellowbrook out on bail. He said Tiger was very depressed and psychotic and was in need of psychiatric help, which he could not obtain in jail. This motion was also rejected. The district attorney was adamant. He had circumstantial evidence—the confession and the cab driver—which he claimed refuted the contention that Tiger was psychotic. The district attorney also referred to the report from the city psychiatric hospital, which said that Mellowbrook was sane. In view of the contradictory opinions of his mental condition, the judge had decided to move the case quickly for a sanity hearing —or, as we know it, a Pre-Trial Huntley Hearing.

Whenever there is doubt about a defendant's mental condition, a sanity hearing can be held at any time—before, during, or after trial. Since his mental status has a bearing upon his criminal responsibility, the problem of insanity has to be solved first.[2] This question was particularly relevant to Tiger's case. With the sanity hearing approaching, I told Taylor I would try to see Tiger within the next few days.

If Tiger had been somewhat inaccessible before, he was now more so. I had to remind him of what he had told me about his experiences with Teddy before the murder took place. He only nodded. I had the distinct impression that he now wanted to have all of what had occurred with her pushed out of his consciousness.

---

2. In particular it is essential to determine *at what time* the offender became insane. For further details see David Abrahamsen, *The Psychology of Crime* (New York: Columbia University Press, 1967), pp. 252–57.

I mentioned that he had told me he had many fears. Could he elaborate on them? Was he afraid of any particular person? Or was it a general fear?

Tiger sat for a long while and thought. "I like to live," he finally said, "but I am afraid of dying."

"When the time comes, everyone has to die."

"Yes," he answered, "but who wants to die?"

"There are those who wish to die. Do you have any comments?"

No answer.

Not wanting to pursue this particular line of questioning, I asked him how he had got along with the other patients in the hospital.

"Nothing to say."

"Did you talk or become friendly with anyone in particular there?"

"Only the nurses; they were nice. They knew their job," he answered curtly.

"Are you hypersensitive?"

"Yes, you can say so," Tiger answered.

"Have you seen your mother?"

"Yes." An awkward silence followed. It was painful to watch the sadness on his face. His eyes focused on the floor without expression.

"It was horrible," he said after some time. "I'm sorry to have put her through all this. Sorry for all the trouble I have caused. She offered me money, but what's the use? If I could only leave this place!" He had raised his voice.

"What would you do then?" I asked.

He shrugged his shoulders.

After waiting a while, I ventured, "You know Teddy is dead." There was no answer. "Did she ask for it?"

"Maybe. Your guess is as good as mine. You're the doctor. You should know. What's going to happen to me?" This was the first time that Tiger had shown any concern for himself. He had become somewhat reality-oriented.

"I cannot say for sure. But there will be a sanity hearing, which your lawyer has told you about. What will happen after that nobody knows."

"Will it be soon?" he asked. "Can I get out in the meantime?"

"You will have to talk to your lawyer about that. I am sorry but I cannot say anything more about it."

"Will I have to stay here for the rest of my life, doctor?"

"I hope not. Are there any other questions you would like to ask me, Tiger?"

"You couldn't even answer my last question. I'm trapped. What's the use?"

"Have you been given any medication?"

"No."

"I shall talk to the prison doctor and see if you can be given something. Do you sleep at night?"

"No," Tiger answered.

"Do you dream at night?"

"Yes, sometimes."

"What do you dream about?"

"People are after me. I'm afraid of them. I run away. They try to get me."

"What kind of people?"

"A gray mass—many faces—large—without features."

After a long while he said, "How can I stay here? I have to walk around here holding up my pants so they won't fall down. They won't even let me have my belt. I'm not an animal. I am—or at least I was—a human being with ideas. Now look at me. What do you think?"

Instead of answering him, I asked, "How did you get into this trouble? Why?"

"I don't know, doctor, but I'm here now."

"Don't you remember anything of what happened with Teddy just before you left the apartment?"

"I have tried to, but I don't."

"Did you take anything with you when you left the apartment?"

Tiger raised his head and his deep brown eyes looked at me quizzically as though he didn't understand my question.

"Take something with me? What?"

"I only asked," I responded. "Have you tried to remember what took place in Teddy's apartment?"

"Tried and tried. What's the use?"

Tiger was beginning to verbalize some bitterness about his situation which until now he had repressed. During the interview he had been relatively quiet, but I could discern a great deal of restlessness, fear and anxiety. He was shy, evasive. He did not welcome my interview, although he had not refused it.

Preoccupied with his own thoughts, he had not paid complete attention to what I asked or said. To the untrained observer Tiger might appear dull on the surface, but beneath this dullness was a great deal of alertness and hypersensitivity. He spoke as though under great strain, Although he was rather hesitant and incoherent, his voice was well modulated and steady. There were no illusions, hallucinations, or delusions. There were some paranoid feelings which had become intensified, possibly due to his being locked up in jail without much possibility of getting out. Yet judging from what he had told me, and from his writings, he had definite death wishes for himself and against his parents. He had had dreams which might be characterized as nightmares. He did not think that there was anything wrong with him. While undoubtedly he felt guilty, he didn't admit to it. This refusal to deal with his emotions indicated that he lacked substantial insight into himself. His memory was intact except for the actual incident of Teddy's death which seemed to be completely buried in his mind. The neurological examination was negative.

Although his behavior during the interviews had been by and large controlled, I believe that there was a certain impulsiveness present, particularly if a question was put to him which threw him off guard. Throughout the interviews he showed a great deal of stubbornness, not wanting or not being able to talk or mention events or express his feelings; at other times, however, he felt the need to talk. One cannot describe him as having been uncooperative because this uncooperativeness was related to his mental control, which was a psychological defense. While he was hesitant to relate details of his past history, or of the particular crime of which he was charged, this hesitation was possibly related to his defensive attitudes and to the fact that his mind blocked out the events that actually took place. His running away from Teddy's apartment was almost like running away in a homosexual panic.

The case of Tiger Mellowbrook was not one to be locked into

a tightly bound diagnostic frame or stereotype. I must state that he had brought me closer to new insights regarding the psychodynamics of murder and the murderer's relationship with his victim than had other cases I had studied. There was little doubt that he had been trying to use all the forces he could summon—his own intelligence, his knowledge of the world the way he saw it, and his sense of social responsibility—to explain himself. He had utilized his reading to develop a philosophy, a life style, to defy the irrational and the violent tendencies in himself, of which, however, he was not fully aware. In his own narcissism he had become his own doctor. If it was true that he had murdered Teddy, he had failed thoroughly in his attempt to gain control over these violent tendencies. In contrast to so many other murderers I had seen, whose minds were incoherent compared to Tiger's, he was confounded by his unconscious violent tendencies. Undoubtedly he was desperate—desperate, I think, to explain to himself what had happened; thus he had tried to save himself. On the other hand, he was proud—terribly proud—as well as being uncommunicative and resigned. From my first interview with him, I felt there was something foreboding about Tiger. At one time he had mentioned that he was something of a rebel, a revolutionary. During our last talk he was angry, though I had the feeling he thought he could sublimate his anger. But if he was that angry, it might well be that he was trying to work out his bitterness and frustrations, trying to overcome his hate in order to reconstruct his weak ego.

The most predominant features in Tiger's mental condition were his depression, his self-destructive tendencies and his monomaniacal behavior. While he had within him a great deal of hostility, he did not bring it out unless challenged beyond the point of being able to tolerate it. He was afraid of being found out; one felt he harbored within him a secret which he couldn't share with anyone. On the surface his attitude seemed to be one of defiance, but I had a suspicion that deep down he didn't care what others thought about him. He was, in short, the classic loner.

How many times had I compared him in my thoughts with the highly gifted Viennese philosopher and psychologist Otto Weininger, who during his short life published a large book, *Sex and*

Character (1903), and then about six months later killed himself.[3] He, too, had a secret he couldn't share with anyone. He too was unconcerned about what people thought of him. Following his own bent, he was strong in character, strong in pride—the classic loner.

Tiger knew the law, but he didn't understand himself. He felt that he had not received a full share of his life, one reason for his low self-esteem. Since childhood he had been hypersensitive to hurt, to insult, to the aggression of others, particularly that of his mother. As a child he suffered most from the conviction that he didn't deserve such treatment. This feeling he had transferred to Teddy. He felt she was unfair to him. She threatened him and was cruel. And now this treatment was going to continue in prison, he thought. He carried his conviction over into adulthood to the point where he, just as Weininger, was no longer able to distinguish cause and effect, was oblivious to his own acts of hate and aggression, until—perhaps—it erupted in murder.

3. See David Abrahamsen, *Mind and Death of a Genius* (New York: Columbia University Press, 1946).

PART THREE

Court

— 6 —

Three weeks had passed. The day of the sanity hearing had come. I entered the courtroom shortly before 10 A.M. It was empty except for a court clerk, who was thumbing through a book. When he saw me he nodded pleasantly, and then became absorbed in his work again. The courtroom was large, bare; the American flag was in the front of the room, and on the wall, "In God We Trust." I wondered why the court had to call upon God, since "In God We Trust" would indicate that God had something to do with the court. To my mind, the court was man-made, not God-made.

I wondered how long I would have to wait. In court one has to learn great patience. Promptness among judges is by no means the rule. Through long experience I have learned always to bring ample reading material.

The sanity hearing, which usually does not attract much public attention, is conducted and heard by a judge, not a jury. He decides whether or not the defendant is legally sane and able to stand trial. In cases where the defendant obviously is psychotic, the sanity hearing will take only an hour or so, but where there is considerable doubt about his mental status it may last longer. (The longest sanity hearing I took part in lasted three months.) Tiger's hearing, I thought, would last for several days.

In a sanity hearing, the psychiatrist can testify to anything about the case or the defendant he deems necessary, even to the point of guilt or innocence. This is in contrast to a trial, during which his testimony is limited to the specific questions asked. If during a trial the psychiatrist does mention information relating to the defendant's guilt or innocence, a mistrial can be called.

Al Taylor, the defense attorney, arrived at precisely ten o'clock, carrying in each hand a large briefcase filled with papers. He was followed by the district attorney, who was a young, heavy-set man, with friendly blue eyes, bushy blond eyebrows and a booming voice. "Mr. Samson," he said as he introduced himself to me. He opened his briefcase at the table a few feet away. I saw one of my books. Here we go again, I thought. Undoubtedly Samson was ready to point out the possible discrepancies between my testimony in Tiger's case and what I had written in the book.

Knowing that any district attorney is eager for a conviction that, from his point of view, is very humane, I have learned from long experience that testifying as an expert witness and being cross-examined in court is largely a matter of strategy. The findings are one matter, but the way they are interpreted and how they are selected by the opposing side is something else. The district attorney is not trying the defendant in order to put him in the best possible light. His main purpose is to obtain a conviction. My main purpose is to bring into full view the psychological dimensions of the case.

Mellowbrook, followed by two marshals, entered the courtroom, handcuffed. He sat down at the table reserved for the defense and the marshals removed his handcuffs. He glanced over at me, his sad eyes catching mine. I acknowledged his gesture with a nod.

After a while there were the customary three heavy knocks on the door leading into the courtroom. Everyone stood up and the black-robed judge entered and sat down on the bench. When the usual preliminaries—"Hear ye, hear ye . . . and everyone will be heard"—had been sounded, the defense lawyer stood up and asked for permission to approach the bench. The two attorneys and the judge whispered together briefly. Then the defense lawyer talked about specifications which I—and I am sure Tiger—didn't understand. The district attorney objected and the judge managed to calm them down. After Taylor had stated for the record that Dr. David Abrahamsen, a psychiatrist, was present in court, Samson summarized the prosecution's case: Tyros Mellowbrook was charged with murder first degree. He allegedly had killed Teddy Gladstone by strangling and stabbing her. (He had inferred she was stabbed from the search warrant, but this proved to be incorrect.) By order of the state, Tyros Mellowbrook had undergone a psychiatric examination at the city psychiatric hospital, and the report indicated that he was sane and was able to stand trial.

The defense attorney made the objection that his psychiatrist's findings of Mellowbrook's mental status differed from those in the hospital report. The district attorney replied that since Mellowbrook's private psychiatrist had not submitted a written report, he had no knowledge of the findings. A heated discussion ensued, whereupon finally the judge banged down his gavel, looked sternly at both attorneys and ordered them to be quiet; as experienced lawyers they should know the rules by now. "Let us proceed with the case," he concluded.

Samson went on to say that The People had a confession from Mr. Mellowbrook, the defendant, and he would like to introduce this as People's Evidence No. 1. Taylor rose to his feet and objected strongly. He stated that the confession had been taken without legal counsel being present and, furthermore, it was not signed. The district attorney responded that he would introduce not only the confession, but also the search warrant and the reasons why the defendant had been arrested and charged with murder first degree.

The defense attorney repeated his objection and the judge announced, "Overruled. I will permit the witnesses who were present at the time of the alleged confession to testify, but in the meantime I will reserve decision with regard to admitting it into evidence." The defense attorney again stood up and objected strenuously. "Overruled."

This verbal dialectic had been going on for almost an hour. Tempers were running high. Both attorneys were slowly jockeying for position. Judging from the way the district attorney had reacted in court, it would seem as though he had an open-and-shut case. Tiger's case exhibited the courtroom "adversary system" in all its splendor.

"Your Honor," the defense attorney said, "may I be heard?"
The judge granted permission.

"I cannot see what the confession has to do with the defendant's mental status. Confession of the crime has not been put into evidence. I must object that the district attorney be allowed to examine the witnesses who were instrumental in bringing forth his alleged confession."

The district attorney rose from his chair and began waving his hand about in the air. "Your Honor, Your Honor."

"Go ahead," the judge said.

"Through the examination of these witnesses we will be able to verify that the defendant was sane and coherent. This is one reason why I would like to bring up the confession now."

At that point the judge became impatient. "If both of you attorneys are going to interrupt the proceedings the way you are doing now, we may well go on until Christmas. You are both intelligent and experienced. You both know the rules of law. Previously I have ruled that I am reserving decision upon the admission of the alleged confession, and we must go along with that decision. Mr. District Attorney, present your witnesses."

The defense attorney at once voiced his objection. "Overruled," the judge answered.

"Exception," the defense attorney exclaimed.

Detective Joseph Curran of the Homicide Squad took the stand. He began to read a long statement which was taken at the precinct on May 15, commencing about 9 P.M. Present at the interview were Lieutenant Paul Monahan, Shield 0016, Detective Frank Washington, Shield 6625, Detective Joseph Curran, Shield 8793. The defendant was questioned by Assistant District Attorney Clarence Newman; Hans Kurtzer was hearing reporter.

Tyros Yarnell Mellowbrook had been advised of his rights, that he could remain silent, that any statement he made could be used as evidence against him, and that he had the right to have a lawyer present when he was questioned. Mellowbrook seemed to understand all this.

Asked whether he knew that Teddy Gladstone was dead at about 11:30 P.M. on Saturday, May 12, Mellowbrook did not know. He did not answer the question whether he had killed her. He did not remember any such thing. He admitted that he had quarreled with her about everything, but denied that he had hit her, or that he was in her apartment when she died. He admitted that Teddy Gladstone was alive when he came to her apartment and that she was wearing a gold necklace. What happened to it he did not know. He admitted that they had had a heated discussion. The questioning went as follows:

Q.   What was the discussion about?
A.   She blamed me for not having given her anything . . . and I told her I had given her a necklace.
Q.   What kind of necklace?
A.   It was a gold chain necklace.
Q.   Was it heavy with thick links?
A.   Yes, sort of.
Q.   Did you take the necklace with you?
A.   I don't know.
Q.   Did you choke her? Did you try to pull it off?
A.   I don't know.
Q.   Did you choke her?
A.   Maybe, if you say so, but I don't remember.
Q.   Had you had problems with Teddy?
A.   Yes.
Q.   What was the trouble?
A.   I was going to marry her.
Q.   Did you love her?
A.   Yes, very much.
Q.   Did Teddy love you?
A.   Yes, she did—that is what she said.
Q.   What was the trouble between you?
A.   She put me down—and my mother.
Q.   What did she say specifically?
A.   Can't remember.
Q.   Did you ever think of killing Teddy?
A.   NO.
Q.   Did you choke and stab her on that afternoon or evening you were in her apartment?
A.   I don't remember.
Q.   Did you have a knife with you?
A.   Yes, one for my pipe.
Q.   What did you do with the knife?
A.   I don't know. I used it for my pipe.

Q.   Do you have your knife with you now?
A.   No.

The defendant ransacks his pockets. No knife.

Q.   Is it in your apartment?
A.   I don't know.
Q.   Did you use it that evening when you were with Teddy in her apartment?
A.   Yes.
Q.   What did you do with the knife?
A.   I cleaned my pipe.
Q.   How large was the knife?

The defendant indicates about five inches.

The assistant district attorney continued his interrogation, filling in the objective facts about Tiger—his age, his address, occupation. Then:

Q.   Do you know why you are here?
A.   I'm not sure.
Q.   Do you remember the name of any people here?
A.   No.
Q.   Do you know who I am?
A.   Yes.
Q.   Who am I?
A.   The district attorney.
Q.   What is my name?
A.   New—man.
Q.   Why did you kill Teddy Gladstone?

Mellowbrook refused to answer this question because his lawyer was not present (he had left to attend another case).[1] He complained about answering questions while his lawyer was absent. Finally, he refused to sign the confession. The statement ended at 11:30 P.M.

1. It may perhaps be surprising to learn that a lawyer may have to leave his client while he is being interrogated by the police. In one famous murder case, the lawyer of the suspect had to leave him while he was being questioned. After the accused had been found guilty of murder and sentenced, the conviction was successfully appealed and reversed, since it had largely been based upon his confession, which in part had been obtained during the absence of his lawyer.

The defense attorney rose slowly. "Your Honor, this alleged confession is not any confession at all. The most it says is that the defendant was in Teddy Gladstone's apartment. There is no description of any psychiatric findings. I move that this alleged confession read here in the court be stricken from the record."

"Motion denied," the judge replied.

"Your Honor," the defense attorney said, "may I please make a statement?"

The district attorney was on his feet.

"What statement?" he asked curtly.

"The statement as to the state's case here."

"Objection," Samson boomed. "We are dealing here with the defendant's sanity; other matters are irrelevant."

Taylor answered, "Before the question about sanity or insanity can be raised, the charge of the prosecution as to the defendant's guilt has to be raised."

"Objection," the district attorney interrupted.

"Let us hear what the defense attorney has to say," the judge answered.

"The case of the prosecution," the defense attorney began, "depends not even upon probabilities, but only on some possibilities. The defendant is high-minded and honest. When he says that he does not remember what took place in Miss Gladstone's apartment, I think he should be believed. That the defendant allegedly was in the dead girl's apartment does not mean that he killed her. As a matter of fact, another man was suspected. Even the building superintendent was under suspicion. The prosecution has only circumstantial evidence to go on. The district attorney has only noncorroborative evidence for his case. At this point I would like to move that the charges against the defendant be dismissed."

"May it please the court," the district attorney retorted in his booming voice, "the defendant was the last one to see the deceased alive."

"Objection. There is no proof of that."

"The confession," Samson continued, "shows that the defendant was in the apartment when she died. She was alive when he arrived, they had a serious argument, and when he left the apartment she was dead. The autopsy report, when it is presented, will also show justification for the murder charge against the defendant."

"We will take a break," the judge said dryly. "Fifteen minutes."

I looked at my watch: a quarter to twelve.

Very little progress had been made as to the question of insanity. So far only some facts had been brought out. In court there is rarely room for interpretation. The law deals only with facts, or so-called facts. From the confession it was clear that Tiger, feeling he was in "enemy territory," an alien and hostile environment, had not divulged what he later related to me.

During the cross-examination of the detective, the defense attorney asked whether or not he had given any thought to the kind of relationship that existed between the defendant and the dead girl. After thinking for a second, the detective said that he had to stick to the facts.

Later, when the prosecution wanted to introduce the search warrant into evidence, the defense attorney objected, saying that it contained the erroneous statement that the defendant had stabbed the girl. "The autopsy report," Taylor continued, "does not contain any evidence that the girl was stabbed. There were bleedings only in the larynx and the pharynx."

"But they resulted in her death," the district attorney interrupted.

At that moment the judge used his gavel and admonished the prosecutor not to interrupt. He would have his say in court anyhow, as the proceedings so far had shown, the judge added, smiling wryly.

"And you, Mr. Taylor, I admonish you too. We are present at a sanity hearing. The question here is whether the defendant is sane or not, if he is able to stand trial, and what his mental condition was at the time of the alleged offense. Address yourself to that point so we can move ahead."

After the defense attorney had inquired about how long the detective had been on the police force, he asked him if he had ever seen an insane person. The witness replied that during the time he had been on the police force he had seen many. He added that Mr. Mellowbrook had made a good impression on him. He was quiet and self-contained. Of course he was upset, but he also seemed somewhat relieved after the questioning. "I found him to be normal," the detective concluded.

"But," Mr. Taylor interrupted, "you did not see him on the night of the alleged crime," to which the detective only answered, "That is correct."

"Then you don't really know how he behaved."

"No, sir."

The defense attorney then dismissed the witness.

At a quarter to one the judge looked at his watch and asked the district attorney how many witnesses he wanted to examine. Six or seven. Mr. Taylor would have four or five, including one psychiatrist.

Samson asked for permission to approach the bench. Both lawyers and the judge whispered together, until finally the judge said, "One witness for the prosecution is not present and will not be available until this afternoon. We therefore will recess until two o'clock."

During the lunch recess Taylor told me that he had almost given up the idea of having the charges against Tiger dismissed. To his mind there were no plain or simple facts in this case. So far the truth, the whole truth, and nothing but the truth had not come to light regarding Tiger's alleged part in the crime. But at the moment it was more important to try to establish that if he had committed the murder, he had not been "sane." Nobody had seen him at the time of the crime. This was a most significant point. I reminded Taylor that a man's disturbed condition may be more acute at one time than at another, that the way a person appears on the surface doesn't necessarily correspond to the way he really feels. Tiger's inner condition couldn't be ascertained merely by observing his outward appearance.

When we returned to the courtroom after lunch, Tiger was already present. During the first session I had observed him carefully. He sat slumped over in his seat, his head bowed. Only once, when the alleged confession was read, did he look up, surprised; then he glanced over at me as if he vaguely remembered my question about Teddy's necklace. At the beginning of the recess I had passed where he was sitting, but he said nothing either to me or to his lawyer. He looked sad; his face reflected a passivity and resignation, as if all were lost.

The prosecution's first witness that afternoon was the superintendent of the building in which Teddy had lived. He related substantially the same story that Taylor had told me; he had opened the door with a passkey, had found the dead girl and called the police. His explanation was smooth, too smooth perhaps. The district attorney then asked him whether he had seen any of Teddy's friends. He mentioned two men who had come to see her quite frequently.

"Do you see one of them here in court?"

The superintendent pointed his finger at Tiger, who still sat with his head bowed. He did not look up until the district attorney told him to. Samson then questioned the superintendent about the time the defendant broke down the door of the dead girl's apartment. The district attorney always used the words "the dead girl's apartment." I felt this allusion introduced a deliberate bias into the case which tended to reduce the complexity of Teddy's role in the murder. In Samson's presentation, Teddy no longer existed. She was a nonentity. As far as I was concerned, of course, Teddy was as central to my case as was Tiger.

"He was violent then," the prosecutor continued, more as a statement than as a question.

"Yes, you could say so."

"Was he or wasn't he?"

"Yes, he was violent," the superintendent answered. The district attorney looked satisfied.

During the cross-examination, the defense attorney brought out Teddy's apology for Tiger's behavior. She had told the superintendent that he was drunk, that he couldn't cope with his problems any longer and was afraid of losing his job. The superintendent also stated that aside from that one episode, Mellowbrook had always been a quiet fellow, pleasant and self-respecting. The witness recalled another man, by the name of Clark, who had come to see Teddy quite frequently. She was a popular girl and had attracted many men.

The next witness was the policeman who had responded to the superintendent's call. Finding Teddy dead, he had called the

Homicide Squad. An ambulance had arrived to take the body to the city morgue for an autopsy. The defense attorney did not cross-examine this last witness.

As the policeman stepped down from the witness stand, the district attorney called back the superintendent. He questioned him further about the dead girl's habits. Did she go to work every day? Did she go out often? Did she have many callers? The witness replied that she was hard-working, and as far as he knew she went to her office every morning. Because this was her routine, he had become suspicious when he didn't see her for a couple of days.

"Did she have high moral standards?"

The defense attorney rose and requested that this last question be stricken from the record. The superintendent had no way of knowing whether Teddy Gladstone's morals were good or bad. The judge acceded to this request, and asked the district attorney for his next witness.

I had already recognized the medical examiner sitting in the courtroom. He was a man of vast experience, very kind, quite heavy-set, with light blue eyes, thick black hair, a beard and a resounding voice. When the district attorney asked him about his education and training, the defense attorney immediately conceded his qualifications.

The medical examiner began his testimony. External observation indicated a marked line, between the chin and the larynx, around the neck of the dead girl, clearly visible in the front—a sign of strangulation by a thick wire or perhaps a string. The face was calm, somewhat cyanosed, no saliva in mouth. There were small bleedings in both larynx and pharynx. The hyoid bone and laryngeal cartilages were not broken. The findings in the lungs, which were dark and congested, also indicated signs of strangulation. Asked what the instrument of strangulation could be, the medical examiner guessed that it might be a metal necklace of some sort.

"A silver or gold necklace?" the district attorney interrupted.

"Something of that nature, I think," he answered smilingly.

"Your witness," Samson said, directing himself to the defense attorney.

"Doctor," Taylor began, "you have just stated that a necklace could have been used to choke Teddy Gladstone to death. Could this strangulation have taken place if a person tried to grab or pull the necklace abruptly in a moment of anger?"

The doctor thought for a moment and then said slowly, "The only sign we have is a distinct rough line around her neck, the bleeding in her larynx and pharynx, all indicating strangulation by something resembling a necklace. Whether this strangulation was accidental, I cannot say."

"But it could have been accidental? Could they have been arguing, perhaps actually fighting, and during the fight someone tried to grab at the necklace, with a fatal outcome?"

"I cannot say for sure."

The defense attorney persisted. "Couldn't there be such a possibility or probability?"

"Everything is possible, but I have no proof of it."

Taylor repeated his question, which now was more of an affirmative statement. "In the heat of an argument, couldn't the defendant have ripped off the necklace because he wanted to have it, and couldn't the deceased in resisting him have put up such a struggle that he accidentally strangled her? Couldn't this be a possibility, doctor?"

The medical examiner stroked his beard. "There always is a possibility."

The district attorney interrupted. "The defense attorney has now asked the same question three times, and the medical examiner has answered him. I don't think that he should badger the witness any longer." Whereupon the judge ordered the defense attorney to proceed with his next question.

"Do you think, doctor, that this strangulation, as accidental as it may have been"—the defense attorney always tried to use the word "accidental"—"could have been carried out in the heat of passion? May I also add for your orientation that the room was in great disarray, with pillows scattered about, and overturned glasses. Obviously a fight had taken place. In the course of the evening the defendant had had several drinks. He possibly may have also taken a few pills."

At that moment the district attorney jumped to his feet. "So far there has been no evidence that the defendant had been drinking or taking any drugs."

"I stand corrected. Later on we will show that Mr. Mellowbrook had been drinking a great deal during that evening. May I change my question? Suppose, doctor, that the defendant had been drinking a great deal during that evening and this was not a normal pattern of behavior for him. In addition to this, suppose he had also taken one or two Dexedrine tablets. Do you think that the combination of these two intoxicants could have influenced the mind of the defendant to such an extent that he used so much force in pulling off the necklace that he accidentally strangled Teddy?"

"I cannot say for sure," the medical examiner began.

The prosecutor interrupted. "My learned opponent is asking a psychiatric question of a man who is not a specialist in that field."

Taylor responded, "Even if he is not a psychiatrist, the medical examiner has had so much experience with similar cases that his opinion here would be of value."

"I still must object to the question."

"Objection sustained," the judge said, and then he advised the defense attorney to change his question.

"Do you believe that ripping off the necklace could have been done in the heat of passion?"

"This is possible," the medical examiner conceded.

On rebuttal, the district attorney said, "In order to strangle someone, doctor, isn't it true that the defendant must have used a great deal of force?"

"Yes."

"Then it wasn't accidental," the district attorney insisted.

"I object," Taylor protested vigorously. "He is leading the medical examiner toward a definite answer."

The prosecutor retorted that Taylor had done the same thing.

"Your Honor, I must object to this question."

The wrangling between them continued for a few minutes until Taylor asked upon re-rebuttal, "Do you think that this act could have been carried out by an insane man?"

"Objection," boomed the district attorney. "The medical examiner is not a psychiatrist. He cannot know whether the defendant was insane or not."

"But it could have been accidental?" asked the defense attorney.

"Possibly."

"May it please the court," said the prosecutor, "to proceed with my next witness."

The next witness was a male nurse, Isidore Stone, who had been working at the city hospital for fifteen years.

The district attorney asked, "Will you please state your job, and what happened at a particular time on the ward when you acted in the capacity of a supervisor?"

After having described his job and his duties, Stone stated that early one morning when he was making the rounds at the hospital with the night nurse, a patient had come over to ask him a question. Stone told him that he would talk with him later on when he was through with the rounds.

"And who was this man who came over to you and wanted to speak to you?" the district attorney asked with his voice rising. "Do you see him here in court?"

The witness replied in the affirmative.

"Can you point him out?"

The defendant was pointed out.

"What happened when you talked with him?"

"He said that he was depressed and that he had not talked with any doctor there. He wondered when the doctor would examine him."

"What did he talk to you about?" asked the prosecutor.

"He talked about his mother. He was upset about how she would react to his arrest."

"Was he concerned about himself?"

"No, he wasn't."

"Did he say anything to you in particular?"

"He said that he had had a fight with his girl friend, and that there had been a great deal of quarreling, that she was dead, and that he was accused of killing her." Stone paused. After a while, encouraged to go on, "I had the feeling that he wanted to say something, but he stopped and seemed to withdraw into himself."

"What happened then?" Samson asked impatiently.

"He walked away."

"Did you find the defendant to be normal?"

"Yes, I think so. I didn't think that he was psycho."

"What do you mean by 'psycho'?"

"That he was off the beam—that he was psychotic."

"Then you did not find him psychotic?"

"No. He made a good impression on me. He seemed intelligent but it was hard to get to him."

This testimony troubled the defense attorney. It didn't seem realistic in terms of the hospital report. He began by asking the witness on which day this conversation with Tiger had taken place. Stone didn't remember.

"You certainly must have made some notes in the hospital records. Could I see them, please?"

"I didn't make any notes on the records, but I told the other nurse to do it."

"Is this the usual custom? Don't you make notes about the patient if anything happens, or if there is something unusual to write down?"

"Yes," he stammered, "but that morning, or that noon hour, I didn't have the time."

"So it is a fact, then, *you don't have any notes with you.*"

"No, I don't."

"Then what you have been saying here this afternoon is only from memory."

"Yes."

"Did anyone see you talk with the defendant, Mr. Mellowbrook?"

"I don't know," Stone replied.

"So what we have here then is only your own observations, which were not written down, and nobody saw you talk with him. Is that correct, sir?" There was an edge in Taylor's voice.

"Yes," the nurse answered.

"Was the patient depressed or agitated in any way?"

"Not that I could see."

"Was he given any medication? Do you know anything about that?"

"Yes, he had been given something."

"What?"

"He was given paraldehyde, ten cc, at night."

"What is paraldehyde?"

"It is a medication we give in order to sedate a patient."

"Then Mr. Mellowbrook must have been agitated or disturbed, or else there wouldn't have been any reason to give it to him. Isn't that so?"

"Yes."

"Despite his being depressed or being agitated, you didn't see anything else wrong with him? He was quite normal in accordance with what you have said?"

"Yes."

"Thank you," Taylor retorted curtly.

These last questions invalidated Stone's original statement about Tiger's mental condition. Tiger had not admitted anything to the nurse. Although he apparently was on the verge of telling him what had happened on the night Teddy was killed, he somehow stopped himself.

The defense attorney spoke up again, "May I direct the court's attention to the fact that the hospital records indicate the defendant was given ten cc's of paraldehyde for several evenings, and that Mr. Stone's dialogue with the defendant is not recorded on the hospital chart."

"So ordered," the judge replied.

It is quite instructive that the nurse had neglected to write down his conversation with Tiger. It could mean that he didn't want to recognize that Tiger was highly disturbed.

On rebuttal, the district attorney asked Stone if the defendant had told him of any wrongdoings during his life. When the witness answered affirmatively, Taylor rose and asked if he had specified what "wrongdoings" he had been guilty of. Stone shook his head.

"Do you mean no?" Taylor asked.

"Yes, the answer is no."

Just as I was beginning to feel the tedium of these proceedings, the judge announced adjournment of the case until the following morning at ten o'clock.

"Your Honor," said the district attorney, "I have two psychiatrists here in court from the city psychiatric hospital. Could we continue the proceedings?"

"Impossible," replied the judge. "Please have the psychiatrists here at ten o'clock tomorrow morning, if they are your first witnesses. I understand that as professional people they are busy, but this time I can't help it. Court adjourned."

The psychiatrists looked at each other unhappily. If they had had more experience as court witnesses they would have known that they have to be present at the pleasure of the court and that as a rule no one knows how long court proceedings will last. While most judges are glad to take into consideration the psychiatrist's time, there are others who, for reasons known only to themselves, do not. There are sinners in every profession.

Back in the office, I pondered on the defense attorney's attempts to have the murder charge against Mellowbrook dismissed. With the exception of the taxicab driver, nobody had seen him near Teddy's house on the night of the murder. So the evidence was at best only circumstantial. If it had been a straightforward confession, the situation would have been worse for Tiger. But to my mind, his statement to the police was not a confession at all. The prosecution did not seem to have much basis for the murder charge.

The testimony of the male nurse I felt was contradictory. He and the two psychiatrists had thought that Mellowbrook had been rational and clear during his hospitalization though the fact that Mellowbrook had been on strong medication, as Taylor had brought out, indicated that he was highly disturbed. Most important of all, the nurse had not talked with Tiger either shortly before or shortly after the murder. And why hadn't the prosecutor called in as witness the doctor at the detention center?

Around nine o'clock that evening, Taylor came to my office. I expected him to be tired, but to my surprise he looked very eager and alert. We were deeply concerned about the case. My testimony, I told Taylor, would depend upon my findings and it might be at variance with what he had stated or tried to advocate in court that day. One reason why he had introduced his motion for dismissal of the murder charge against Tiger was to bring the district attorney around to reducing it. The prosecutor had mentioned to him as they left the courtroom that the murder charge might possibly be reduced if Mellowbrook pleaded guilty.

"But I can't plead him guilty because he hasn't admitted to committing the crime."

"There is little doubt," I said, "that the district attorney has a definite opinion about how this murder took place, but, as you know, things are not always the way they seem, and I hope to show the circumstances surrounding the homicide. If I were to postulate here, I would say that there are two people Tiger wanted to kill, at least in his own unconscious mind—his mother and his father. Not being able to do that, he had to find a substitute. But there is more to it than that and I will try to bring it out tomorrow in court."

The crucial circumstance I would emphasize was the close love-hate tie between Tiger and Teddy, which I felt served as an instigation for the killing. The roots of this crime lay not only in *male psychology* but also in *female psychology.*

"You know," Taylor said, "the whole case really depends upon psychiatry—what you have to say, and also what the other psychiatrists will testify."

After learning what witnesses Taylor planned to put on the stand, and having assured him that the case depended upon the lawyer as well as on the psychiatrist, I asked him how he saw the case. He thought that tomorrow we would probably get somewhere, but, "You are never entirely sure about cases before they come to trial."

I mentioned that, as he very well knew, we treat in a special way the *excusable homicide*—one committed by accident or in the heat of passion; or under threats sufficient to show there was reasonable cause to endanger the person's life; or when no advantage was taken or no dangerous weapon was used; or when the killing was not carried out in a cruel manner. Asked whether all these conditions wouldn't apply to Tiger's situation, Taylor nodded, but added that the prosecution was determined to establish that the killing was the second type of murder, *felonious homicide,* one committed willfully, and punishable by law.

I mentioned to Taylor that Tiger had felt threatened by Teddy and that without being aware of it, she may have felt threatened by him. I suggested then that when I was on the witness stand the following day I would present the case in accordance with what

I had told Taylor so far, stressing in particular the deep love-hate relationship between Tiger and Teddy. I hoped it would be considered an excusable homicide, committed by accident or in the heat of passion, or upon sufficient provocation. One element which might have provoked him to kill was his low opinion of himself in relation to Teddy. If at times he thought himself important or displayed an almost exalted opinion of himself and presented himself with a sense of dignity, this was a compensatory reaction to his own feelings of worthlessness. The question of whether or not he was insane, and to what degree, I told Taylor, was not an easy one, but I would have to raise it in the form of a psychosis, and possibly in the form of diminished responsibility. The latter I would describe as an abnormal condition in which his consciousness was restricted to or diminished to such a degree that he was unable to think rationally of the act or the consequences.

The defense lawyer looked at his watch. It was almost eleven o'clock. Faintly suppressing a yawn, he bade me good night.

The next day, just as I was preparing to leave for court, Taylor called. The case had been adjourned until the next day because the prosecution's psychiatrists were not available. This gave me additional time to think over my testimony. I began to make more notes about the case, and mentally started to go over the most prominent features in the personalities of both protagonists.

Was Tiger guilty? The important factual element in the case was that the cab driver had picked him up that Saturday night near the house where Teddy lived, thus placing him close to the scene of the murder. It surprised me that the prosecutor had not presented the driver as a witness. But perhaps he was afraid that his testimony would raise questions about Tiger's sanity. If the driver testified that Tiger had been in the vicinity of Teddy's apartment that Saturday night, then he would also have to state that Tiger had run off without paying his fare, indicating that he was confused, bewildered, irrational. I had asked Tiger about this, but he had no memory of it. Not in any of my interviews with him, not to his mother, his lawyer, or Neil, had Tiger admitted that he had strangled Teddy. I would have to testify that his amnesia could have resulted from the use of drugs and alcohol, which combined act as a strong depressant. As to the possible use of drugs, particularly amphetamines, I doubted that I would ever get a clear answer from Tiger, because of his pride. From experience I knew that amphetamine abuse may elicit paranoid reactions resulting in violence, assault and homicide. The most significant factor was still the highly sexual, symbiotic relationship between Teddy and Tiger. Each in his own way had been hungry for affection, Teddy more than Tiger, for while he had an almost compulsive impulse to be alone, she walked around with outstretched hands to catch whatever affection came her way.

From the psychoanalysis of a great many cases I had learned that it was next to impossible through the examination of the murderer alone to map out accurately the road which led to the killing. The meeting of the murderer and the murderee has many decisive aspects, the most important being *how* the victim invites his doom. There are people who, as mentioned earlier, are accident prone and unhappiness prone. We have also shown that there are murderees—people who expose themselves to murder. In all probability Teddy was such a one. Both Tiger and Teddy participated in the *homicidal process,* during which the sadomasochistic relationship between the murderer and his victim kept intensifying, and ended in a climax. The ego-disharmonious homicide originated in the homicidal process between them, their personalities and life styles determining the outcome. In all probability Tiger did not have any superego defect, but he was unable to satisfy consistently his aggressive needs, being capable of gratifying these feelings only suddenly and explosively. It would be difficult to prove my assumption in court, particularly since so much would depend on whether the judge would permit me to elaborate on it to demonstrate that my interpretations provided the strictly factual evidence which the law required.

Delving deeper into the evidence presented so far in Tiger's case, I wondered whether it was an oversight that the medical examiner had failed to mention that Teddy was pregnant, or hadn't there been any evidence of the pregnancy in the autopsy? A call to Taylor revealed that Teddy had *not* been pregnant at the time of her death. However, if Tiger believed that Teddy was pregnant it would be reasonable to assume that in murdering her he had been motivated by jealousy.

If Teddy was having affairs with other men, how strong and how close had the tie of love been between Tiger and Teddy? Their mutual attraction ran hot and cold. Even though she attacked his virility in a sadistic way, she felt an underlying sexual attraction to him. But from *his* passive tendencies arose desires of wanting to hurt, to punish her, as a way of asserting his damaged ego. Tiger may have said to himself, "You killed me [my self-esteem, my virility] and I'm going to kill you in return." Unconsciously Teddy exposed herself to Tiger's desire to hurt, thereby becoming a masochistic victim. Her guilt stemmed not only from her hostile feelings toward Tiger, but from her actual accusation that he was not a real man. It was this guilt which impelled her to accept punishment. Teddy invited attack—a common pattern found in many cases of murder.

Another aspect of the homicide was Tiger's strong suicidal inclinations. These self-killing tendencies may very well have brought him to say something to the effect: "When you hear that I killed myself, you will know it was you who killed me, and so will everybody else."

Another feature of the murder was Tiger's claim that he had returned to Teddy's apartment after the crime when he was in a completely confused state. In view of his fantasies and his nagging guilt he could very well have done so, or *wished* to. If he really did return to the scene of his crime, we know that his reaction— his guilt at the realization of his act—impelled him to help in his capture. Tiger said he lost his eyeglasses; they could have fallen off during his struggle with Teddy, and he missed them only later.

But there is another, deeper psychological factor involved here. When he left Teddy's apartment after the murder, in his state of panic and terror he could not see because unconsciously he did not want to use his eyes. Sometimes the eye sees what it wishes to see; more frequently it sees what it expects to see. By putting himself in an "unseeing" condition, Tiger shut himself off from what had happened. Blurring of the vision is not unusual in a person under acute stress. Tiger's guilt or imagined guilt about Teddy or about other illusory acts may have triggered off "blindness," which he thought had been caused by "losing" his glasses, naturally putting him into a frenzy.

There was a further aspect of the case that particularly plagued me—Tiger's amnesia about Teddy's death. That because of repression or suppression a person is unable to remember what actually took place in the heat of an argument resulting in violence is well known. What is not so well known is that proof that a murderer suffers from what he has done can often be discovered in that fact that—quite honestly—he cannot remember how it happened. (Of course amnesia cannot be used as evidence that a man has committed a murder.) Tiger suffered from the consequences of his act, and that is one fundamental reason why he could not recall what had taken place that fateful night.

— 7 —

The next morning when I returned to court the two psychiatrists from the city psychiatric hospital had already arrived. I was not permitted in the courtroom during their testimony, so I waited in the corridor outside. Later, Taylor told me that the first psychiatrist held to the opinion, given in his report, that the defendant had been sane at the time of the murder and was able to stand trial. He had found Mellowbrook guarded, evasive and depressed, but not more than could be expected under the circumstances.

In the cross-examination, Taylor had gone into great detail about the psychiatrist's limited qualifications and experience. Then he asked him whether the lack of a *formal thinking disorder* —whose presence generally is a sign of psychosis—could not be due to the fact that Mellowbrook had been depressed and guarded during the psychological test. The psychiatrist agreed that this was possible. He said that the defendant had shown paranoid ideas, and that he was exceedingly preoccupied, at times almost cut off from reality.

The second psychiatrist agreed with his colleague. The defendant was able to appreciate and know the wrongfulness of his alleged crime, was responsible for his criminal conduct and able to stand trial. During the cross-examination the defense lawyer got this man to admit that Mellowbrook was extremely concerned with himself, to the point of being compulsive, that he was hostile and depressed, but that he did not appear to be anxious. I had told Taylor that it was important to show that Mellowbrook was anxious and fearful in order to counteract any idea that he was a psychopath, a type of individual who displays few anxieties and lacks a sense of guilt regarding his actions.

Taylor began to shoot questions at the psychiatrist. A short verbal battle ensued.

Q. This man did have anxieties, didn't he, and fears too, didn't he?
A. Yes, he did. [The answer came hesitantly.]
Q. Did you ask him whether he had any fantasies?
A. No, not directly.
Q. What were the indirect questions you asked?
A. I don't remember.
Q. Don't you think that ascertaining fantasies in a person accused of such a serious crime is an important question to ask?
A. Yes.
Q. You have previously stated that the defendant was preoccupied and showed obsessions in his preoccupation. Do you know what he was preoccupied with?
A. It was impossible to find out what his preoccupations were.
Q. In attempting to find out those obsessions, what questions did you ask?
A. I cannot remember.
Q. And when you found that the defendant had shown obsessions, don't you think this should have been in your diagnosis?
A. I didn't think they were that important.
Q. But you have stated yourself that he was preoccupied, that he had obsessions. Wouldn't it be fair to mention it in your diagnosis?
A. Maybe.
Q. You have stated that in your examination, Mr. Mellowbrook was depressed.
A. Yes, he was depressed, but nothing out of the usual.
Q. Of course you didn't see him at the time of the alleged crime, did you?
A. No, I did not.
Q. So in the course of ten days or so, his mood and his temper, and his whole mental condition, may have changed. Couldn't that happen?
A. Yes.
Q. Did you know he had been self-destructive, maybe suicidal? Did you go into his early history?
A. No.

Q. Did you read some of his writings where he states he doesn't want to live?
A. Not to my knowledge.
Q. So far this man is far from being normal. He has obsessions, he is preoccupied, he has been depressed or he has a depression, and he has been suicidal. Isn't that a fair account of the defendant's mental condition?

The psychiatrist was hesitant in answering. The district attorney interrupted and said that the witness had answered this question before. The judge agreed. The witness was dismissed.

The prosecutor made a short announcement: "Your Honor, the state rests its case."

The defense attorney collected some of his papers, went over to the stand and began a statement. "If it pleases the court, I would like to make a motion to dismiss the charges against the defendant for the following reasons:

"Your Honor, this defendant has been charged with murder first degree. Murder or, to use the general name for murder, homicide as it applies to this case is defined as follows: 'Homicide is the killing of a human being by the acts, procurement, or omission of another.' Murder in the first degree, which the defendant has been charged with, is defined according to the statute as follows: 'The killing of a human being is murder in the first degree when committed from a deliberate and premeditated design to effect the death of the person killed.' In order to establish the crime of murder in the first degree, the prosecution has to prove beyond a reasonable doubt that the defendant killed the deceased with a premeditated or deliberate design to effect her death.

"Premeditation is the formation in a person's mind of a specific intent to kill.

"Deliberation is consideration and reflection upon the preconceived intent to kill.

"As Your Honor knows, premeditation and deliberation express the defendant's mental processes and the only way we can ascertain them is by his behavior or by his acts, by his manners or by his verbal expressions.

"The premeditated and deliberate design to kill must precede the killing by some period of time, whether long or short. Nowhere has there been any iota of proof that the defendant had made any premeditated or deliberate design to kill. The surrounding circumstances at the time of the alleged killing and his behavior do not at all warrant the conclusion of any premeditation or deliberation. My client did not show or make any design to effect death with premeditation and deliberation. For all these reasons I submit that the charge of murder, first degree, is out of order and should be dismissed. There is no proof that the defendant committed the crime for which he is charged.

"Even if one goes so far as to say that my client did kill, not even murder in the second degree would be fair since there is no proof that the killing of Teddy Gladstone was done with the design to effect the death of the person killed, but without premeditation and deliberation. There was no design to effect the death of the person killed, which the law requires.

"Furthermore, Your Honor, manslaughter in the first degree is not even applicable in this case. Manslaughter in the first degree is defined: 'Such homicide is manslaughter in the first degree when committed without a design to effect death, in the heat of passion, but in a cruel and unusual manner, or by means of a dangerous weapon.'

"It would then seem," the defense attorney continued, "that in manslaughter in the first degree there is no premeditation. There is no deliberation, nor is there any design to effect death. It is committed in the heat of passion, but in a cruel and unusual manner, or by means of a dangerous weapon. There is no element of intent to kill in manslaughter in the first degree.

"There is no proof that the alleged killing in this case here was committed in a cruel and unusual manner. If it is true that the girl was strangled by having the necklace pulled off her neck, it cannot by any stretch of the imagination be stated that this necklace was a dangerous weapon.

"Then, as to the words 'heat of passion,' what does the law mean by these words? The law does not refer to 'heat of passion' in the usual, technical sense. We mean by it an excited, excitable and hypersensitive unstable mental condition in contrast to a cool or sober state of mind. 'Heat of passion' does not mean a passion or anger which arises from old hate, but the passion of anger that suddenly arose at the time of the alleged killing.

"And, Your Honor, if I may be permitted to add, in order for the killing to be cruel and unusual, it must be carried out in some extraordinary manner—in a dreadful or shocking way.

"Then, too, may it please the court that I call to your attention the provision of our law applicable to all homicides. Section 1041 of the Penal Law provides that no person can be convicted of murder or manslaughter unless the death of the person alleged to have been killed, and the fact of the killing by the defendant as alleged, are each established as independent facts; the former— that is, the death of the person alleged to have been killed—must be proved by direct proof, and the latter, beyond a reasonable doubt."

At this point, the district attorney rose and stated that what the defense attorney had said so far had little, if anything, to do with the matter of insanity, which was the question here. The defense attorney replied that if the defendant had not been charged with a crime, the question of either his sanity or his insanity would not have been raised. There would not have been any case at all.

The judge listened intently for a while and then ruled that for the time being he would permit the defense attorney to continue his argument for the dismissal of the charge of murder first degree.

Tiger's lawyer replied that a girl had been killed in her apartment. "I shall not go into what the medical examiner has stated, only mention that she was strangled, possibly by a necklace. No stab wounds were found."

"But," Taylor continued, "the killing of the deceased by the defendant has not been established at all, and certainly not established beyond a reasonable doubt. I would like to call your attention here to the word 'intent,' that is, 'criminal intent.' 'Intent' means that the person has a purpose to obtain a certain or definite effect of his act. Nowhere can it be ascertained from the actions and conduct of the defendant that he had any intent of killing Teddy Gladstone. The weapon used here—the necklace—cannot be considered as a weapon to be used in order to carry out the intent of killing.

"May I remind Your Honor that it is a general rule of law that a man's actions and behavior reveal what his mind thinks and feels. A man does not express his intention only by words. Let me please state that it is a fundamental rule of evidence that a man is presumed to intend the consequences of his deed unless the act was carried out under circumstances which preclude the existence of such an intent. From what the prosecution has established about the defendant's actions and his conduct, we cannot conclude that the defendant intended to commit the deed that caused Teddy Gladstone's death.

"Mr. Mellowbrook did not intend to kill, in the event that he was in the apartment of the deceased. He had no reason for wanting to murder Teddy. He was in love with her. He wanted to marry her. Therefore, he did not plan to kill her.

"Whatever the question of motivation was, it might not have been of so much importance. What is essential here is 'criminal intent.' Motivation is the spring of action which prompts a man to commit a criminal act. The motivation attributed to a defendant in any case must have a logical or legal reason, and be associated with the criminal act, according to the rules of human behavior. If there is no connection, or if the motivation is not single-minded, but rather ambivalent, it cannot be considered as an integral part of the proof.

"While I do know that the evidence of motivation to commit a crime is decisive or essential to a conviction, the law does not require motivation. Here, in the case of Mr. Mellowbrook, there is an absence of motivation for the commission of the crime of which he is charged.

"On the basis of what I have said here, I ask that the charge of murder, first degree, be dismissed and that the defendant be set free on bail, and that in the meantime the degree of the charge be placed in abeyance."

During the last few minutes of the defense attorney's speech, the prosecutor had been pacing back and forth. Now he said, "If it pleases the court, the confession states that Teddy Gladstone was killed while she was visited by the defendant, and for that reason I ask that the defense attorney's motion be dismissed."

The defense attorney objected. "The confession has not yet been admitted into evidence. When my client made this confession he was not represented by counsel. I shall not argue with the prosecution about this anymore. I appeal to Your Honor that the degree of the charge against my client, Tyros Mellowbrook, be dismissed and that it be kept in abeyance, and that in the meantime the defendant be released on bail."

The judge replied that he would reserve decision and asked that witnesses for the defense be heard.

The district attorney immediately rose to his feet. "Your Honor, this defendant has been indicted after due examination and investigation by the grand jury."

"My learned colleague certainly must know," the defense attorney replied, "that an indictment is not proof that a man is guilty. If I may direct myself to the court," he continued, "the defendant and I repeat my appeal at this time for the dismissal of the indictment and for a direction of verdict in favor of the defendant, Tyros Mellowbrook, first on the grounds that the evidence as a matter of law is insufficient and highly inadequate, and secondly on the grounds that as a matter of law The People have been unable to prove the defendant guilty beyond a reasonable doubt. Further, that as a matter of law the prosecution has failed to refute the presumption of innocence. Further, on the grounds that the evidence is weak, improper and untrue to the facts, reached only on fantasy and suspicion, and as demanded by Section 389 of the Code of Criminal Procedure, it is highly inadequate."

"The court has reserved decision on these motions," stated the judge.

"May it please the court," the district attorney interrupted, "to move that the defendant be bound over to trial."

In the same curt voice he had used in reserving decision, the judge retorted, "The defendant is remanded. Case adjourned until ten o'clock tomorrow morning."

Taylor had done well. The judge at least had not dismissed the motion, which I considered a good sign. Apparently he wanted to think over the matter, which was quite natural, particularly since the evidence brought out so far had not been very damaging to the defense. I was surprised at the district attorney's insistence upon the indictment as the basis for his murder charge. Apparently he had forgotten that an indictment is not evidence. The prosecution had presented statements before the grand jury which might or might not be evidence in the case. In general, before the grand jury he can present facts, or what he thinks are facts which would not be permitted in a trial. Mellowbrook had not appeared before the grand jury, particularly because he could not be permitted to be represented by counsel.

Since so much misunderstanding exists in the mind of the public about the nature of an indictment, it is necessary to point out that if a person is indicted it is an accusation only, it is not a proof of guilt, nor is it evidence of the crime. In discussing an indictment we often hear people say, "They indicted him though." And sometimes they add, "Where there's smoke there's fire, so it looks suspicious." An indictment is not like that at all. It is like a summons in a civil case. A man presents a person with a summons and says, "You have to pay your debt to me." This is the way through which a defendant is brought into court. There is no difference between a summons and an indictment.

Thus it can be understood that the defense attorney's motion to dismiss the charge against Tiger could not be called empty words or gestures. It was based on facts.

When I returned to my office late in the afternoon and reviewed what had taken place, I realized with surprise that the prosecutor had not asked the medical examiner for the time of Teddy's death. Determining the time of a person's death is easily done by measuring the body temperature and the degree of rigor mortis. Experience has taught that rigor mortis appears at a certain time and then disappears at another time. The temperature of the body drops a certain number of degrees each hour following death, and by counting back to the normal temperature of 98.6 degrees, the time of death can be stipulated approximately—that is, within three hours.

There was still another aspect of the case which had not been touched upon. The medical examiner had stated that the cause of death was asphyxiation due to strangulation by the necklace. If this was the case, it certainly showed that the murderer, whoever he was, had torn off the necklace and in so doing had choked the girl without touching the back of her neck. This would indicate that the crime had not been committed with any criminal intent or with malice or with forethought, but that it had come about in the course of the killer's ripping the necklace from the neck. If this had occurred, and I thought it had, then certainly the murder charge should be reduced at least to manslaughter first degree, if not second degree.

There was yet another factor which had not been brought up at the sanity hearing by either the district attorney or the medical examiner. Could the cause of death be associated with alcohol or carbon monoxide? Death by carbon monoxide is a more frequent cause of death than people realize. If there had been a large enough amount of carbon monoxide in the air, it might have induced asphyxiation. I remembered that Tiger had told me something to the effect that it had been raining and windy, maybe chilly, and Teddy might have lit a fire in the fireplace.

I put in a call to the weather bureau. A girl informed me that from six to twelve o'clock on the evening of the murder the temperature range was between 56 and 64 degrees. "It was windy with some rain."

"What was the temperature after midnight?" I asked.

"I will have to look it up," the girl answered.

The temperature later that night until six o'clock in the morning proved to have been 57 or 56 degrees, cloudy and windy.

From psychiatry to weather. My thoughts wandered to the time when Teddy actually was killed or died. The time period was not given because there were several unknown factors. Teddy was found lying on the bed and covered by a blanket. It was a cool evening and the window was closed. All these factors influenced the timing of her death, which could only be approximated.

More important, though, was the cause of death itself. The evening was cool. There may have been a fire in the fireplace. Teddy was a chain smoker and Tiger had been smoking both cigarettes and a pipe. The fireplace in her apartment may have been lighted for at least a couple of hours. The room may well have been filled with carbon monoxide as a result of a faulty flue or because of their smoking.

People usually think of carbon monoxide as a deadly gas coming from the exhaust pipe of an automobile. The smoke stream of a cigarette contains not only warm air, nicotine and tar, but also large amounts of carbon monoxide whenever there is incomplete combustion of carbon. If a smoke-filled room contains 0.25 percent of carbon monoxide, it would prove fatal to an adult in about four hours;[1] and a 1 percent concentration of carbon monoxide in the air is rapidly fatal.[2]

Tiger had told me that at one time during the evening he had opened a window in her apartment, and had later closed it. If the living room was poorly ventilated, the amount of carbon monoxide—which is odorless, tasteless and nonirritating—could have risen to the danger point without their noticing it.[3]

Could it be that in addition to alcohol they had been exposed to the lethal gas, and that Tiger in pulling off Teddy's necklace had temporarily knocked her out, and that the carbon monoxide finally had closed off whatever was left of her impaired respiration?

The more I thought about the murder, the more certain I became that Teddy's death had been accidental despite Tiger's unconscious wish for it. There was the necklace. The district attorney had not mentioned it at all and apparently it had not been found either. If Tiger *had* taken it from Teddy's neck, he could have thrown it away in anger or disgust, in bitterness or embarrassment. But he had been in her apartment, he had left, and Teddy was dead. The circumstances surrounding her death were too enigmatic for comfort.

During dinner that evening, my wife noticed that I was very preoccupied. She tried to divert me, but I was lost in my thoughts. When my wife knows that I am busy with a difficult case, she always goes out of her way to make the dinner appealing; she is an excellent cook. By the time I had my coffee and my cigar, I felt much better, though the case was in the back of my mind.

1. *Modi's Textbook of Medical Jurisprudence and Toxicology*, ed. N. J. Modi (Bombay, India: N. M. Tripathi Private Ltd., 16th ed. 1967), p. 758.
2. D. M. Pryce, M.D., and C. F. Ross, M.D., *Ross's Post-Mortem Appearances*, 6th ed. (London: Oxford University Press, 1963), p. 41.
3. Edward F. Wilson, M.D., Terry H. Rich, M.D., and Henry C. Messman, "The Hazardous Hibachi, Carbon Monoxide Poisoning Following Use of Charcoal," *JAMA*, vol. 221, no. 4 (July 24, 1972), pp. 405–6.

I excused myself to make a telephone call. I wanted to tell Taylor about my thoughts on the carbon monoxide, the fireplace and the weather. He listened attentively and said he thought I'd done some good detective work. All this had a bearing upon the case, and he felt that the district attorney hadn't mentioned these factors for tactical reasons. They would be taken up at the trial.

"Of course I'm far away from my own field," I said, "but I couldn't help thinking that maybe he doesn't want to show his hand now. The assistant district attorney who interrogated Tiger about the murder," I continued, "is a gentleman, I would assume, and very busy. Even if he was interested in facts only, he knows what he was after."

I asked Taylor if he was going to call to the stand the doctor who had examined Tiger in the detention center when he screamed for help and had to be sedated. He answered, "It may be necessary, but I'll wait to see first how my own witnesses make out tomorrow. And you will be on too."

When I entered the courtroom the following morning, the first witness for the defense was on the stand. Milton Bridges, a tall, thin man with a small mustache, was office manager for the public relations firm Petterson & Schatz, where Teddy had worked full time and Tiger had worked on a temporary basis. I had thought of talking both to him and to the president of the firm, but had refrained. Mr. Bridges told the court that during the few weeks before the murder he had noticed that Tiger was nervous and erratic in his behavior. He didn't come in on time, and then one day, just before that fateful Saturday, he had asked Mr. Bridges if he would lend him some money. Mr. Bridges was quite surprised at this request because he knew that Tiger was very careful in managing his finances and always carried some money with him.

"How much did he borrow from you?" the defense attorney asked.

"Twenty-five dollars."

"Did you think this was unusual?"

"I thought that he had been out drinking and needed money, or maybe he wanted to buy something, but I didn't press him."

Upon further questioning, the office manager admitted that

everyone knew that Tiger and Teddy were spending a lot of time together, that they were a steady thing. When asked to describe Teddy, he said that she was bright and good-looking. She was not easy to work with because she always wanted things her own way, but she had many good ideas, and the people around her were very fond of her, although at times she teased quite a bit.

"Was she a teaser?" Taylor asked.

"Yes, you could say that."

The witness had not seen Tiger in the office the Monday after the alleged murder. He called him at his home to find out whether he was sick, but there was no answer. On Tuesday Tiger came in very late—around twelve o'clock. He looked awful—unshaven, hair uncombed, eyes bloodshot, clothes wrinkled. "I went over and talked with him, but he was reluctant to speak. I asked him where he had been, if he was angry at someone, or if anything had happened, but he didn't say anything. He accepted a cup of coffee, and then half an hour later when I returned to his office I saw that he had not touched it. He just sat there. I tried to joke: 'Too much to drink?' 'Is it a new girl?' He acted despondent, and did not answer. We were concerned because Teddy hadn't shown up either that Monday, nor on Tuesday. We tried to call her apartment but didn't get any answer, so we assumed that she was out of town, though she usually left word where she could be reached. It all seemed so mysterious, and of course we were upset a bit. We hadn't put the pieces together yet."

"What happened then?" the defense lawyer asked.

"In the afternoon the police came, identified themselves and said that they wanted to talk with Mellowbrook, and that was the last I saw of him."

The defense counsel went over Mr. Bridges' testimony again, stressing in particular Tiger's erratic behavior when he came to work that Tuesday and that he had been upset, disturbed and depressed a few days before the alleged homicide occurred.

Dismissing Mr. Bridges, the district attorney remarked only, "No cross."

The next witness was Mr. Petterson, a heavy-set, stocky, short man in his early fifties. As he took the stand, I saw that he had a cigar in his hand. The clerk admonished him to put it away, which he did. Petterson spoke in a rather guttural voice. He had known Teddy for several years, considered her very capable, and had hired Mr. Mellowbrook as an idea man. He thought that he was gifted, very talented, "but he only thought about finishing his book. Tiger was a hard worker, but much too serious. He was inner-directed."

"Did you notice anything in particular about him?"

Petterson thought a bit. "I really never saw him smile. He always seemed to be lost in his thoughts, and he talked very little with the rest of us in the office, but you could surmise that he was perceptive."

Had Tiger ever mentioned to the witness anything about Teddy?

"No, there was no need for it," he answered in a self-assured voice, "because everyone knew that they were going together."

"Do you have anything else to say about Mr. Mellowbrook?"

The witness mentioned that he had been thinking of promoting Tiger, but because of his personality— He interrupted himself. "You like to get results—and get them fast. I need people I can depend on when the pressure gets high. He was a risk, an unknown quality. I thought it best to leave him where he was."

When the lawyer for the defendant was about to call Tiger's mother to the stand, the prosecutor interrupted him and asked whether he could please recall to the stand Mr. Bridges, the office manager, because he had one or two questions to ask him. He apologized for his request, but Taylor graciously acceded, and so did the judge.

First Samson asked Mr. Bridges whether he had talked with Dr. Abrahamsen, Mr. Mellowbrook's appointed psychiatrist.

"No, I have not," the witness answered.

"Did you receive a call from Dr. Abrahamsen?"

"No, I did not."

I had expected the prosecutor to ask such a question, which is why I had not called Bridges. I knew that the district attorney might imply that I had influenced his testimony. A psychiatrist can never be too cautious.

The district attorney then asked the witness how he could tell that Tiger had been depressed. He answered that this was easy because he—Mr. Mellowbrok—could not concentrate on his work. He spent a great deal of time at the water cooler, drinking water as if he were very thirsty. "But I don't think he was that thirsty. It was a way to relieve his preoccupation. He was agitated —depressed, I would say."

"If it pleases the court, may I submit that since this witness is not a psychiatrist, and certainly not a professional witness, little or no credence can be placed in his testimony about the defendant."

The defense lawyer objected. The witness had the right to express an opinion about Mellowbrook's behavior, particularly since he had worked with him for some time and had come to know him and his habits.

The judge interrupted and asked the prosecutor if there were any further questions. "No more questions," he mumbled.

The next witness was Mrs. Mellowbrook. During his gentle questioning of Tiger's mother, the defense attorney tried to bring out that Tiger had been her main source of support for many years. She had found it necessary to take in roomers, and when business was bad her only income was what her son sent her. She repeated that he was a 'good boy,' and he could never have committed this crime.

When asked if he wanted to cross-examine Mrs. Mellowbrook, the district attorney demurred, apparently out of compassion.

As she left the stand, Tiger's mother implored the judge, "Let my boy go free; let him go home." When she returned to her seat she began to sob and moan quite loudly. The judge stopped the proceedings for a few moments, then motioned to the defense counsel to continue.

To my surprise the next witness was a pretty, wholesome-looking girl in a tight-fitting jersey dress, her hair styled in high fashion. Her name was Jane Willow. I had noticed her earlier in the courtroom, talking with Tiger's lawyer, but I didn't know anything about her. Now I saw her glance over at Tiger, who looked at her rather attentively. Then I noticed that she was wearing a thin gold necklace around her neck. Immediately I thought of Teddy. I heard the court clerk ask her where she lived, and I caught the last part of it: borough of Queens, New York City.

After she had testified that she was a hairdresser working at a midtown hotel, Taylor asked her how long she had known the defendant in this case, Tiger Mellowbrook. She replied that she had met him in a hotel bar one night, that is, May 12.

"Do you see him here in court?"

"Yes, sir."

"Can you point him out?"

She pointed to Tiger. I noticed on her hand a ring with a large stone. She seemed aggressive, someone who knew how to get what she wanted.

"Tell me what happened the night of May twelfth."

"Well, like I said, I was sitting at the bar with a girl friend, and he came over and began to talk to us. He was quite good-looking, but he looked out of it. I think he was high; his eyes were blood-shot and he seemed tense."

Asked what she was doing in the bar, she said that she was going to get married, so she was out for a good time while she was still free. She thought Tiger looked sensitive—someone who would be interesting to talk to—and he looked as if he would pick up the bill. Of course he wasn't that attractive, but he looked interesting. They talked for an hour or possibly an hour and a half. The defense attorney pursued his question. Did she note anything particular or unusual about him? He knew so much about psychology. He seemed like an authority, someone to respect. "I wanted to touch him. I know people better when I can touch them. I guess I'm intuitive."

The judge interrupted her and said, "Will you kindly answer only what you are asked, and try to answer to the point without giving any outside information, please."

"Sorry," she answered, and blushed.

Asked again how long she had known Mr. Mellowbrook, she replied that she had only met him that night and she wanted very much to be with him. She always tried to live for the moment. I saw Tiger look up. The girl continued. He had given her his address so that she could call him. Taylor asked in a pointed voice, "Did he write this down, or did you?"

"No, he couldn't. I wrote down his name, address and telephone number."

"What happened then?"

"You see, I like intelligent men, and I really went for him. I remember there was some sort of painting over the bar and he was looking at it too. He said that he couldn't see anything, and I told him to put on his glasses, and he said he didn't have any, but I could see that there were glasses in his shirt pocket, I think."

"Are you sure about that—that he had glasses in his pocket?"

"Yes, sir, I think so."

"By the way," Taylor asked, "how many drinks did you have?"

"I can't remember exactly. Maybe three or four martinis. Single martinis, I mean, not double."

"Do you remember what time it was when he left?"

"I can't say for sure, but it possibly may have been about four o'clock or so, something like that, or maybe three-thirty. I don't know."

"You stated it was your impression that he was quite high? Would you say that he was drunk?"

"Yes, I think you could say that."

"Objection, Your Honor. Counselor is leading the witness," the district attorney interrupted.

"Sustained."

"I'll change my question. Miss Willow, how would you describe Tiger Mellowbrook's condition at about three-thirty that morning?"

"He was drunk."

I caught Taylor's eye as he smiled.

"Did he talk about anything else?"

"Well, he talked about dancing and a girl, but he was babbling so that I couldn't understand what he was saying. I wanted him for myself, but then my girl friend was there and she wanted him too, so we had a sort of a fight between us, but I think I won out because he liked me." At this point the judge, the lawyers and the clerk began to laugh. The witness noticed the reaction and said, "Seriously, I think he liked me."

The defense attorney asked, "Are you sure that he had his glasses?"

The witness answered that she thought so. But then in a hurried voice she continued, "Somehow I felt that he couldn't see. What the reason was, I don't know. Now I remember that he told me he saw all kinds of bottles behind the bar and in all kinds of colors —red and green, yellow. It occurred to me that if he could see those things he must be able to see other things too. But I was high myself, though not as far gone as he was. Then I felt sorry for him and I thought I should take him to my apartment, where he could sleep it off, but he didn't want to. He seemed to be thinking about something else, and I just let him alone."

"May I please ask you . . ." Taylor thought for a while. "Can you state to the court here how you came to be a witness in this case?"

"I called Tiger's apartment and someone answered the phone and asked who I was. I gave my name and address and my phone number, and asked that he should call me back. And then one day a man came to the place where I work and asked me what I knew about Tiger Mellowbrook. I told him that I had met him at the bar on May twelfth, but that I didn't know very much about him. It turned out that the man who questioned me was a detective because I now remember that he showed me his identification card."

"What happened then?"

"He told me that the man I had been with was in serious trouble. I asked, 'What trouble?' and he told me about the murder, and I couldn't understand this at all because this man had looked so nice and so kind and he was so nice-looking. I felt sorry, really sorry, that he was in trouble, that he had killed anyone. Even when he was drunk he was nice to me. He listened to what I had to say."

"Well," Taylor continued, "what else happened with the detective?"

"I asked him who Tiger Mellowbrook's lawyer was, and he gave me a name, Albert Taylor, but he wasn't quite sure, and then I asked again because I felt a certain bond toward this man even though he was really more a stranger than a friend. I hadn't seen anything in the papers, so I looked his name up in the phone book. I called the office and found out about the trial so I told Mr. Taylor I would like to come here."

"Your witness," the defense attorney said to the prosecutor.

After some hesitation Samson asked whether she had seen the defendant drink anything. She was more than eager to testify that he had been drinking bourbon, one glass after the other, but also that he had been drunk when he entered the bar. "He was quite unsteady, and I seem to remember now that he said he had been in several bars before. I think he also told me that he had been in the subway, or in the movies, or somewhere. He had his tie in his pocket, and when he saw me he tried to put it on, but he couldn't. It was too complicated for him, so I helped him, but I can't do those knots. It looked sloppy. I have never tried to do a tie before."

The judge interrupted gently. "Please only answer the questions."

The district attorney moved that her remarks be stricken from the record, but Taylor protested loudly.

"Overruled," the judge intoned.

The prosecutor said, "I see that you are wearing a necklace. Do you wear this necklace every day?"

"I do. I wear it all the time, even when I take a bath. I never take it off."

Samson conferred briefly with his assistant and then said, "No more questions."

The defense attorney rose slowly, and after thinking for a while asked, "Can you remember whether the defendant looked at your necklace very much?"

"I think that he even touched it. I wanted him to. That is all I can remember."

Taylor thanked her for coming to court and she was dismissed.

After a short recess, Neil O'Brien was put on the witness stand.

The defense attorney began by asking Neil about Tiger's childhood and youth. Neil began by saying that although they had been friends from their first day at school, he felt that Tiger was often quite secretive about himself, particularly when it came to talking about girls. He would act very shy and change the subject. Neil fancied that Tiger had a rather unhappy childhood since his father had left him and his mother when he was a little boy, and she had been forced to take in roomers in order to support them. Later, Neil said, Tiger took on whatever jobs he could find in order to help his mother. He recalled the episode of the cat and the attic window.

Had Tiger ever been in trouble? Neil replied that sometimes he had difficulties with his teacher. On one occasion she became so angry that she hit him, and he hit her back.

"What was his opinion of himself?" Taylor asked.

"I believe he thought well of himself. He always knew what was right. He was very interested in politics, in social problems, like welfare."

"Was he at any time violent?"

"No, not usually . . . except for the cat. Even though nothing happened to it, Tiger was conscience-stricken, and brooded about it for a long time."

"How did Tiger come across to you, Neil?"

"Tiger never argued. He didn't like to argue. He believed that it was petty and he didn't want to get involved in pettiness. He supported his mother, but I don't think that he always got along with her. He felt that it was his duty to help her. It was my impression that she nagged him a great deal, which he hated, and that he might have been afraid of her. She was convinced that her boy was going to be great, and more than once she bragged to me that he had such a good brain. He sometimes was moody—a daydreamer. He was difficult to reach then."

"Did Tiger have any particular habits?"

"What do you mean by habits? Tiger read a great deal. I remember particularly, when we were children he talked about Darwin. I had never heard of him and was quite impressed."

"What was your relationship with Tiger later on?"

"He went to college and I went into public relations. Later, when I came to New York, I wrote to him and told him to come up here. I introduced Tiger to Teddy."

"How would you describe Teddy?"

"She was intelligent, she had a good brain; very good-looking —high cheekbones, blue eyes that sometimes seemed green and hair that was auburn. She was aggressive around men and some were turned off by her. I liked her. She was a dynamo and lots of fun."

"What did Tiger do after work?"

"He wrote a great deal, but I'm not sure what he was writing about. Sometimes he would show me pages from his manuscript —a novel expressing his ideas on politics and social issues. I brought a few notes with me. Would you like to read them?"

"Yes."

"Objection," the district attorney bellowed. "Nobody knows that the defendant actually wrote these notes."

"Your Honor, my witness is under oath and I am sure that he would not perjure himself by saying that these notes were written by the defendant if in fact they were not. Furthermore, these notes should throw some light upon his mental condition."

The judge took a deep breath. "First let us hear the contents of these notes, and then I will decide whether they shall be included in the record. Objection overruled."

Neil began:

"What is mortal seeks to be immortal. Death is the separation of the mind, the spirit, from the body.

"Some people wait to be slauhgtered. They wait to die.

"Who that can conquor life will be a man.

"Man is the most ferocious of all animals, more than a tiger, more than a shark.

"A man kills his own species, not for pleasure but because he wants to.

"Who that can conquer his own desires can or will be a man.

"There is a time to despair, and a time to enjoy.

"Emotional infidelity is worse than sexual infidelity.

"To step on one's soul is criminal.

"Do I love you, do you love me? You cannot love what you don't know."

The witness stopped.

I noticed that Taylor had almost winced when Neil read, "A man kills his own species, not for pleasure but because he wants to." But he was too astute to let the prosecutor know about his consternation. My thoughts were interrupted when Taylor continued, apparently unruffled. "You say that Tiger was interested in politics? Do you have any specific information about it?"

Neil answered that Tiger used to compare himself to Georges

Clemenceau, who went under the nickname "Tiger." "He read everything about him he could get his hands on. Tiger really wanted to become a doctor, but he thought that the world of medicine was too narrow for him. He wanted to be out in the real world, the world of politics. It really amazed me when he told me that Georges Clemenceau originally had been a physician, but later became a statesman. Tiger was ambitious."

"Did he have any definite ambitions?"

Neil said that he couldn't be sure, but Tiger certainly was ambitious.

Asked about the relationship between Teddy and Tiger, the witness had the definite impression that they were in love with each other but that they argued a great deal, and he could never understand why. It was like a lovers' quarrel. Were they dependent on each other? Neil thought so. The defense attorney again returned to the question, Was Tiger violent, or had he been in the past? Neil didn't think so, because Tiger refused to argue. How can a man be violent if he can't stand conflict?

"Do you think that Tiger could carry out the crime of which he has been accused?"

The district attorney arose and shouted, "Objection."

"Sustained," the judge announced.

Taylor returned to his yellow papers, looked at them and then said quietly, "You've said that they seemed in love with each other —Teddy and Tiger. Do you believe they intended to get married?"

"Tiger talked a great deal about her, said that he wanted to marry. But she was seeing someone quite prominent in the international business world. I didn't think it was serious, but of course Tiger was jealous. Thinking about it now, he was more than jealous; he was hurt, and felt betrayed."

"Did he ever seem upset or disturbed?"

"Yes, sometimes he was upset, especially when he hadn't heard anything from his mother, and then he would call her. But I also think that it was quite difficult for him to make a go of it with Teddy. She was willful and impatient. I remember that Tiger was able to calm her down, but it wasn't easy for her to give in. When she found something to argue about, she could argue until dawn. I felt sorry for him, and sorry that I had brought them together.

I'd thought that Tiger might have a good influence on her—moderate her energy and help her relax more."

"Do you use drugs?"

"Once in a while."

"Did Tiger use drugs?"

"Sometimes he used Dexedrine or amphetamines, but very little. With his independent mind he wanted to stay away from drugs. He wanted to be his own person. That's why he drank so little."

On cross-examination, Neil said he hadn't actually seen Tiger take any drugs.

"No more questions," the prosecutor said.

During the recess we discussed Neil's testimony, which we felt had helped the case considerably. We also felt that Jane Willow, even with all of her assertiveness, had been decisively helpful in her testimony, which was sincere and honest.

"Things are getting brighter," Taylor said smilingly.

"I am glad you are optimistic now, but remember the case is not clear-cut. Tiger was traumatized—psychotic, or at least in the twilight of a psychosis—when he was in Teddy's apartment. He may have been predisposed to becoming suspicious or paranoid, all of which very well could have been instrumental in leading him into his legal difficulties." I was cut off by three knocks on the door leading into the courtroom. We all stood at attention while the judge entered and took his seat on the bench. "Next witness?" he asked.

The defense attorney arose. "At this point I would like to call Max Golden." Max Golden had been a taxicab driver for over thirty years. He was around fifty-five, short, with thick black hair and brown eyes that were bright and shrewd. He obviously was nervous. Taylor asked the witness to sit back and think carefully before he answered.

"Do you remember that you were on duty the evening or the night of May twelfth or May thirteenth, and that you picked up a certain passenger? Do you see him here in the courtroom?"

The cab driver looked around and said, "Yeah, there he is," pointing to the slumped figure of Tiger.

"Will you please tell the court what happened, Mr. Golden?"

"My name is Max, but they call me Moishe. You can call me Moishe." He already had become familiar, covering over his anxieties.

"Will you please tell the court what happened that night when this man was a passenger in your cab?"

"I picked him up around Sixtieth Street or so."

"Try to remember as well as you can what took place."

"I picked this man up, it was around midnight, and he said that he was going to Forty-second Street. I asked him where. He didn't know where, he just said, 'Drive.' "

The defense attorney asked if he had noticed anything in particular about him.

"Yeah, I think he was gooky."

"What do you mean by 'gooky'?"

"Oh, off the beam."

"What do you mean by 'off the beam'?"

"He looked spaced out."

"Did he say anything?"

"No. He looked upset—angry. I still can remember his eyes. They were red and watery. I tried to talk to him, but I never should have said anything, because he told me to shut up, so I shut up, but I looked at him in my mirror. He sat there. He looked tired. I figured he had had a hard night."

"You said he looked wild. Can you describe it, please?"

"He looked drunk."

"Did he smell of alcohol?"

"Yeah, yeah, he sure did. He smelled of alcohol and at that time of night I am very careful about who I pick up. You never know what crackpots are on the street. But then, business has been lousy and I have to take what comes along."

"So what happened then?" the defense attorney asked. "You drove down to Forty-second Street and what then?"

"Then he asked me to go up Broadway. I told him that I couldn't go up Broadway, it's a one-way street. So he said, 'Go wherever you want.' 'Where to?' I asked. 'Go down to Fortieth Street.' 'And then?' I asked. 'Turn left.' So we went down to Fortieth Street and turned left. 'Where do we go now?' 'Turn left,' he said. So we went up Sixth Avenue, and I asked, 'Where do we go now?' 'Turn left,' he said. I thought to myself, 'This man must be nuts.' I looked for a policeman but I couldn't see one. You know the police have to have one day off, and this was it."

"Do you know why there were no police?"

"No, but now I remember it was raining."

"Was it cold?"

"Yes, sort of."

Taylor asked, "What happened after you had turned left?"

" 'Go up Forty-second Street,' he said. 'Where then?' 'Up Eighth Avenue,' he said. 'Where then?' 'Turn right,' and so I turned right three times, and there was some sort of a movie or something like that, and before I realized it he jumped out of the cab. You know he didn't pay me. I was mad as hell."

"Did you find a policeman?" Taylor asked.

"Yes, but it was too late. The man had run away from me, and I was four dollars and fifty cents short, without tip. A man has to make a living. Some living!"

"Now, Mr. Golden—"

"Moishe," the cab driver interrupted.

"You said that your passenger was 'off the beam.' Did he threaten you in any way?"

"He didn't threaten me. He just seemed mixed up."

It surprised me that the district attorney didn't object.

"Was he frightened?"

"You're damn right he was frightened. When I now think about it, yes, that's what he was. He was frightened."

"Do you know what he was frightened of?"

"Look here," he answered, "I am no head doctor. I don't know, but nuts he was."

Taylor asked, "Have you received any payment for coming here?"

"Yeah."

The prosecutor looked up intently.

"How much did you receive?" the defense attorney inquired quietly.

"Four-fifty for my fare."

"Have you received anything else?"

"No."

"Who paid you this four-fifty?"

"You, mister."

A subdued wave of laughter followed, and the judge, trying to suppress a smile, banged down the gavel. "Continue, counselor," he said.

"That is right. I paid you out of my own pocket—four dollars and fifty cents. Did I promise you anything else besides the fare?"

"No. No promises."

"Good. Your witness," Taylor said to the district attorney.

The prosecutor looked at his watch and said, "May I suggest, Your Honor, that we take a luncheon break now."

"If it is agreeable with the defense attorney we will adjourn until two o'clock," the judge replied.

8

At two-thirty that afternoon the court clerk called the court to order. The cross-examination of the taxicab driver Max Golden began.

First the prosecutor asked about the witness's education. Grade school and high school, that's all. What did he do when he finished school? Odd jobs. Then he learned how to drive, and after driving a truck he began driving a cab for a fleet, and he had been doing this ever since. What did he know about people who were insane or, as he put it, "crazy"? He had seen many of them. He even had one in his own family. Who was that? Oh, an aunt. She was crazy and had to be hospitalized. Taylor looked concerned, and so, no doubt, did I. I wondered if she was a member of his own family or merely related through marriage? I hoped that Taylor would question him about this.

The district attorney asked Golden to repeat his story about the evening he drove the defendant around the city, and he told exactly the same story. "He didn't pay me either, damn it," he concluded. "Sorry, Your Honor, I know I shouldn't swear in court."

The judge looked at him and smiled.

Outwardly it would appear that the cab driver was calm, but I could see that he really was angry. Suddenly he blurted out, "The man was mad. I could see it in his eyes that he was mad. Don't you understand? He was mad—that's what he was—mad." By this time Moishe had become quite agitated.

The prosecutor turned to the judge. "If it pleases the court, I request that this last statement about the man being mad be stricken from the record."

Tiger's defense lawyer protested vigorously. Mr. Golden had seen the defendant very shortly after the alleged murder. He had the right to be heard and to relate what he had observed. One doesn't necessarily have to be a psychiatrist to be able to say whether a person is "mad" or not.

The judge thought for a moment and then, looking at the prosecutor, announced, "Overruled."

The district attorney asked for the court's indulgence while he conferred with his assistant. They talked together for a long while and finally Samson asked, "How come you remember so much about the defendant? You pick up many people, don't you?"

"Yes, but this man didn't pay me," the witness retorted.

The prosecutor interrupted. "No more cross-examination."

After the defense attorney had asked the judge for permission to question Mr. Golden again, he turned to the witness, who by this time had regained his composure and was smiling broadly at Taylor.

"You told the court that you had an aunt who had been mentally ill. Was she a member of your family?"

"Yes, she was in my family."

"I mean," interrupted Taylor, "was she your real aunt? Was she a blood relation?"

"Oh, no," he answered quickly, "not a real aunt. We couldn't have such a nut in our family. No, she was married into the family."

Taylor looked relieved. He continued his reexamination. "And you had seen this aunt for some years?"

"Oh, yes," Moishe answered. "At least fifteen or twenty years."

"Can you describe her for us?"

The district attorney objected.

The judge stated that it was important for the court to know what experience this witness had, so he would let him answer the question.

"Where is your aunt, Moishe?" the defense attorney asked.

"She's in the hospital. I drove her over there last year. I'm the only one in the family who has a car, so I told them I'd drive her over."

"So you have seen people who are 'off the beam,' to use your own expression?"

"Oh, yes, many of them at the city psychiatric hospital."

"No more questons."

The defense attorney had handled this matter very well. He had exposed himself to a definite danger in asking about Moishe's aunt. She very well could have been his aunt by blood, and the cabby's judgment could have been invalidated as that of one with "madness" in his own family. From the way the examination had gone, I did not think that the defense attorney knew beforehand that the aunt was related only through marriage.

The court clerk had been whispering with the judge, who now announced a fifteen-minute recess and hurried from the courtroom.

The case was building up for Tiger. Both Taylor and I agreed that Dr. Foster, his former psychiatrist, should testify since he was the only professional man who had examined Tiger a few days prior to the murder.

After the recess, Foster took the stand. Taylor asked him the usual questions about his qualifications. He had graduated from the Berlin Psychoanalytic Institute and later had come to the United States, where he had held staff positions in various hospitals. He had written quite a few papers and several books, particularly about certain phases of psychoanalytic treatment and the handling of transference. "Did you say transference?" asked the judge. Dr. Foster explained the meaning of transference.[1]

---

1. By "transference" we mean the transfer to the psychiatrist of feelings, impulses, wishes and fantasies which the patient has experienced in the past related to people to whom he was emotionally close, such as parents or siblings. During psychoanalysis, the patient unconsciously considers the psychiatrist as the object of his repressed impulses.

We differentiate between the positive and the negative tranference. In the positive transference, the patient will praise the psychoanalyst and frequently will fantasize about him and his private life, or dream that the analyst visits his house, etc. The negative transference is expressed by the patient's consistent lateness in coming to his sessions, by not paying his bills, by bringing in very few dreams, or by constantly complaining.

The defense attorney took a deep breath and said, "Now, doctor, it has been stated that you saw the defendant, Tyros Mellowbrook, or, to use his nickname, 'Tiger,' in your office. Will you please tell the court in as much detail as you are able about your examination of him?" Dr. Foster had seen Tiger in the beginning of May. At that time Tiger was depressed, disturbed and suicidal. The doctor wanted to admit him to a psychiatric hospital, but the patient refused. He was not responsive or communicative. He was preoccupied. He thought he was a failure and hadn't been able to sleep for several nights. Finally he admitted some trouble with a girl whom he wanted to marry. He was deeply in love with her, and several times had made hints about his desire to marry her, but he wasn't sure how he should go about it. He repeatedly claimed that he had no time for his own writing because he was involved in press relations for a political campaign, and was working for a public relations firm. It was strange that even though he was very depressed and agitated, he struggled for control of himself, and somehow did seem to be in control.

The district attorney was on his feet. "Your Honor, may I please be heard? The witness has been reading from something. What is it?"

The doctor hesitated, perplexed.

"Please answer the question," the judge told him.

"These are some notes I took at the time I examined the defendant."

"May we please continue the interview?" asked Tiger's lawyer.

"I gave the patient a prescription for some sleeping medication, but when he returned I learned that he had not filled it. He was depressed, had not eaten anything, and looked hurt, as if he were in agony. I advised him to go into a psychiatric hospital for

---

A person who had a harsh, dominant father may become rebellious and defiant of all authority. Unconsciously he identifies the analyst as a father figure. The analyst by understanding the patient's situation will try to make him accept the fact that his defiant behavior is unrealistic, show him that these were feelings which he originally felt toward his father, but that now they are no longer valid. When the transference is interpreted, the patient's resistance is reduced and he gains understanding of himself. The working through of a transference is essential in bringing about a successful psychoanalysis.

treatment, and while he agreed at first, he later changed his mind."

"Did you notice anything else about his behavior?"

Dr. Foster replied that despite Tiger's emotional problems, he was very gifted, highly intelligent. "My main impression of him was that he was depressed, self-destructive and angry at himself and the whole world."

"How would you classify his mental condition, doctor?"

"Definitely a severe depression, possibly of a schizophrenic nature. He was ill—suicidal, I felt. I repeatedly insisted that he be admitted to a psychiatric hospital."

The defense attorney then asked the doctor whether Tiger's mental condition at that time had any bearing upon what allegedly took place on May 12 in Teddy Gladstone's apartment, resulting in her death.

He thought for a while. "It is my belief that Tiger's mental condition had a definite connection with what took place in her apartment. Of course, I do not know whether he strangled or killed her, but whatever happened, he was in such a state of confusion that his mental condition must have influenced his actions, whatever they may have been."

Taylor busily thumbed through his papers. "Suppose, doctor— and I am raising here a hypothetical question—suppose that Tiger was in Teddy Gladstone's apartment and suppose that he had no memory of what had happened at the time of her death—"

"Objection," boomed the district attorney. "There is no evidence that the defendant did not remember anything of what took place in the dead girl's apartment."

Taylor said to the judge, "I will prove this point later, Your Honor."

The judge answered, "You know very well that you cannot bring up this or anything else unless it is first admitted as evidence, so we will have to omit it for the time being."

Tiger's lawyer asked the doctor whether he had reached any opinion as to the defendant's mental condition at the time of Teddy's death, in the event Tiger had been in Teddy's apartment at that time.

The witness replied that he had reached an opinion.

What was it?

"My opinion is that at that particular time Tiger lacked substantial capacity to appreciate the wrongfulness of his behavior."

"Do you believe that this man should be in a mental hospital?"

"Yes, this man is in need of psychiatric treatment, and he should be transferred to a psychiatric hospital."

"Your witness," said Taylor, nodding to the prosecutor.

The district attorney requested a short recess so that he could study the notes the doctor had been using. The defense attorney had no objection.

When the recess was over and the doctor had again taken the witness stand, the prosecutor stated that there were several words in the handwritten notes which he was unable to decipher. The defense attorney responded that the psychiatrist had made the notes for his own use, not for the district attorney. At this point the judge became impatient. "Go on with your cross-examination."

The prosecutor asked Dr. Foster if, in view of the fact that he considered the defendant to be severely depressed and in need of hospitalization, he had contacted his family. Foster explained that Tiger had no family in the city, and there was no one to call. This was one of the reasons why he wanted to hospitalize the patient.

Was it possible that the defendant could have faked his illness?

The doctor replied there was no malingering involved here. Tiger, he thought, was an honest man—almost too honest for this world.

Had the doctor testified in court before? "Very rarely."

Was he being paid? Dr. Foster replied he didn't know.

The district attorney exclaimed with feigned astonishment, "Are you telling the court that the counsel for the defense didn't discuss with you how much you would be paid for testifying?"

"Yes, we talked about it, but there was little or no money involved. Possibly the state might refund something for my services."

The prosecutor looked through his papers, and then asked the witness in a calm voice whether he had known or ever seen the dead girl.

The doctor shook his head.

"Does that mean no?" asked the district attorney.

"That's right."

It was now four-thirty. The judge interrupted. "Do you have any more witnesses?" he asked the defense counsel.

"Only one more, I believe."

"Court adjourned to tomorrow at ten-thirty," the judge announced.

Afterward Taylor told me that the district attorney had taken Dr. Foster's testimony quite seriously and was going to direct his firing guns against me the next day, Friday. When I told him it was important to get through with my testimony tomorrow, he made it quite clear that for tactical reasons he did not want to carry over the cross-examination until Monday.

From long experience I have learned that unless I have submitted a written report, it is best not to use any notes while I am on the witness stand, since they might be put into the evidence and made part of the court record. Once this happens, it is impossible or difficult to retrieve them. To prevent this I merely jot down a few facts on a piece of paper which, if necessary, I have in my pocket ready to use.

At ten-thirty the next morning we stood around in the courtroom waiting for the judge to appear. Following the ritual knocks on the door, he finally entered.

Mellowbrook, seated alongside a marshal, looked tired and old. His face was pale, almost gray, and his sad brown eyes were sunken in a face that looked emaciated and drained of expression. He appeared detached, oblivious to what was going on around him. I talked to him, trying to offer some encouragement. Things weren't as bad as he thought. His lawyer would do his very best for him.

"But, doctor," he said in a weak voice, "you don't know what it means to be in jail. I am trapped."

"I can only imagine how you feel, but I understand."

The judge banged down his gavel. "Defense counsel, present your next witness."

The defense attorney said that his next witness was a psychiatrist, and nodded in my direction. I took the stand and was sworn in, after which he asked about my qualifications.

At that the prosecutor rose. "We concede Dr. Abrahamsen's qualifications."

Taylor replied that this was agreeable to him, but he would like the record to show that the witness had served as a member of a commission to study legal insanity, and he wanted to question him about the work he had done on that commission.

I testified that I had been appointed by the governor to study the problem of legal insanity and to modify or change the M'Naughten Law—the classic knowledge-of-right-and-wrong test.

The defense lawyer asked what the M'Naughten Law was.

"The M'Naughten Law states that a mentally ill person unable to understand the difference between right and wrong is declared not guilty because of insanity. Since the right-and-wrong test did not cover the conscious or unconscious emotional aspects of behavior, it was inadequate. In 1959 the commission tried to overcome the defects of the M'Naughten rule by making the following changes: 'A person may not be convicted for a crime or conduct for which he is not responsible. A person is not responsible for criminal conduct, if at the time of such conduct, *as the result of mental disease or defect,* he lacks substantial capacity to know or to appreciate the wrongfulness of his conduct or to conform his behavior to the requirements of law.' "

The defense attorney queried, "And you were a member of the commission?"

"Yes, I was."

"What kind of doctor are you?"

I was a little startled by this question. It reminded me of the time a colleague had been asked exactly the same question on the witness stand, and he had replied, "I am a good doctor." Not wanting to stir up any laughter in the courtroom, I only replied, "I am a psychiatrist."

Asked what a psychiatrist was, I explained that he is a graduate of an accredited medical school with a Doctor of Medicine, and he has received several years of specialized training in the examination, diagnosis and treatment of people who are mentally and emotionally disturbed.

"This is your specialty?"

"Psychiatry is my profession. The study of criminal violence is my specialty."

"You are acquainted with the defendant, Tyros Mellowbrook, aren't you, doctor?"

"Yes, I am."

"Will you please tell the court the circumstances under which you were called into this case, and what the results of your examination were?"

I told the court that late one night in May, Dr. Foster called to ask me to take over the case of his patient Tyros Mellowbrook, who was in jail charged with murder. That same night in my office he gave further details about the murderer and the murderee, Teddy Gladstone. Having been appointed by the court to examine the defendant, which I did at the detention center, I also talked with Mellowbrook's mother and his closest friend, Neil O'Brien, and I studied his alleged confession.

"And you have also been present here during these court proceedings?" asked Taylor.

"Yes, and I have read through the court records of the proceedings I may have missed."

"Now can you please tell the court—and try to speak loudly enough to be heard in the back of the courtroom—about your examination of the defendant."

"May I perhaps be permitted to say, counselor, that I also have read through some parts of Mellowbrook's manuscript, entitled *The Silent Man.*"

"Continue, please."

"My first impression of Mellowbrook was his extreme reluctance to communicate. He was guarded, denied defiantly that there was anything wrong with him. Behind his defiance I sensed a man of great dignity. Despite his inner turbulence, he managed to hold himself together. It was difficult, on the surface at least, to fathom his severe depression. He had been accused of intimidating people. He elaborated by saying that he didn't like small talk, that he was reserved. He never was aggressive. He had seen two psychiatrists four or five years ago because of depression, fears and inability to work, but he soon terminated treatment.

"Mellowbrook said he felt his lawyer wanted him to be classified insane. But he told me, 'Long ago I decided that I couldn't become insane.' He believed that people could control their sanity, which indicated how little he really understood about how the mind works. His attempt at being rational was a defense against becoming mad, which really means that he was afraid of losing control of himself and becoming insane. He was in the throes of suicide, insanity and homicide. Realizing the gravity of his situation, I warned the correction officer that the inmate needed to be watched.

"When I returned to the detention center the next morning, Mellowbrook's appearance had undergone considerable change. He was haggard, seemed to have lost several pounds overnight. No belt, no tie. He was confused, contradictory; not sure whether he wanted to live or die. When the guard finally came, he accused Mellowbrook of screaming and said that he was insane. Mellowbrook thought his cellmate wanted to kill him, so he was transferred to another cell.

"Mellowbrook was agitated. 'Life is punishment,' he told me, and I presumed that this observation was based on his own experiences. After a while, when he had calmed down somewhat, I asked him about the events leading up to the evening he visited Teddy's apartment—the night of her death. Instead of answering my question, he became evasive and said he wasn't sure whether he had taken some Dexedrine or speed. I then asked him to give me in as much detail as possible an account of his actions that day. He had been working on a public relations job which he had obtained through Teddy Gladstone's efforts.

"That Saturday morning turned out to be crucial for him. Instead of working on his book, he found himself spending long hours on research for the political campaign of Senator Callahan. Mellowbrook, thinking that it might help his book, had arranged for dinner that evening with Teddy and the senator. But she had called late that morning and said she had a date for that evening, but Tiger could come over in the afternoon for drinks. He became furious, jealous. Why did he allow Teddy to treat him like a doormat—something to be used?

"I am sorry, Your Honor," I said, turning to the judge, "that

I have to go into all the details of Mellowbrook's examination, but without it I am afraid the court may not learn the full story, as far as I have been able to piece it together."

"If any material you bring out is irrelevant, doctor, you can be sure there will be objections," he replied with a smile. "Proceed."

"I had of course read the search warrant, which stated that Teddy had died by strangulation and stabbing. I asked Mellowbrook about it, but instead he began to talk about his childhood; he seemed to be trying to find out who he really was. He was angry at himself, in fact hated himself and, as I have said before, angry at Teddy. He brought out that ever since childhood he had had many fears which he was unable to cope with, and which now seemed to reach a climax in his fears of Teddy.

"After many frustrating attempts, I finally got Tiger to talk about that night at Teddy Gladstone's apartment. He wanted to marry her, but that was all over, she said. When he announced that he wanted to go to bed with her, she only laughed at him, mocked him. She made fun of him—he wasn't really a 'tiger,' only a 'paper tiger'—a Chinese paper tiger—and this made him more furious. She berated him for not giving her anything, to which he retorted that he had given her a gold necklace, and she snapped back that he had given his mother a necklace too. Whether it was the same type, I don't know. So he left and was told to come back at ten o'clock. Later, while waiting at the hotel for the senator, he saw Teddy and the senator enter arm in arm, completely engrossed in each other. Tiger spent the evening at the hotel bar, and when he returned to Teddy's apartment he was quite drunk. He was angry but controlled, perhaps more annoyed than angry. He could not verbalize his anger, and that was to a large extent his undoing. Apparently he was afraid of her. Then Teddy announced that she was pregnant. Tiger was stunned. He felt sure he wasn't the father. He was humiliated. He looked at her face and it looked yellow.

"I would like to call this manifestation to the attention of the court because it indicates that Mellowbrook was at that time not only disturbed but even psychotic. Seeing a face take on a different color is not necessarily a commonplace manifestation in an emotionally disturbed person. Certain patients suffering from a psychosis, or those who have taken mescaline—which was not the case with Mellowbrook—may see a change in color or a distortion in the face of others; or upon looking into a mirror, the reflection will be altered, perhaps appear markedly older or even grotesque. In this instance, where drugs were not a central factor, Tiger's observation that Teddy's face had turned yellow reflected his hate of her, which probably had taken on psychotic dimensions.

"But to continue Mellowbrook's story, he accused Teddy of being a troublemaker. First she asked him for money so she could have an abortion. When he offered it, she changed her mind; she was afraid to have the operation, particularly since her mother had died in childbirth.

"Tiger's recollection of their dialogue that evening was impressive—up to the time of the alleged killing, which he did not remember. He was angry at Teddy for humiliating him, but I think he was—strangely enough—more angry at her for first wanting him to help her get an abortion. He is, as you understand, a man of high moral standards, naïve maybe, idealistic, and Teddy's behavior and attitude offended him.

"But after all this is said, he loved her, and she loved him, and despite their frequent and heated arguments, they both needed each other desperately. A lovers' quarrel, you might think. Not so simple. It was a gradual destruction of the self day by day, almost imperceptible things happening. Although Teddy wasn't the only one to play on Tiger's aggressive impulses, she was the main trigger. She tantalized him. A multitude of vibrations arose, all bringing out deeply buried feelings of hostility and fear and frustrated hopes.

"It was a strange, frantic, *symbiotic* relationship. Mellowbrook remembered that after his heated argument with her he found himself on the street. I asked him point-blank whether he had choked or stabbed her, and he denied this vehemently. He had been walking around in the streets, he told me, and then had taken a taxi without remembering where he had been driven. The taxicab driver has described the ride here in court. Mellowbrook had been in several bars; in one he met the girl who already testified. He wandered around in a daze, was frightened, and was on the verge of giving himself up to the police. But then he said to himself, 'I haven't done anything wrong.' Undoubtedly he was in a state of panic, as illustrated also with the odd situation in the bar when he was talking to Jane Willow and then suddenly discovered that he didn't have his eyeglasses. Strange as it may sound, he returned to Teddy's apartment without meeting anyone, he says, found his glasses and then quickly left again without meeting anyone. Whether this was only a figment of his imagination or whether he dreamed it, he couldn't say for sure.

"At that point I felt it was best not to force the interview; the relationship—transference—between Mellowbrook and myself was so brittle that I decided just to let him talk on in the manner in which he most easily could express himself. He mentioned that Teddy was successful and he wasn't; without much emotion he described her as being selfish, domineering, quarrelsome and jealous. One time while in a man's apartment, she had found some contraceptives in a dresser drawer and had pierced holes in them with a needle. It would seem that unconsciously she wanted to become pregnant because she desired to have something—a child —which belonged to her and to her alone.

"Tiger talked as though he were dealing with prescribed destiny, as if he and Teddy were meant for each other. An additional factor which may have strengthened this belief was that both their first names began with the same letter—T—and had two syllables —Teddy, Tyros or Tiger. A name gives shape or form to a person. It may not necessarily define him, but it delineates in a very special way his personality frame. In Tiger's mind their names proved that they belonged to each other. It was childish and superstitious, but he took it seriously. Here were two people caught up in what one would describe as a sadomasochistic relationship. Teddy apparently was the sadist, and Tiger the masochist. In one murderous moment the tables were turned. They both loved and hated each other, and yet they felt attracted to each other—in a crucial way.

"In my several interviews with Tiger, he left me with the impression that he had pronounced death wishes and self-destructive tendencies. I believe that without these self-destructive tendencies there could not have been any relationship with Teddy. In a way, she responded to what he didn't have rather than to what he did have, and Tiger on his side responded to what she lacked rather than to what she had. Whatever happened between them, the one was as important for the act as the other. I finally had to conclude that Tiger was involved in a *compensatory murder.* He was only a part of the act. It was caused by both, with each bearing responsibility. Remember, he was naïve, idealistic, and therefore had placed Teddy on a pedestal. To some extent, at least, he may have felt that he had found a mother, even though in reality Teddy lacked any maternal qualities in her personality. On her side she may have felt that she had found a man in Tiger, when in fact he lacked masculine self-confidence. It was a compensatory or symbiotic relationship, in which the invisible tie between them became as inevitable as the murder itself. While initially he was her victim, she later became his. This relationship is a page, an important page in the book of *victimology,* in which the victim, having seduced and stimulated the victimizer to attack, serves the end for the aggressor.

"There is another aspect of Mellowbrook's personality that I would like to go into. He either denied any personal drug abuse or tended to minimize it. In examining him, I found him to be tense, but I couldn't detect any withdrawal symptoms, such as excessive perspiration or shakiness. But even if he had been taking drugs—amphetamines or Dexedrine—his personality makeup would not permit him to escape the consequences of his conduct, nor would he deny using drugs because he was ashamed to admit it. His high sense of morality prevented him from wanting to hide behind anything which might be used to excuse his behavior."

The defense attorney interrupted me and asked what bearing those drugs would have upon a person's behavior.

"While until recently we did not have any inkling that amphetamines may elicit violent aggressions, we now have learned that violent aggressive acts, often leading to death, have been caused by the use of this particular drug."

I spoke of the possible presence of a high content of carbon monoxide in Teddy's apartment, a fact not mentioned by the medical examiner, which could have been a contributing factor to her death.

"As to the alleged killing, I would like to recount an incident which took place when Tiger was very young, possibly fifteen or sixteen years old. I received this information from his friend, Neil O'Brien, but it wasn't brought out when he testified. On this occasion Tiger had either dreamed or fantasized that he had killed someone. He and Neil had become drunk, and in the morning Tiger asked whether he had killed anyone the night before. Neil, of course, was surprised by his question and reassured him. During his interview with me, he told me that as far as he knew, Tiger had not killed anyone.

"While there were times when Mellowbrook spoke freely about himself, most of the time he was not emotionally accessible. Throughout most of the interview with me he was preoccupied, or almost asleep, not quite sure about what was going on. At other times he was alert. His attitude was that of fear, self-destructiveness and depression. No delusions or hallucinations could be elicited. He felt that at times people were against him. He was suspicious, which might lead one to believe that he had some paranoid inclinations which could not be rectified through persuasion. He was obsessed with intricate ideas, the nature of which were often difficult to ascertain. Apparently he was preoccupied with Teddy, although he didn't verbalize this. I was struck by the fact that throughout my many interviews, Tiger *never* gave me any physical description of Teddy. He had given me a mental picture of her, personality traits, but nothing physical. It is remarkable too that during the interviews, which lasted almost two and a half days, he did not utter one word about the killing or mention that Teddy was dead. To him this was an alien thought, as though by erasing it from his memory the deed could be undone. By not remembering what had happened, he was denying that he killed Teddy.

"Tyros Mellowbrook is a man of superior intelligence. But because of his emotional turmoil he tries to repress or deny within himself his true feelings so that he does not have the self-awareness, the insight which one would expect from a man of his intelligence. With the exception of Neil, he grew up practically without any close friends. Since he had to work to support his mother and himself, his social activities were limited. Very early in life he withdrew from any religious affiliation. He has no past record of being involved in either antisocial or criminal activities. During his schooldays he was different from his classmates since he had no father, and I would venture to say that he enjoyed this feeling of being different from others. He carried over this sense of distinctiveness—superiority, you might say—into his adulthood. Without doubt, the loss of his father was strongly traumatic for him, even though he never mentioned this to his mother. The effect of an absent or a weak father in the family is crucial in the development of the child. Tiger didn't have any stable male figure to identify with, so he identified with his strong, dominant mother, bringing about a distorted identification. Unable to drain off his grand fantasies, he became so preoccupied with them that he almost thought he could command people to do his bidding. A startling example of this was his relationship with Teddy. Because of his own overwhelming wish fantasies, he believed that she in turn was genuinely in love with him. Tiger's distorted identification led to an ambivalent closeness to his mother resulting in a love-hate relationship, which later, possibly, was transferred to his relationship with Teddy Gladstone. His traumatic childhood and his dependency on his mother resulted in his not being able to develop a free, natural relationship with a woman with whom he could share his life. His twisted identification led to his stunted sexual development, and he became shy and secretive, fearful about sex, and apparently did not have heterosexual relations until quite late in life. Mixed in here were deeply entrenched homosexual leanings.

"All his life Mellowbrook has lived in a world rich in fantasy. He wanted to become famous and dreamed of becoming a politician, or of doing something worthwhile which would benefit society. He had, however, great difficulty in adapting himself to a given situation. His mood, temper and actions would be either higher or lower than what the actual circumstances represented.

"These very fantasies were also to cause Mellowbrook untold suffering in that instead of giving him gratification, they were anxiety-provoking. Through his fantasies, nebulously connected with reality, he exaggerated greatly the extent of Teddy's love for him, and thereby unconsciously created a dangerous condition where he and others could be hurt. Through his fears and anxieties he unwittingly exposed himself to danger, very much like the accident-prone psychosomatic person. As a child he would climb high trees from which he would fall, or defy the ocean waves so that he could barely get back to the beach, or cut himself 'accidentally' with a knife to such an extent that the wound required stitches. In courting danger in this fashion he was driven by his unconscious desire for self-punishment, which in turn was prompted by his feelings of guilt. This behavior also carried over in his relationship with Teddy. In fact, I believe Mellowbrook unconsciously manufactured an anxious, almost psychotic guilt-ridden situation with Teddy from which there was no return.

"At the core of Mellowbrook's maladjustment was his ego-disharmonious mind—technically termed dystonia. It was not in harmony with itself, nor with its environment. This disharmonious mind expressed a state of abnormal tension which arose in the main from his inability to identify with male figures.

"This inability to identify with a male person may also have been increased by his unique name—Tyros or Tiger. People with peculiar names often show more severe personality disturbances than those having more widely accepted names. The child's future emotional development is linked to his name more decisively than is generally acknowledged. It is interesting to note that a psychosis due to psychogenic factors is more prevalent among those with unusual names than those with common names.[2] Tiger's name undoubtedly may have interfered with his relationships, going back to his schooldays. No wonder that his name made him feel unique among his peers in particular, and later on among people in general.

"Because of his early traumatic experiences he became withdrawn, aloof, dependent and fearful, all of which were instrumental in his involvement with Teddy. He entered into this relationship with the anticipation that she would respond to his needs, and that he in turn would respond to hers. Although he appears strong on the surface, inwardly his ego is weak, and this has led him to

2. See the study made by A. Arthur Hartman, Robert C. Nicholay and Jesse Hurley at the Psychiatric Institute of the Circuit Court of Cook County, Chicago, 1972.

withdraw from people. He became hypersensitive, suspicious and vulnerable, and in his relationship with Teddy, this vulnerable hypersensitivity was greatly accentuated by her provocation, which resulted in acting out, often leading to paranoid-colored schizophrenic outbursts.

"Tiger was afraid of his strong sexual impulses. He had symptoms of passivity, fears of a homosexual nature, he was uncomfortable with women, all possibly a result of his wish that his mother would seduce him and of his sense of triumph that his father was not around as a competitor.

"For some time, particularly in the last fourteen days prior to Teddy Gladstone's death, Mellowbrook was preoccupied with strong death wishes, directed against himself, his parents and to a lesser degree toward Teddy. His mind was clouded with hateful thoughts which he could not control, rendering him helpless as he hovered in a state of mind between suicide, psychosis and homicide.

"Teddy, by provoking and goading Tiger, instigated her own murder that Saturday night. Unconsciously she herself played a predominant part—a seductive role in her own death in the process of victimology.

"The diagnosis of Tyros Mellowbrook is that he has developed a reaction of withdrawal, suspiciousness, marked depression, self-destructive and paranoid traits, all in the nature of a schizophrenia."

During my lengthy exposition of the psychiatric aspects of Mellowbrook's case for the court, I was impressed by the way the judge, to whom I had directed myself, listened carefully to my comments. It was good to see how seriously psychiatry was being taken in the courtroom. As a matter of fact, at times when I brought in certain technical terms, the judge asked me for clarification and then wrote down my explanation. More importantly, though, when I had brought out the fact that they had both played a part in the murder, the judge, sensing the complexity of the case and the shared guilt, reacted almost imperceptibly with his eyes and seemed to nod his head slightly.

The district attorney had surprised me during my testimony by not raising certain objections, and he had made copious notes.

As for Mellowbrook, he sat quietly, lost in his thoughts. I wondered how much of my explanation he could comprehend.

Finally the defense counsel stood up. "Based upon your diagnosis and findings, did you ascertain whether or not Mellowbrook is responsible for his alleged criminal behavior?"

"Based upon my examination, Mellowbrook is not responsible for his alleged criminal conduct. At the time of his conduct, as a result of mental disease or defect he lacked substantial capacity to know or to appreciate the wrongfulness of his behavior, and was unable to conform his conduct to the requirements of law."

"And this," asked Tiger's lawyer, "is based upon the findings we have just heard?"

"That is correct."

"Your witness," said the defense lawyer, nodding in the direction of the district attorney.

The judge interrupted. "It is now almost one o'clock. We will take a recess until two o'clock."

The district attorney was on his feet. "The doctor's testimony has been quite detailed. If it pleases the court I would like to ask that the cross-examination be postponed until Monday morning so that I may discuss this testimony with my own psychiatrists."

That the opposing attorney wanted to have time to discuss my testimony with his psychiatrists was not a new experience for me. An attorney cannot, as a layman, be familiar with all the psychiatric aspects of the case. In order to counteract effectively the opposing psychiatrist's testimony, he must acquaint himself with the intricacies of the psychiatric aspects of the case, and he needs professional guidance in preparing his cross-examination.

The defense attorney stated that the prosecutor had one hour to discuss these matters with his own psychiatrists. After a whispered conference, the judge called for a recess until two-thirty that afternoon. That, he said, should give the district attorney sufficient time to consult with his psychiatrists and prepare his cross-examination.

9

It was a long recess. I could not talk with the defense attorney because as long as a witness is on the stand, and consequently under oath, he cannot discuss the case with anyone during a recess. So I had luncheon by myself and was back in court at two-fifteen. Nobody was around. To sit and wait alone in a large empty courtroom is not a pleasure. To sit waiting to be cross-examined is even less of a pleasure. It is an emotional strain even for a psychiatrist, who at times has to be a masochist in the line of service.

The courtroom filled slowly, and I noticed the district attorney and the hospital psychiatrist talking together.

The judge returned to the courtroom, I took the witness stand and the district attorney began the cross-examination. First, he wanted to know how much I was paid for these services. I told him that I hoped to be compensated by what the state offered me, and that closed the matter. He then continued that in accordance with my own findings, the defendant knew where he was and who he was. Wouldn't this indicate that he was sane? I answered that on the surface he seemed so; but it was only superficially that he was in contact with the real world.

"But he knew where he was?" the district attorney repeated.

"Yes," I said. "He knew where he was."

"Don't you think he knew where he was when he was in his girl friend's apartment?"

"Yes, I think so."

"In your testimony you have stated that Tiger was schizophrenic. Couldn't he also be described as a psychopath?"

"No, he cannot. A psychopath suffers from a character disorder or a character disturbance which is not a psychotic condition."

"Isn't it true, doctor, that many of these so-called psychopaths are highly intelligent, very gifted and sometimes very creative?"

"Yes, they are. People considered to be psychopaths are aggressive and impulsive. Their character has become distorted or deformed and this type of person therefore becomes criminal and antisocial. They are unable to get along with other people and keep forming unhealthy relationships, so that they are constantly at war with their environment. They suffer from inner conflict and use their families and society in general as prime targets in expressing their hostile emotions. Such a person is infantile in his emotional and behavioral manifestations. He is exceedingly egocentric, but he is neither neurotic nor psychotic, nor mentally defective. The most pronounced characteristics of the psychopath are the frequently diminished feelings of anxiety and guilt. But this cannot be said about Mr. Mellowbrook's personality makeup. This man shows a great many guilt feelings. In all probability he has always felt guilty about one thing or another."

"Doctor, on the witness stand today you stated that the defendant had amnesia about the death of his girl friend, Teddy Gladstone. Wouldn't this amnesia point to the fact that he had repressed what took place because it was too painful for him?"

"Yes, this could be the case, but it was strange that he had such a block for what happened with her, or between them."

"We have a confession, you know," he interrupted.

"Yes, I do, but the confession did not state in a straightforward manner that Mr. Mellowbrook had committed a murder. Furthermore, as I am sure you are very well aware, a confession is not sufficient to warrant guilt, or a conviction, without additional proof that the crime with which the suspect has been charged was committed, and committed by him. Of course this is a legal question and I can only give my impression from the point of view of a psychiatrist."

"What is a schizoid person?"

"A schizoid person is isolated, shut in, introverted, encapsulated in his own egocentric world. His outlook is turned inward, manifesting what we call 'autism.' Such a person daydreams to such an extent that his own thoughts become much more real to him than the reality around him. Living in his own fantasy world, he is to a high degree out of touch with his surroundings. His thoughts and feelings are contradictory, and he demonstrates emotional leveling in his lack of affection and in his cool manner. Crucial for such a man's life is when the connection between his ego and his environment is broken off, leading to the development of schizophrenia. As a matter of fact, the schizophrenic person is developed from this schizoid personality."

"Doctor," the district attorney asked, "couldn't this defendant be psychopathic?"

"No, I do not believe so because this isn't consistent with Tiger's personality."

"Doctor, I would like to quote something from a book I have: 'Like the juvenile delinquent, he [the psychopath] has usually been raised in a family having poor emotional relationships, emotional deprivation (usually real, sometimes imagined), inconsistent upbringing (alternating between rejection and overindulgence).' Then the book goes on to say: 'His poor'—that is, the psychopath's—'relationship with his parents, plus the lack of any other stable force in his environment with which he could identify, resulted in a faulty development of his ego and superego structure, which made it impossible for him to form an emotional tie, that is, an object relationship, with anyone.' Now, doctor, wouldn't you say that this description fits the defendant, Tyros Mellowbrook?"

"Before I answer your question, may I ask the source of your quotation?"

"As a matter of fact, this is from one of your own books, *The Psychology of Crime,* and I have quoted from the first and second paragraphs on page 137. What you say here seems to fit the defendant very well indeed," the district attorney noted somewhat triumphantly.

After a while I answered, "My books and my letters are my worst enemies. Of course, I shall have to explain what I mean. I am glad that you brought this up because to a certain extent you do have a point, but only to a certain extent. When you consider Mr. Mellowbrook's personality in terms of his childhood and early youth, it is completely different from that of a psychopath. It is during this time that the personality is formed. Keeping Tiger's childhood and early development in mind, you will find we have no information of any stealing or lying. During his school years there was no truancy, no pilfering. These are traits frequently found in the boy who very often later becomes a psychopath. If Tiger had been a psychopath, it would already have revealed itself in his childhood years, but this didn't happen in his case. Furthermore, the psychopath in general does not have much if any remorse or any conscience, and this is in *strong* contrast— I emphasize strong—to Mellowbrook, who has both conscience and deep feelings of guilt. These overwhelming guilt feelings you don't find in a psychopath."

The district attorney asked, "But doesn't the psychopath have *some* conscience?"

I answered that he did have some, but his superego development has been incomplete, and it is for this reason that even as a child the psychopath is, so to speak, driven into both antisocial and criminal acts as if compelled. His actions are almost instinctual, impulsive, carried out only from his own self-centeredness, with little forethought. "If I may be permitted to continue, your honor, I would like to say that a psychopath is a person who tries to obtain immediate gratification, to get what he wants at any cost, even by means of bribery and extortion."

"Doctor," Samson said, "you have brought out in your testimony that this defendant has amnesia about what happened at the apartment of the dead girl, Teddy. Can you please explain this?"

"Amnesia is," I said, "either organic or psychologically conditioned. In this case it's psychological. If it should be organically conditioned one might think of epilepsy. It is well known that an epileptic seizure is followed by some degree of amnesia lasting for a short while, but we have no information that Mellowbrook has suffered from epilepsy. The other explanation must then hold: that his amnesia is psychological, that somehow whatever took place in Teddy's apartment had such a traumatic effect that every memory of it has been erased."

"Doctor, isn't it so that when amnesia is present, there must be some painful experience behind it?"

"Yes, there is, but it may well be that this painful experience may not be basically related to this particular case. The deed could have been carried out by somebody else. I realize of course that this is only speculation, but nevertheless it has to be taken into consideration. Remember that fundamentally Tiger's mental attitude is one of being secretive, of consciously suppressing or unconsciously repressing. For him to forget something or to keep it to himself would then be natural. Furthermore, remember that this is a man who always has had a great many fears, who always has been fearful, which may in part explain his secretiveness and his suppression or repression, particularly of painful experiences."

"What is a thinking disturbance?" the district attorney asked.

"A thinking disturbance is a disorganization of the personality with impairment of reality relationship, disturbances in thinking and concept formation, all of which bring about disorders in behavior and intellectual functioning, ambivalence, paranoid ideas, autism, hallucinations, or delusions. It may express itself in a hallucinating person who believes in the validity of his hallucinations without understanding that they represent wishes and impulses coming from himself. Such a condition may be present in a schizophrenic or a manic-depressive psychosis, or in other types of psychosis—toxic, arteriosclerotic."

"In the hospital report written by two psychiatrists," Samson interrupted, "there is no evidence of a formal thinking disturbance in the defendant. Did you find a thinking disturbance in him?"

"I did."

"You did?" the prosecutor exclaimed, feigning surprise.

"Are you really surprised, sir?" I asked.

"How do you explain the discrepancy between their opinion and yours?"

"The explanation is very simple. When you mention that in the hospital record there was no proof of a formal thinking disturbance, I believe you should include all of what the psychiatrists state on that point. The fact is that they wrote, as I recall it: 'There was no evidence of a formal thinking disturbance. This may be because we are dealing with a very intelligent person who is able to guard his answers.' In other words, Mr. Mellowbrook was guarded in his answers, which prevented the psychiatrists from discovering the thinking disturbance. In my mind, Tiger's emotions *are* interfering with his thinking, often resulting in acting out."

"What do you mean by 'acting out'?" the district attorney asked impatiently.

"A person who is unable to withstand frustration or discomfort likes to be satisfied at once, that is, likes to obtain immediate gratification. To do so he must 'act out' his wishes in order to obtain this satisfaction. In other words, acting out is a mobilization of his unconscious feelings and fantasies into an aggressive or violent act. If I may be permitted to give an example, a child tries to express his unconscious angry feelings against his parents by fighting or quarreling with his brother or sister. If he does not fight with his brother or sister he may discharge his hostile aggressions by acting them out in some form of impulsiveness, or through an antisocial or criminal act. What I would like to point out is that all acting out comes about as the result of an underlying frustration with which the person cannot cope. When we are not satisfied, or are unable to postpone gratification, we all have a tendency to act out in one form or another."

"Isn't it so, doctor, that people who feel frustrated have a tendency to act out their violent inclinations?"

"Yes."

"Don't you think, doctor, that this could also be the case here?"

"It possibly could be."

"It is possible, doctor. Could it be probable?"

"I don't know. It would depend upon the situation. The person who acts out has to be impulsive, but Mr. Mellowbrook is not generally the impulsive type. He seemed rather controlled. On the other side I would like to add that beneath his apparently controlled state of mind he has aggressive or hostile suspicious tendencies which, as your own psychiatrists have stated, 'at times seem to reach paranoid proportions.' "

"In the report from the psychiatric hospital, the diagnosis of the defendant has been given as a depression of a reactive nature. Don't you think that his depression is reactive?"

"I don't think so. His mental condition is more than a reactive or situational depression because Mellowbrook has been mentally depressed for a long period of time, possibly all of his life from early childhood, without his realizing it. A reactive depression is a condition which passes after a little while, in a day, or a few days. A genuine depression is different. The patient has a psychotic reaction, is moody, has difficulty in thinking and shows either a decreased or increased psychomotor activity. This depression becomes his inner nature and is always present. It becomes a significant part of his whole being."

"Can it lead to a psychosis?" the district attorney asked.

"Yes, it can." I told the court that to my mind there was little doubt that Tiger was disturbed and confused. "While his self-esteem is low, he also has a high opinion of himself to the point where he at times may well have felt he could be his own doctor —a point about which he was gravely mistaken. He is not able to explain to himself or to others what happened at the time of Teddy's death. This is a proud man, and because of his pride he is somehow uncommunicative. He doesn't try to convince you, or anyone else, about his condition. His mind goes in one direction. He is defiant, fearful, secretive and angry, yet unable to express these feelings in words. This repression reduces his awareness of what is going on around him, such as, for instance, his relationship to Teddy, which went beyond his conscious awareness."

I didn't want to say any more, but I had challenged the district attorney. He was quick to begin his counterattack.

"Doctor," he began slowly, "you have stated that the defendant is highly intelligent and talented. If this is the case I think it is strange that this man wouldn't be aware of what was happening around him—to be specific, to remember what he did to the dead girl." He emphasized "the dead girl."

"Are you asking me a question, sir?"

"Indeed I am."

"A person's intelligence doesn't completely govern his ability to remember; Mellowbrook's emotions, over which he had little or no control, interfered with his memory."

"I object to the form of the district attorney's question," the defense attorney said belatedly.

"Overruled. The witness has already answered the question," the judge stated disapprovingly.

The defense attorney sat down quickly.

"Continue, doctor," the judge urged.

"When Tiger's mind was confused and disturbed, this condition most certainly became aggravated under the influence of liquor. He is a man who wasn't used to alcohol, and therefore couldn't tolerate it. I've come to the conclusion that when he committed the deed, he was not responsible for it because he lacked substantial capacity to know or to appreciate that he did wrong."

"Do you believe, doctor, that the defendant was under the influence of alcohol?" the judge asked.

I felt the judge's question was sympathetic, so it was easy for me to confirm it.

"And this was an additional factor to his confusion that evening and night the murder took place?"

"Yes," I replied.

"Proceed."

At this moment I felt it would be worthwhile to bring in the point that Mellowbrook showed *diminished responsibility* for his alleged crime; that is, even if the court found Mellowbrook to be legally sane, he could not have planned or intended the crime because he lacked substantial capacity to do so. I mentioned this to the judge, but the prosecutor, fully aware that we had no precedent for it,[1] demanded that my remarks be stricken from the records, which the judge promptly ordered.

On rebuttal, the defense attorney asked how a mental depression came about. A depression, I stated, arises chiefly because of a great loss, either real or fancied, that a person has suffered in early childhood. He feels the loss as a rejection, which in turn precipitates anger. Not able to tolerate it, he turns his anger toward himself and this makes him feel guilty and unworthy, leading to suicidal thoughts. With feelings of guilt comes the

1. It is of great interest to notice that a modified version of the new concept of "diminished responsibility" has recently been introduced by the U.S. Court of Appeals, for the District of Columbia Circuit. *Psychiatric News,* Washington, D.C., July 19, 1972.

depression. As a matter of fact, guilt is the most important cause of a mental depression.

"Now, doctor, does this depression follow the patient constantly as an integral part of his personality?"

The prosecutor arose. "I object to the form of the question. Counselor is leading the witness."

"Overruled."

I continued by saying that a depression can be an integral part of the person's behavior, and while on occasion it comes to the surface and is experienced very keenly by that person, it also is always present as an undercurrent in his mood and attitudes. In the case of Mellowbrook, he had come into psychiatric treatment about one to two weeks prior to Teddy's death. His suicidal tendencies, which Dr. Foster had mentioned in his testimony, may have been an *early* symptom of an impending psychiatric disturbance.

"What kind of psychiatric disturbance, doctor?"

"A psychosis."

"Thank you, doctor."

"Any rebuttal?" asked the judge.

The prosecuting attorney sprang to his feet and asked, "Can a man have a mental depression as part of a neurosis?"

"Yes."

"Can he be suicidal?"

"Yes."

He sat down. Now it was Taylor's turn. "But a mental depression can also take place in a psychosis?"

"Yes," I answered, wondering who was going to have the last word. As it turned out, it was the judge. He looked from the district attorney to the defense attorney and back again, and since neither of them had anything to say, he turned to me and said in a soft voice, "You may step down."

I was relieved. As I passed Taylor at the defense table he thanked me, and when I went over to say good-bye to the district attorney he whispered, "I hope you'll be on my side next time."

"I wonder where I've heard that before," I responded quietly. "I'm trying not to be on either side." We shook hands.

Tiger followed me with his sad brown eyes as I left the stand. (Those eyes had made quite an impression on me.) I went back and talked with him. He seemed grateful for my help. He thanked me and then asked how I could know so much about him.

"Oh, it is my profession," I answered with a smile.

Tiger didn't take the stand in his own defense; Taylor agreed that we would first see how things went. Personally I didn't want Tiger to take the witness stand because it might be too traumatic. Then, too, his honesty and self-destructive tendencies might be damaging in his case. That he did not take the stand could not be held against him. It is a matter of court procedure that a person charged with a crime has the right to refuse to take the witness stand without being considered guilty.

These factors, plus the fact that Taylor had succeeded in presenting the case to Tiger's greatest advantage, spoke in favor of his not being his own witness. And there were some additional reasons why he should not testify.

If he took the witness stand, the prosecutor could either cross-examine him very artfully so as not to put him under a stress or strain situation, and later try to claim that his ego was strong and that he was not likely to become psychotic; or he could cross-examine him intensely, hoping that Tiger would react very well without becoming unduly disturbed, which would indicate a stronger ego and less proneness to becoming psychotic than had been suggested by the defense attorney. Whatever way one looked at it, cross-examination by the district attorney would not serve any fruitful purpose for Tiger.

—10—

Late that evening, Taylor called to say that he again had submitted a motion for dismissal of both the murder charge against Mellowbrook and his confession. The judge had given both attorneys one week to prepare their briefs on the legal and psychiatric aspects of the case, and then he would make a decision. Both Taylor and I felt that the prospect of an extensive reduction of the felony charge seemed reasonably good. As to the confession, I thought that since it placed Tiger on the scene of the crime, the judge would permit it to be brought in as evidence.

I could hardly free myself of the thought that Tiger was preoccupied with the idea of suicide. He was so detached. He was now in the detention center waiting for the outcome of the sanity hearing, and he would be watched there, I hoped, although one never could be sure. Naturally, I would have liked to talk with him, for possibly I could help him along a little in the days ahead. A psychiatrist's job was never finished.

Even when a patient is successfully through with his treatment, he stays, along with others, on my mind. It is a professional liability. Soul-searching goes on almost eternally. A psychiatrist is not blessed with the doctrine of infallibility. Could I have done better by changing the treatment procedure a little, bringing up something to the patient of which he was unaware? Or would the intended new element disturb him so much that he couldn't continue the thread of his thoughts, or be of such a nature that he wouldn't understand it emotionally, so that nothing would be gained anyhow?

It was in such a mood that I began to think back on my presentation of Tiger's case in court. I had known, of course, from the outset that I had to be selective, that my testimony to some extent depended upon the judge's discretion and the questions the district attorney put to me. Obviously, time had been a factor here, and with due consideration to the important facts, I had felt somehow that I had to play it by ear. It was fortunate that the presiding judge had given me leeway in the presentation of my findings, and thereby had given me a chance to elucidate Tiger's psychopathology and its bearing upon his behavior. The purpose of the psychiatric testimony was to explain and provide insight into the offender's conduct, to help rehabilitate him so that he could become a useful human being.

In my testimony I had tried to show that since early childhood Tiger had been violated by the desertion and subsequent absence of his father. When a child's parents are divorced, the father may still see him and show the child that he cares for him. But Tiger's father had left him and the boy could only fantasize about the sort of person his father had been. Tiger never revealed his hurt feelings but instead, unable to defend himself by giving verbal expression to his anger, he allowed himself to be continually hurt by other people. He couldn't withstand the dormant and hostile feelings present in those around him, and withdrew into himself to that place where he was king and where nobody—so he thought —could hurt him. He built around himself a wall of immunity, but it could not protect him. He became sensitive and suspicious to the point where he could not even stand arguments. To him it seemed that the slightest emotional infringement upon his mind was a sort of mental violence, as devastating as physical violence.

Today, with hidden and manifest violence an almost integral part of our daily life, it is worthwhile to remember that among us are many, many people who like hunted animals receive and accept blindly emotional hurt and injury to their soul. While it may be that hidden hate and aggression do not physically destroy the person, they inflict wounds that cripple him and turn his existence into a kind of living death.

Wounds. Suppose I had dwelt more in my testimony on the hidden psychological violence Tiger had been exposed to—would it have made more of an impression? I'm afraid not. Not because the prosecutor might not have mercy in his heart, nor the judge understand that a hurt person might do harm to himself or to others, but because the law is mechanical and has to be carried out to the spirit of its letters, not to the spirit of life.

As the day approached when the opposing attorneys had to deliver their briefs to the judge, I was kept busy in my office. Neil called me. He had visited Tiger in jail, and he voiced concern about his friend's condition. Mellowbrook seemed terribly depressed by his continued incarceration.

Taylor called too, to talk with me about some of the psychiatric aspects of the case which needed clarification. "A central core in his personality makeup are his death wishes and self-destructiveness, and this ought to be stressed," I told him, "because from this arise many of his abnormal tendencies—his guilt and depression, his suicidal and homicidal inclinations. And then you have her part, her seductiveness, provocation and manipulative behavior."

"I have it," Taylor replied, and hung up hurriedly. I called him back and said that I wanted to talk with Tiger. Taylor himself had tried to see him the previous day but Mellowbrook had a cold and had been sent to the infirmary.

"In a few days we will know anyhow how things stand, so why don't you wait?"

And I didn't have to wait long because three days later, the judge called in both the prosecuting attorney and the defense lawyer and gave them his decision. The confession of Mellowbrook was *bona fide* insofar as it placed him on the murder scene, and therefore it had to be admitted in court. The judge had reduced the indictment from murder first degree to manslaughter second degree. The defense attorney implored him to release his client on bail in his custody because the defendant needed psychiatric treatment, which he would not get in jail. He could stay with his friend, Neil, and if the judge felt so inclined he could in his condition of bail stipulate that Tiger was not to leave town without the court's permission.

The district attorney made well-pointed objections to letting the defendant out on bail. The judge retorted that *this* decision was up to him. Furthermore, as to the question of insanity, he was going to postpone the insanity decision, which was legally possible. He decided to let the defendant be tried and let the jury, or the judge if he didn't want a jury, determine during the trial whether or not the defendant was mentally able, and whether he had been sane or insane at the time of the murder. He set bail at $10,000, and Taylor succeeded in having it reduced to $7,500.

"Well done," I told Taylor. "This is the best news I've had in a long time."

"I couldn't have done it without your meticulous work," he replied.

"You're too generous."

Before hanging up, he told me that Tiger's mother had bought a bond for her son, and he would be out of jail the next day.

"I took it for granted that you will treat him," Taylor said.

"Of course. Have him call me for an appointment."

I was pleased that I would be able to continue Tiger's treatment. He needed my help. The judge most certainly had understood that the indictment had gone too far. His decision to postpone the insanity problem to the trial seemed at first glance Solomonic. At second glance, though, he had cleverly passed on the decision of this crucial matter. Whatever the motivation, though, he had acquitted himself in an admirable way.

The following day, late in the afternoon, Tiger called for an appointment. Since I was with a patient, I told him that I couldn't say much to him except that I was glad of the outcome and that I would be seeing him the next day. He sounded nervous and upset on the phone and I asked whether he needed something to help him sleep at night. I should have anticipated his answer, because he said he would be able to live through the coming night without sleeping medicine. But then he added, "It has been intolerable to be locked up on the inside. But it is intolerable to be on the outside." This philosophical observation—almost like a formula —was characteristic of Tiger. I asked him to go to a nearby drugstore and have the pharmacist call me so that I could prescribe some medication.

When my patient had left, I called Neil. No answer. I must admit I felt uneasy. I left a message with my telephone service to call Neil every half hour and have either him or Tiger call me. The following morning Neil returned my call.

"I just wanted to find out how Tiger was," I told him.

"Depressed," Neil answered. "We took in a movie last night. I don't think he slept a wink."

"Tiger was supposed to have the drugstore call me so that I could prescribe some medicine for him. Did he mention this to you?"

"No. When it comes to keeping secrets, Tiger is a master. He told me that he was going to see you at noon today."

I thanked Neil for calling me. I admired his concern for his friend.

That morning I had several patients and it was with a certain uneasiness that I looked at my watch—twelve o'clock. I waited, became restless, uneasy. If Tiger had been eager to come to my office, he would have been here already. Maybe he had been delayed for some reason. The minutes ticked by. I thought of his defense lawyer's remark in my first talk with him. When I had asked him whether Tiger would escape, he had answered, "One never knows." Then I recalled that Tiger had told me about the melody which had gone through his head during that fatal night: *Slow, fast, escape, disappear.* Could he have carried out his wish? The thought chilled me.

I had to do something, call someone—the police, the Bureau of Missing Persons, Neil. I had a funny feeling which I couldn't explain. Intuition, maybe. It was now twelve-thirty and no Tiger. I called Neil at his office. He was out to lunch.

Late in the afternoon Neil returned my call. I told him that Tiger had not kept his appointment. Had anything happened to him? Had he left town? Neil was dumbfounded. My call to Taylor was fruitless. He was in court on a case.

The following day I learned from Neil that Tiger, in crossing against the light on heavily trafficked Broadway, had been struck head on by a large black fast-moving car—a hearse. He was thrown to the pavement and brought to the hospital unconscious. He died within hours of a fractured skull. His wandering straight into the middle of heavy traffic and disappearing from the view of the horrified onlookers reminded me again of the last link in his mysterious melody of the night Teddy died: *escape—disappear.*

EPILOGUE

Does Murder Have an End?

Red light. Struck down. Obviously it was a suicide—indirect, you may say, but nevertheless suicide. Somehow Tiger felt guilt about Teddy's death, even if he didn't remember that in pulling off her necklace—as I had come to believe—he had choked her. The murder, caused by the sudden lessening of his self-esteem, was an extension of his suicidal impulse. Suicide is an act of aggression against the self, and homicide is an extension of aggression which includes not only the self but those who are closest to the self. In our case, Teddy, the victim, was a part of Tiger's self.

Many times people don't feel guilty unless they fear retribution. The guilt Tiger already felt about Teddy's death became more manifold *because he feared retribution.* While he himself wanted to die, he killed, in a way, because he was afraid of dying. And it was possibly this fear of dying which kept him from insisting that Teddy have an abortion. Tiger may very well have felt that *he* was Teddy's child, and killing the baby would be the same as killing himself.

This fear of dying, as generally is the case, was rooted in his fear of sex. Not only was he afraid of sex in itself, but he also feared his strong sexual impulses, which he felt could overpower him— as at times they had. We are aware of the intimate connection between sex and violence; Tiger had through his sexual repression experienced violent actions. His fear of sex might well have been the reason for his marked compulsion to be alone. Being with or sharing something with somebody else was never easy for him, and being in love was even more difficult. Prior to the murder he could hardly look at Teddy without experiencing feelings of hate toward her, but after the killing, in spite of guilt feelings, he could think of her more easily since she was no longer a threat. Tiger had lured himself into a paradoxical victim-victimizer situation. Trying to overcome his extreme sense of helplessness, he turned his intense anxiety-loaded passivity into angry, violent aggression, seeking the revenge against Teddy which he originally had directed against his mother.

As a matter of fact, the helpless impotence associated with the feelings of revenge that had been with him since childhood days, and other special traits—hypersensitivity to rejection or injustice, suspiciousness—so common to the actual or potential killer were present in Tiger. He did not exhibit, however, as most murderers do, irrational hate for others or inability to withstand frustration. To some extent he was able to cope with hate and disappointment by covering up his emotions—until the fateful night with Teddy. He was obsessed with a wish to retaliate, and subject to his anxiety-ridden emotional outbursts, he fell victim to his own ferocity.

These are the symptoms we find frequently in the individual who murders in a fit of passion, such as might have been the case with Tiger, who, unable to stand his intense rage feelings, had to act them out. But, as mentioned earlier, these same feelings are also generally present in murderers of the more calculating type.

Another factor worth noting in the reactive mechanism between homicide and suicide is that suicide is, in a sense, considered psychologically a homicide in that the person is killing the parent within him. Tiger felt close to his mother, too close in fact for his own comfort and emotional health. Through his Oedipus situation he had, in both his own and in her eyes, completely replaced his father and become his substitute, unleashing resentful and hateful feelings against his mother and bringing him into a love-hate relationship with her such as he was later to have with Teddy. In wanting to kill himself, he wished through his fantasies to kill off what there was within him of his hated mother and father. But this to him was taboo, so instead he fantasized—and this may well have been completely unconscious on his part—that if he couldn't kill, he could become powerful and outdo his father. It was a dream of grandiose accomplishments—a characteristic found in many murderers. Supported by an identity and ego strength which was more developed in Tiger than in the majority of murderers, he tried to control his fantasies. Yet finally fantasy overruled reality.

He became a prey to brooding, doubting—and sleeplessness.

What sleeplessness—or insomnia—amounts to is living in the dark half of one's life, enduring a secret terror from which one arises depleted and unsure to face the real world. Many patients have told me that they are able to tolerate nightmares far better than insomnia. Nightmares bring you fear, yes, but they also have a fascination, a power, and then there is an end to them. Insomnia has no end. It is a kind of never-never land between life-reality and death-fantasy.

Tiger didn't want to take sleeping pills for his insomnia. His refusal to acknowledge need for help made him reject any advice. He wanted total control of himself. Besides, like some patients, he was afraid of adverse reactions from sleeping pills. He refused to combat his sleeplessness with medication. He used books. I am sure they filled his nights. Apparently they gave him lines of inquiry that were definite and rational. They gave him certainties, but also uncertainties and confusing thoughts. His lack of ego strength often made his thinking defensive and distorted. The masochistic, negative part of him was another person, a separate matter having nothing to do with the image of himself he carried in his mind. Unconsciously he wanted to hurt himself, to stay in misery, which was in tune with his past.

Tiger's death wish and suicide seemed ironic. He was on the verge of being cleared of the murder charge. His defense lawyer had succeeded in reducing the charge Murder I to Manslaughter II, and such a reduction might mean that Tiger very well would have been acquitted when the case came to trial. It was possible that the district attorney, because of lack of evidence and the crowded court calendar, would have refrained from prosecuting Tiger.

But, in the end, why had Tiger killed himself, however unconsciously? I think he had lost all hope and felt there was nothing left to live for. Even if he went on living there would be no gratification, because his main object of gratification—Teddy—was dead.

Tiger had committed the sin for which there is no forgiveness: He murdered the love in himself and Teddy, as she had killed the love in him.

Tiger's story—the experiences of one young man in a losing battle for a dream—reveals, however pathetically, our human predicament. We fail ourselves when we fail to acknowledge and deal with our deepest emotions. Tiger's case dramatizes tragically how we are brought down by our fears and guilts. Many of us, in whom the death instinct is stronger than the life instinct, seem to wish—unhealthy as it is—to spend our existence in misery. But knowing that when a murder has been committed we all suffer, we must all become more sensitive to the power of our own emotions. As Pascal said, "We know the truth not only by the reason, but also by the heart."

But Tiger could not accept this truth. His death instinct was well defined, and he fell victim to his own unconscious desires to hurt himself. He could only be there where his pain was. He preferred misery to the point where he could neither remember nor understand reality. Notwithstanding his gallant effort to create a life for himself and for the girl he, in his own way, loved, death came to both of them. The secret of their last evening he took to his grave. Only he knew.

His had been a life—and a death. And somewhere in between —in his isolation—he had in vain tried to find the bridge of love.

Bibliography

ABRAHAMSEN, DAVID. *Mind and Death of a Genius.* New York: Columbia University Press, 1946.
————. "Psychosomatic Disorders and Their Significance in Antisocial Behavior." *Journal of Nervous and Mental Disease,* 107 (1948).
————. *The Psychology of Crime.* New York: Columbia University Press, 1967.
————. "A Study of Lee Harvey Oswald: Psychological Capability of Murder." *Bulletin of the New York Academy of Medicine, Second Series,* 43 (1967).
————. *The Emotional Care of Your Child.* New York: Trident Press, 1969.
————. *Our Violent Society.* New York: Funk & Wagnalls, 1970.
————. "The Murderer and His Victim." Lecture given at the Society for Medical Psychoanalysts, New York, 15 November 1972.
BRIGGS, L. VERNON. *The Manner of Man That Kills: Spencer-Czolgosz-Richeson.* Boston: The Gorham Press, 1921.
BRODY, SYLVIA, AND AXELROD, SIDNEY. "Anxiety, Socialization and Ego Formation in Infancy." Lecture given at the New York Psychoanalytic Institute, 1966.
CARDOZO, BENJAMIN. *Law and Literature.* New York: Harcourt Brace Jovanovich, 1931.
CASSITY, JOHN HULLARD. "Personality Study of 200 Murderers." *Journal of Criminal Psychopathology,* 2 (1942).

FEDERAL BUREAU OF INVESTIGATION. *Crime in the United States.* Reports, 1971. Washington, D.C.: Government Printing Office, 1972.

FENICHEL, OTTO. *The Psychoanalytic Theory of Neurosis.* New York: Norton, 1945.

FORTAS, A. "Implications of Durham's Case." *American Journal of Psychiatry,* 113 (1957).

FREUD, ANNA. *The Ego and the Mechanisms of Defense.* New York: International Universities Press, 1964.

FREUD, SIGMUND. *Civilization and Its Discontents.* London: Hogarth Press, Ltd., and the Institute for Psychoanalysis, 1946.

————. "Analysis Terminable and Interminable." In *Collected Papers.* Vol 1. London: Hogarth Press, Ltd., and the Institute for Psychoanalysis, 1950.

————. *Group Psychology and the Analysis of the Ego.* New York: Liveright, 1951.

GLUECK, SHELDON, AND GLUECK, ELEANOR. *Unraveling Juvenile Delinquency.* New York: The Commonwealth Fund, 1950.

GREENACRE, PHYLLIS. *Trauma, Growth and Personality.* New York: Norton, 1952.

————. *The Quest for the Father.* New York: International Universities Press, Inc., 1963.

LEWIN, BERTRAM D., ed. *On Character and Libido Development: Six Essays by Karl Abraham.* New York: Norton, 1966.

MACDONALD, JOHN M. *The Murderer and His Victim.* Springfield, Illinois: Charles C. Thomas, 1961.

MENNINGER, KARL. *The Crime of Punishment.* New York: Viking, 1968.

MODI, N. J., ed. *Modi's Textbook of Medical Jurisprudence and Toxicology.* Bombay, India: N. M. Tripathi Private Ltd.

PALM, ROSE, AND ABRAHAMSEN, DAVID. "A Rorschach Study of the Wives of Sex Offenders." *Journal of Nervous and Mental Disease,* 119 (1954).

PRYCE, D.M., AND ROSS, C.F. *Ross's Post-Mortem Appearances.* London: Oxford University Press.

ROSENTHAL, A. M. *Thirty-eight Witnesses.* New York: McGraw-Hill, 1964.

Violence in America: Historical and Comparative Perspective. Report to the National Commission on the Causes and Prevention of Violence, June 5, 1969. Washington, D.C.: Government Printing Office, 1969.

VON HENTIG, HANS. *Crime: Causes and Conditions.* New York: McGraw-Hill, 1949.

_____. *The Criminal and His Victim: Studies in the Sociobiology of Crime.* New Haven: Yale University Press, 1947; New York: Anchor Books, 1967.

WEININGER, OTTO. *Sex and Character.* Vienna and Leipzig: Wilhelm Braumuller, 1925. New York: Putnam's.

WEISSMAN, P. "Why Booth Killed Lincoln." *Psychoanalysis and the Social Sciences.* Vol. 5. New York: International Universities Press, 1958.

WERFEL, F. *Nicht der Morder, der Ermordete ist schuldig.* Munich: Kurt Wolff Verlag, 1920.

WILSON, EDWARD F., RICH, TERRY H., AND MESSMAN, HENRY C. "The Hazardous Hibachi: Carbon Monoxide Poisoning Following Use of Charcoal." *Journal of the American Medical Association.* 221 (1972).

WOLFGANG, MARVIN E. *Patterns in Criminal Homicide.* Philadelphia: University of Pennsylvania Press, 1958.

_____. *Crime and Race: Conceptions and Misconceptions.* New York: Institute of Human Relations Press, 1964.